Sensing the Future:
Moholy-Nagy, Media and the Arts

Photographer unknown (Lucia Moholy?),
untitled, not dated. Modern gelatin silver print
from original negative, paper: 25.5 × 20.5 cm;
image: 15 × 10.5 cm.

Sensing the Future: Moholy-Nagy, Media and the Arts

Oliver A. I. Botar

Plug In Institute of Contemporary Art
Bauhaus-Archiv/Museum für Gestaltung, Berlin

avant-garde transfers 2

Lars Müller Publishers

6	**Prefaces**
9	**Introduction**
17	**Sensory Training**
41	**Production–Reproduction**
59	**Gesamtwerk**
81	**Immersion / Participation**
101	**Projection Spaces**
129	**Transparency / Reflection / Motion**
151	**Art as Information / Information as Art**
159	***telehor* 1936 and the Crisis of Media Art**
165	**Commissioned Artworks with Artists' Statements**
179	Chronology
180	Artists' Biographies
183	Notes
187	Reference List
189	Index
190	Locations, Image Credits and Copyright Information
191	Acknowledgments

Sensing the Future: Moholy-Nagy, Media and the Arts is the realization of six years of intensive research, preparation, and international coordination. László Moholy-Nagy, a seminal figure of postmedial art practices, has been inspiring artists since the 1920s. His achievements presented Dr. Oliver A. I. Botar with the ideal platform on which to base an exhibition and a book combining Moholy-Nagy's work with that of contemporary artists. *Sensing the Future: Moholy-Nagy, Media and the Arts* was proposed to Plug In Institute of Contemporary Art's then Director Anthony Kiendl, who took the project on because Botar sought to ground contemporary practice in the work of a particularly prescient member of the historical avant-garde, and because of his intent to present Moholy-Nagy as a pedagogical innovator. This historical and pedagogical approach is in keeping with Plug In ICA's mandate as an Institute of Contemporary Art: to support historical, theoretical and pedagogical research as a means of contextualizing art now.

Our deepest thanks go to Dr. Oliver Botar who conceived of this project and brought it to fruition. The Exhibition *Sensing the Future: Moholy-Nagy, Media and the Arts* opened in March 2014 and is one of the most ambitious exhibitions to be held at Plug In ICA. It would not have been possible without the support of all the staff, including Emily Doucet, Janique Vigier, Graham Asmundson, our team of preparators lead by Aston Coles, gallery attendants, as well as our donors, members, and volunteers. Plug In ICA is very pleased to have been able to partner with the Bauhaus-Archiv, Museum für Gestaltung, The Salgo Trust for Education, and publisher Lars Müller on this project. We are grateful to Hattula Moholy-Nagy and to the Moholy-Nagy Foundation for their support.

Noam Gonick, President of the Board
Heather Laser, Acting Director
Cassidy Richardson, Assistant Curator and Project Manager
Plug In Institute of Contemporary Art, Winnipeg

It has been almost a decade since this book first appeared, and it has been out of print for a few years now. So it is with great pleasure that I introduce this second, corrected printing of the English edition of *Sensing the Future: Moholy-Nagy, Media and the Arts*. I wish to thank Lars Müller for agreeing to this enterprise, to Mickey Salgo for his generosity in making it possible, and to the studio of Olafur Eliasson, to Patrick Harrop, and Lancelot Coar for providing fresh texts and images on the Berlin showing of their respective works in 2014–15. Except in a very few cases where I deemed it important to do so, I have not revised the text. Rather, I have proofread it and have corrected any typographical or other errors that had crept in. I regard this book as representing the state of knowledge as it was in 2013–14 and did not wish to add any new interpretations or much new information that has arisen since then. The book continues to stand on its own as a book, even as it also acts as a document of the exhibition that took place in Winnipeg and Berlin.

Dr. Oliver A. I. Botar
Professor, Art History and Associate Director (Graduate Studies and Research)
School of Art, University of Manitoba
Winnipeg

Curator, The Salgo Trust for Education
New York

With *Sensing the Future: László Moholy-Nagy, Media, and the Arts,* the Bauhaus-Archiv/Museum für Gestaltung present one of the Bauhaus's most experimental masters. To this day, the enormous range of his artistic expression and the visionary power of his multimedia works of art continue to inspire many artists and discussions. While he was head of the preparatory program and the metal workshop at the Bauhaus from 1923 to 1928 his work centered on the ways that different areas of life and work intersect, and on the materials used in the production of art, both of which led him to develop a new formal vocabulary that has maintained its relevance to this very day. His approach to education seems equally contemporary: his notion of exploiting and expanding every individual's potential for sensory experience, as well as his efforts to make art accessible to everyone and to hone human perception, are also issues we pursue in this exhibition at the Bauhaus-Archiv/Museum für Gestaltung.

We consider ourselves very fortunate to have been able to persuade Oliver Botar, a proven expert in the work of László Moholy-Nagy, to act as curator in adapting and expanding the exhibition (first seen at the Plug In ICA) for the Bauhaus-Archiv/Museum. Thanks to his engagement, we are able to present works by many contemporary artists that provide a new perspective on Moholy-Nagy. At the same time, the Bauhaus-Archiv's extensive inventory of Moholy-Nagy's works—in all genres and from all stages of his career—forms the show's indispensable foundation.

We are grateful to Plug In ICA for their smooth efficient, cooperation, as well as to our many international lenders, especially Hattula Moholy-Nagy, The Salgo Trust for Education, and the Theaterwissenschaftliche Sammlung (Theater Collection) at the University of Cologne. Klaus Weber of the Bauhaus-Archiv judiciously realized the concept with the exhibition designers Rodney Latourelle and Louise Witthöft, with assistance from Astrid Bähr, Dina Blauhorn, Berthold Eberhard, Sabine Hartmann, Sibylle Hoiman, Bärbel Mees, Antje Möller, Dagmar Seydell, Monika Tritschler, Katrin Wehry, and Ulrich Weigand. All are heartily thanked. Generous support from the Berlin Hauptstadtkulturfonds (Berlin Capital City Cultural Fund), the Art Mentor Foundation of Lucerne, and The Salgo Trust for Education made this exhibition possible.

Dr. Annemarie Jaeggi
Director of the Bauhaus-Archiv/Museum für Gestaltung, Berlin

Note: Moholy-Nagy's texts are often difficult, and I have found that many translations are inaccurate. For the sake of clarity, I have therefore sometimes slightly altered the available translations into English of Moholy-Nagy's writings that were made after his death. I have not indicated these alterations. Texts by Moholy-Nagy that were published in English during his lifetime are however left unchanged, even when these texts were ostensibly translated from the German (notably *The New Vision*). This is because Moholy-Nagy revised his texts constantly, and so *The New Vision* became, in a real sense, a different book from the German "original," *Von Material zu Architektur*. One exception: If a translation into English from the German or Hungarian original that appeared during Moholy-Nagy's lifetime was too problematic, I have retranslated it. I have also translated texts in German and Hungarian that had not been translated previously. Thus, if a German or Hungarian text is indicated as the source text for a given quotation rendered in English, this indicates that I am the translator.

Oliver A. I. Botar

The biological pure and simple taken as the guide

The last and highest stage of spatial creation is evidently its grasp from the standpoint of biological possibilities.

In the practical evaluation: it does not have to do with a "sculptural", exterior creation, but only with space relationships, which establish the content of experience necessary for a plan of creation. Under certain circumstances, a firm large-surfaced bounding wall can be created on the outside, since in architecture, not sculptural, movable, patterns, but the spatial positions are the building element. Thus the inside of the building is interconnected and is connected with the outside by its spatial divisions.

The task is not completed with the single structure. Even today the next stage becomes manifest: space in all dimensions, space without limitation.

Photo: Weltspiegel

Fig. 156. A street intersection in New York.

A bird's-eye view of the landscape is today a useful guide to the airplane pilot. In the near future views from above, both in representations and in nature, will be familiar to everyone.

Introduction

The enormous development of both technology and big cities has broadened the capacity of our sensory organs for simultaneous acoustic and optical perception. Everyday life itself affords examples of this: Berliners cross Potsdamer Platz. They are conversing. **They simultaneously hear:**

the horns of the cars, the bells of the trams, the honking of omnibuses, the cries of the coachmen, the roar of the subway, the shouts of newspaper sellers, the sounds of a loudspeaker, etc.

and they can differentiate between these various acoustic impressions. A person from the country who had wound up on Potsdamer Platz, on the other hand, was recently found so overwhelmed by the variety of sensory inputs that … he stood frozen in the path of an oncoming tram. It's not hard to imagine an analogous situation concerning optical sensory inputs.[1]

This is a passage from László Moholy-Nagy's first book, *Malerei, Photographie, Film* (*Painting, Photography, Film*), published in 1925. It was the first important book on media theory to appear in the twentieth century, and has been described as "epoch-making."[2] In it, he described both the state of people in modernity and the crucial importance of adapting to this condition. However, he was not only concerned with traffic. By the mid-1920s, Moholy-Nagy had realized that we are placed in a fundamentally new and ever-intensifying condition, one of sensory saturation, stemming from a number of factors: the reproducibility of technically based media (photography, film, print); the easy production of facsimiles of works created in all media, new and old, visual and aural; the proliferation of images, sound, and other forms of information, not to mention advertising and mass-media propaganda (periodicals, posters, books, films, radio, records, even emergent television); the appearance of entire walls of lit advertising in public space; and the concentration of human activity in an increasingly urbanized world. "The new century has overwhelmed people with inventions, new materials, constructions, sciences," as he phrased it in 1930.[3] To make matters worse, education was overspecialized, rather than "organic." Instead of a general education that would help people live happier, more balanced lives, they were trained to fill specific roles within a kind of machine of modernity. As a consequence of this "segmented" educational system, the average person's … "self-assurance is lost. He no longer dares to be his own physician, *not even his own eye.*"[4] (italics added) People were being raised to suppress even their inborn healing and sensory capacities! In his view this was a recipe for disaster, particularly when combined with modernity's sensory overload. Moholy-Nagy, the consummate optimist and utopian, made it his life's project to help rectify this situation.

On the other hand, Moholy-Nagy, like many of his generation, loved modernity. He enjoyed big cities, trains, telephones, roller coasters, radio towers, machines, simultaneity. He was enthusiastic about the challenge that modernity offered to his body and its sensorium. Nonetheless, while enamored of the experience and aesthetic implications of modernity, he took a guardedly critical stance toward it, repeatedly stating that technical progress should be a means to an end rather than the goal.[5] He cast art and artists in the role of helping people adapt to this state, not only through basic sensory exercises such as those he introduced in his classes, but by creating artworks that challenge the senses, both by emulating modernity's sensorial onslaught and by producing art that makes demands on our senses in ways that even modernity had not done. Media art, such as his proposal for a "Simultaneous or Polycinema," he wrote in 1924, "makes new demands upon the capacity of our optical organ of perception, the eye and our center of perception, the brain."[6] This is why a fully reformed pedagogy formed the center of his interest, rather than art making per se. Indeed, he saw his art as an aspect, if not a by-product, of his larger pedagogical project, and did not even consider some of his proposals, such as the Kinetic-Constructive System, the Light Prop for an Electric Stage, or the Polycinema to be artworks in any conventional sense of the term. He viewed them instead as devices for creating situations in which people could have experiences. It was of scant concern to him whether those experiences were art or not.

Street intersection in New York City, in Moholy-Nagy 1932, p. 177.

AEG Film Projector, in Moholy-Nagy and Kassák 1922.

Film stills, Potsdamer Platz, *Berliner Stilleben* (Berlin Still Life), Germany, 1932. 35 mm, black and white, silent, 8'5".

Introduction

While the Hungarian Activists, the Russian Suprematists and Constructivists, the German Dadaists, and the German Lebensreformbewegung (Life Reform Movement) all had a profound impact on Moholy-Nagy, his aesthetic project is rooted in that of the Italian Futurists to a greater extent than has been acknowledged to date. One essential difference did however distinguish Moholy-Nagy's project from the Futurists' vision. As early as 1913 F. T. Marinetti wrote of "multiple and simultaneous awareness in a single individual,"[7] a potentially destabilizing state that the Futurists sought to aestheticize and harness. However, this destabilization was not utopian in impetus. In their responses to modernity, the Futurists sought, for the most part, to instill a sense of discomfort and disorientation rather than adaptation in their audiences. In Moholy-Nagy's scheme, art and artists are accorded the role of educator rather than that of agent provocateur, and it is through this pedagogical prism that art is refracted and projected toward medial experimentation and sensory training/expansion. The range of possible media to be used for artistic expression was greatly expanded by the production of "new, as-yet-unknown aesthetic relations," as he phrased it in his article "Production–Reproduction," and by the endlessly varied means of producing novel sensations through such relations. This was Moholy-Nagy's recipe for new media art, and it resulted in a number of ideas and practices that anticipate what has become standard practice for artists today. It is his prescience in so many respects that inspired me to undertake this project, in which I wish to present the works he realized, his project proposals, and the ways in which contemporary artists have taken up some of these suggestions.

Moholy-Nagy was one of the most influential aesthetic thinkers, designers, and art teachers of the first half of the twentieth century. Photo historian Herbert Molderings writes, "the Hungarian Constructivist Moholy-Nagy belongs among the great universal artists of the modern period."[8] Curator and publisher Oliva Maria Rubio refers to him as "one of the great figures of modernity."[9] "As we move into a world in which technology increasingly shapes cultural sensibility," media artist Eduardo Kac asserts, "Moholy-Nagy's true significance becomes progressively clearer to artists, art historians, and the general public."[10] Photogram artist Floris Neusüss identified Moholy-Nagy's "unique and unmistakable contribution to the history of twentieth-century art," as he put it, in "[the discovery of] light as the primary artistic means of representing space and movement and, in so doing, breaking with the principles of central perspective." By doing this, he continues, "Moholy-Nagy … raised the photographic process … to the level of the latest accomplishments in painting."[11]

During 1920 and 1921, Moholy-Nagy grappled with the development of a pictorial language, a struggle that gave rise to a body of work colored by his own style. Although he was aware of the Futurists' media-related innovations, it was only after encountering the multidisciplinary oeuvres of Kurt Schwitters, Raoul Hausmann, and the Russian Constructivists that Moholy-Nagy began, in 1920–21, to experiment with nontraditional media. This predilection not only very rapidly assumed a central place in his practice, but would, compounded by his pedagogy and theoretical writings, become perhaps his most important contribution to twentieth-century art. His encounters with the work of Lajos Kassák and the Hungarian Activists, as well as with Hungarian art historian Alfréd Kemény's Bogdanovian's ideas, not to mention Moholy-Nagy's engagement—both intellectual and personal—with Lucia (Schulz) Moholy and her biocentric and youth movement connections, sensitized him to a greatly expanded field of possible aesthetic and pedagogical expression and experience. In 1922–23 Moholy-Nagy formulated this as a fairly coherent—if not rigorously systematic—synthesis of thought and practice. In terms of articulating his epistemology and aesthetics, that year marked the most crucial moment in his career and it was essentially this same synthesis that he elaborated until his premature death from leukemia in 1946.

As suggested above, Moholy-Nagy, contrary to his reputation, did not fetishize technology. His leftist-utopian roots in Hungary drew his attention to the stark contrast between the technologically advanced capital and the country's backward rural areas and precluded the uncritical worship of technology characteristic of the 1920s avant-garde:

I am not speaking against the machine or the machine age. The machine is a splendid invention and will form the new basis for a more developed human society. But after the glorious technomania of the twenties, we know today that man cannot master the machine until he has learned to master himself. But how can he achieve this when he even does not know what he possesses, what his abilities and capacities are?[12]

Moholy-Nagy did not leave this question unanswered: "… the injuries worked by a technical civilization can be combatted on two fronts:

1. By the purposeful observation and the rational safeguarding of the organic, biologically conditioned functions (science, education, politics).

*2. By means of the **constructive** carrying forward of our overscientific culture— since there is no turning backward.*

*In practice the two approaches interlock closely, though theoretically step **1** must prepare for step **2**.…*

Utopia? No, but the task is for tireless pioneers. To stake everything on the end in view—the supreme duty for those who have already arrived at the consciousness of an organic way of life.… At this point the educational problem merges into the political.…[13]

He saw his pedagogical program as being political in nature, and was often criticized, even attacked, by his Communist friends and colleagues for this view. As early as 1922, when he contributed to the "Debate on the Problem of New Content and New Form" that was unfolding in the Hungarian Communist-Dada émigré journal *Akasztott Ember* (Hanged Man), his views were controversial among those who held that only partisan art approved by the Communist Party should be made by artists working in the context of capitalism. Moholy-Nagy's response: "Why the big debate over whether a person has a right to express themselves in words or colors, in forms or light? In every one of our gestures, in every one of our manifestations, people express themselves."[14] Furthermore, he held that the artist's role is to enable such expression. This will, consequently, pave the way for revolution, and in any case, people's basic needs cannot be neglected, even within capitalism. Moholy-Nagy's Lebensreform-inspired pedagogical views asserted that people had to be changed now, as such change would help stimulate the revolution. This was in opposition to official Communist policy.

His reference to an "organic way of life" suggests further depths to Moholy-Nagy's thought. Moholy-Nagy's Weltanschauung was firmly anchored in Central European Biozentrik (Biocentrism), and more specifically in biologism. An environmentalist position emerged from this, which he articulated late in life:

One suddenly becomes aware [of] … the incoherent use of our rich resources. Technological ingenuity provides us with gigantic structures, factories, and skyscrapers, but how we use them is shockingly anti-biological—resulting in wild city growth, elimination of vegetation, fresh air, and sunlight … leading toward a biologically right living most probably through a right regional planning; toward a city-land unity.[15]

While congruent with midcentury Modernist city and regional planning movements, there is a biocentric edge to this passage that betrays his intense involvement with the German Lebensreformbewegung during the 1920s. Moholy-Nagy's environmentalism will not be investigated in this publication, but it is another reason to consider his relevance today.

His open-mindedness and enquiring mind led to thoughts and work that anticipated the artistic culture of the second half of the twentieth century, a period he was unable to experience due to his premature death: His practice challenged the traditional media hierarchy, and announced the insignificance of the artist's own hand in producing artwork. He was a pioneer of multidisciplinary art practices that have now become standard; he promoted a process-based and research-based approach to creative production; he recognized the central importance of photography and cinema for art; he theorized what became known as "expanded cinema"; and he began to think in terms of systems in art. By claiming the supremacy of the idea over its execution in artistic production, by promoting the position that any and all media should be considered when realizing an idea, and by thinking about art as a form of information, he came to recognize the dwindling importance of the "original" and the (sometimes concomitant) growing significance of the mass media in art production and dissemination. Kac has pointed out that Moholy-Nagy pioneered strategies anticipating digital artistic thinking in his "Telephone Pictures" (1923). These ideas in turn informed theorists like Walter Benjamin, John Cage, Sigfried Giedion, Marshall McLuhan, and Vilém Flusser, who anticipated or theorized digital culture as it emerged. Should we

Introduction

regard Moholy-Nagy as a pioneer of the digital? How does his work relate to the current debate concerning the turn away from bodily experience that engagement with cyberworlds entails? His aesthetic concern with the technology/body issue— he proposed the first immersive and participatory artwork as early as 1922–28– broached the notions of immersion, interactivity, and bodily participation. In this respect, he was a pioneer of participatory and relational art practices. This, however, seems to run counter to the notion of absorption into cyberworlds and games via avatars. Does this immersive, body-centered early work suggest a critique of today's disembodiment? Was he both a pioneer and a protocritic of the digital? Whatever the answers to these questions, Moholy-Nagy was instrumental in laying the groundwork for the post– World War II digital-medial shift in artistic practices.

Some of his predictions have, of course not, come to pass, or they have taken paths that he did not anticipate. He wrote about the use of pure colored light as the future of art. Such art, despite waves of popularity since the 1960s, has remained relatively marginal. However, immersive events featuring projected or laser lights, strobes, projected and moving images, smoke machines and intense rhythmic sound involving corporeal movement (all in all quite a Moholyan convergence) did emerge, but as a popular art form found in discos, at psychedelic light/music events, raves, circuit parties, festivals, and the like. Rather than a lofty and somewhat esoteric idea, "optophonetics" (simultaneous aural and visual expression of information) is an essential and pervasive by-product of the digital. His view that television would become the bearer of abstract light "painting" proved particularly unrealistic, though he did muse darkly on the possibility of television's complete commercialization, like that of cinema. In a sense, his promotion of the "development" of all art toward "pure energy" did come to pass with the rise of digital technology, which has also validated his conviction that art was a form of information that could be reduced to a code for transmission.

This book, published in conjunction with the exhibition *Sensing the Future: Moholy-Nagy, Media and the Arts*, is organized into chapters that recapitulate the sections of the exhibition. These are thematic in nature, and do not cover the entire oeuvre of the artist as it related to media. Rather, they form an interrelated constellation of essays (and one image/quotation montage) that I hope will illuminate some of the topics I have chosen to cover.

This publication and exhibition constitute a stage in my research on Moholy-Nagy and media. They were preceded by another exhibition/publication project, *Technical Detours: The Early Moholy-Nagy Reconsidered* (2006–2008), which considered the sources of Moholy-Nagy's artistic and pedagogical career. For the most part, that project ended where this one begins, around the time of Moholy-Nagy's annus mirabilis of 1922. *Sensing the Future* is closely related to a project I recently completed in collaboration with Klemens Gruber. We edited the facsimile edition of the most important monograph on Moholy-Nagy published during his lifetime, *telehor* (1936). The republication of *telehor*, and this book, form part of a series on the interconnections of the international avant-garde, entitled "avant-garde transfers." *telehor* was the first publication in that series. This is the second.

With this project, I had the privilege of engaging in collaborative research with artists such as Bernie Miller, who reconstructed one key lost early construction by Moholy-Nagy, and Eduardo Aquino, whose *Text Space* is an attempt to meld the body-focused, experiential aspects of Moholy-Nagy's oeuvre with his extensive written corpus. Lancelot Coar and Patrick Harrop collaborated on an attempt to realize Moholy-Nagy's rather hazily articulated notion of a "Simultaneous or Polycinema." This project–like Aquino's–was funded by a generous grant from the Social Sciences and Humanities Research Council of Canada, a grant that also supported the research and writing of this publication. Collaboration between an historian like myself and artists/architects such as Miller, Aquino, Harrop, and Coar has been an exhilarating experience, as was my earlier cooperation with Peter Yeadon and Naomi Crellin. The research-creation of all these artists/architects has given me insights into Moholy-Nagy's oeuvre that I would not have gleaned by employing traditional scholarly methods alone.

Involving contemporary artists was an integral aspect of this project from the outset. It has been immensely rewarding for me to engage in creative and critical dialogue with artists such as Ken Gregory, Erika Lincoln, and Freya Olafson, with all of whom I had the privilege of spending a month during the 2013 Plug In ICA Summer Institute, where Gregory and I acted as faculty. Eduardo Kac–a scholar as well as a highly innovative

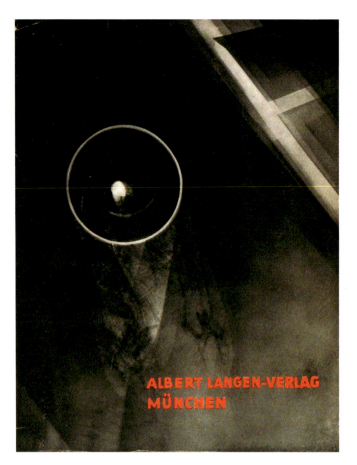
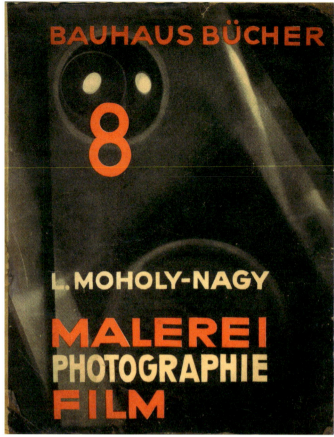
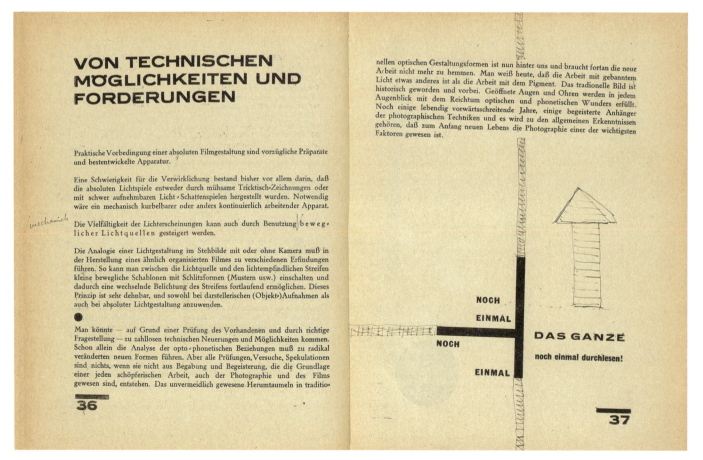

László Moholy-Nagy, *Malerei, Photographie, Film* (Painting, Photography, Film), 1925. Cover design by Moholy-Nagy, using photograms of ca. March 1923– April 1925 (top). Moholy-Nagy's proof copy of *Malerei, Photographie, Film*, 1925 (bottom).

artist–came to the Summer Institute as visiting faculty, and this proved to be a signal event in the project's development, as few people have a deeper understanding of Moholy-Nagy's oeuvre than he does. Discussions with filmmaker Guy Maddin and his work with the other Development Ltd. members (Evan Johnson, Galen Johnson, Bob Kotyk, and Ryan Simmons) led to the production of a gorgeous, erotic, dream-like "evocation," as Maddin put it, rather than a straight realization of one of Moholy-Nagy's 1920s "film scripts." Corresponding with Floris Neusüss and Renate Heyne (authors of the outstanding catalogue raisonné of Moholy-Nagy's photograms) about their work has been satisfying. Neusüss and Kac are living proof that great scholars and great artists can inhabit the same body. Olafur Eliasson, whose highly varied, remarkable oeuvre is informed by Moholyan research-creation practices, has been generous in his contribution to this project. Working with him and with Caroline Eggel of the Olafur Eliasson Studio in Berlin has been an enriching process that has produced wonderful results. It has been inspiring to connect with artists, architects, and art historians such as Francisco Javier Navarro de Zuvillaga (Madrid); Gottfried Jäger and Karl Martin Holzhauser (Bielefeld); the team of Jörg U. Lensing, Gudula Schröder, Jürgen Steger, Thomas Neuhaus, Malou Airaudo and Sascha Hardt (Düsseldorf); and the team of Nike Arnold, Andreas Haus, Aline Helmcke, Frédéric Krauke and Walter Lenertz (Berlin). All of them had previously produced outstanding work of relevance to this project, and I am grateful to them for agreeing to include it here.

Finally, though this book is being published in conjunction with the eponymous exhibition, it is not an exhibition catalogue: the exhibition was too different in its two venues for that format to work fruitfully. Most of the works illustrated were however included in one or both of the venues, and this publication encompasses the majority of the works shown in one or both of the exhibition's iterations. Since the book is also structured as the show was, this, along with the inclusion of the commissioned artists' statements and biographies, should give readers a sense of the exhibitions.

While acknowledgements are listed at the end of the book, I would like to mention a number of key figures and organizations who were central to the realization of the project, in addition to those already cited above. My publisher, Lars Müller (also in charge of design), and his managing editors Rebekka Kiesewetter and Michael Ammann have been both patient and generous in their support of this endeavor. I was fortunate to have an editor as intelligent and rigorous as Helen Ferguson. Anthony Kiendl and Annemarie Jaeggi, directors, respectively, of Plug In Institute of Contemporary Art and the Bauhaus-Archiv, Museum für Gestaltung, took on this project with what I can only assume was blind faith, and have supported it in every way possible. Klaus Weber of the Bauhaus-Archiv has been in every sense a collaborator and a generous colleague, while Sabine Hartmann, Sibylle Hoiman, and Astrid Bähr, also of the Bauhaus-Archiv, have supported the project as well. Cassidy Richardson successfully project-managed the exhibition at Plug In ICA under challenging circumstances. The exhibitions' designers Eduardo Aquino (Winnipeg) and Rodney Latourelle/Louise Witthöft (Berlin) did exceptional work. The Salgo Trust for Education funded my participation in the exhibition and a good portion of my research for the entire project. The Salgo Trust is also the principal funder of this book. None of this would have been possible without the ongoing support of the Salgo Trust's executor, Mickey Salgo. Hattula Moholy-Nagy has been extraordinarily generous and patient in supporting my research, curating and publishing over a long period of time. She is also a major funder of this book and a key partner of the exhibition, as is the Moholy-Nagy Foundation, headed by Andreas Hug. I owe my thanks to all these people and organizations. Above all, I wish to express my deep gratitude to my patient and supportive family, Serena Keshavjee, who read the entire manuscript and made enormously helpful comments, usefully clarifying a number of points, Oliver Nadir Botar, and Devin Gyula Botar. This book would not have been possible without your help and understanding.

Oliver Botar, Winnipeg, July 2014

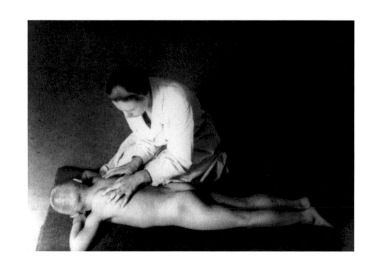

Sensory Training

Oh thou, beloved of my twenty-seven senses, I love thine![1]

In the frontispiece, we see a young man standing tall, a look of intense concentration on his face. His eyelids are lowered. Behind him stands a woman. They are outdoors, under a gray sky. Her tanned right hand is visible as it lightly touches his shoulder, her eyes down-cast. Their contact is intense, but not erotic. His focus seems inward, toward his body. We know that the young man is László Moholy-Nagy, and judging by his age, that this is the second half of the 1920s. However, as we have only the unannotated negative, we do not know for certain who took the photograph or where it was taken, though it may well have been taken by Lucia Moholy at the Schwarzerden Commune, and the young woman may well be Elisabeth Vogler.

Lucia Moholy, *Portrait of László Moholy-Nagy with Hand*, 1926. Concept by László Moholy-Nagy. Gelatin silver print from 1994, authorized by the Estate, 23.3 × 20.3 cm.

Lucia Moholy, Untitled (child undergoing therapy, Schwarzerden), 1927. Modern gelatin silver print.

László Moholy-Nagy, "My right hand kindly placed at your disposal! For Walter Gropius on his birthday, May 18, 1926." Handprint on paper, mounted on paper.

At present, our education is an overwhelmingly intellectual one, ignoring almost everything to do with our sensory experiences.... Bringing education into a state of equilibrium—that is, giving the student enough food for the brain, yet at the same time not neglecting the sensory experience of nose, tongue, eye, ear, and fingers is one way of overcoming ... the present faults of our educational system. Only the total use of the abilities, the integration of the senses, and the intellectual power [sic] will allow an organic development of the individual. A person balanced in both intellect and emotion will be better able to face the complexities of modern life.[2]

It is balance that seems to be at play in the photograph: balance of the body (hence the posture), of the mind (concentration), and of the senses (eyes lowered).

From his biological being every man derives energies which he can develop into creative work. Everyone is talented.... One has to live "right" to retain the alertness of these native abilities. But only art—creation through the senses—can develop these dormant, native faculties toward creative action. Art is the grindstone of the senses, the coordinating psycho-biological factor. The teacher who has come to a full realization of the organic oneness and the harmonious sense rhythm of life should have a tongue of fire to expound his happiness.[3]

"Balance," "psycho-biological," "organic oneness," "harmonious sense rhythm of life," "tongue of fire," even! These are not phrases normally associated with International Constructivists such as Moholy-Nagy. These passages and phrases are typical of kunsterzieherisch (art pedagogical) and reformpädagogisch (reform pedagogical) ideas, which were prevalent in the Pädagogisches Reformbewegung (Pedagogical Reform Movement) of the early twentieth-century German Lebensreformbewegung (Life Reform Movement), and more specifically of the Jugendbewegung (Youth Movement).[4] One might therefore ask once again: What did an International Constructivist, who lived in Berlin and subsequently at the Bauhaus in Weimar and Dessau, have to do with these movements? What was Moholy-Nagy, clad in his jump suit, doing with that woman?

When Moholy-Nagy arrived in Berlin in mid-March 1920, he encountered members of the Jugendbewegung, specifically the Freideutsche Jugend (Free German Youth).[5] As several historians have documented, the Freideutsche Jugend was steeped in utopian "life reform" practices. The concomitant of this was a biocentrically based environmental consciousness.[6] At the Erster Freideutscher Jugendtag (First Free German Youth Day), the movement's founding event in 1913, the philosopher Ludwig Klages, who coined the term *Biozentrik* (biocentrism) and was its most important theorist, delivered his rousing environmentalist manifesto, "Mensch und Erde" (Man and Earth). "Horrible are the effects that 'progress' has had on the aspect of settled areas," he thundered. "Torn is the connection between human creation and the earth, destroyed ... is the ancient song of the landscape.... The reality behind the facade of 'utility,' 'economic development' and 'Kultur' is the destruction of life."[7] Klages railed against the destruction of the environments in which aboriginal people lived and against curtailed diversity in the natural world. *Biozentrik* was the German term for an early-twentieth-century worldview which was based on trends such as Darwinism and biological determinism, and on a kind of materialist Nature Romanticism; it rejected anthropocentrism,

Lucia Moholy, *Portrait of Elizabeth Vogler and Tilla Winz, Schwarzerden*, 1927, modern gelatin silver print from original negative.

Lucia Moholy, *Hands, Peeling Potatoes, Schwarzerden*, ca. 1929–30. Modern gelatin silver print from original negative.

Lucia Moholy, *Gymnastics, Schwarzerden*, 1927. Modern gelatin silver print.

Lajos Kassák, *Horizont* no. 2, "Moholy-Nagy" (Vienna: MA Editions, 1921). Dedication on title page: "Für Paula und Paul [Vogler] / Moholy-Nagy."

Lucia Moholy, *Portrait of Paula Vogler*, 1927. Modern gelatin silver print from original negative.

Komposition, ca. 1923. Linocut or woodcut on velum, paper: 23.7 × 16.7 cm, image: 12 × 8.2 cm. Dedication: "für Paula [Vogler]."

espousing instead a neo-Vitalist and ecological view of the world. It can most succinctly be described as Nature Romanticism updated by biologism. Ranging politically from proto-Nazism to Peter Kropotkin's and Pierre-Joseph Prudhon's biologistic anarchism, yet often seeing themselves as a political third way (the Biozentrik trend was a predecessor to the Green Party), those who espoused the bundle of biocentric positions were situated at the intersection of a wide range of fin-de-siècle movements, groupings, and philosophies.[8]

The left wing of the Freideutsche Jugend was inspired by the writings of pacifist anarchists such as Tolstoy and by the artist Heinrich Vogeler, who had transformed his home, Barkenhoff, in the Worpswede artists' colony, into a nature-centric anarcho-Communist commune by 1918, making him one of the pioneers of the 1920s German communard movement. As well as accommodating what we could term "New Age," Lebensreform, and biocentric ideas, Barkenhoff was a center of left-wing tendencies in the Freideutsche Jugend. A young, German-speaking assimilated Jew, Prague-born Lucia Schulz was actively involved with these ideas during 1919.[9] Her contact to Barkenhoff grew out of friendships that had developed in 1918, particularly with Paul and Paula Vogler, adherents of what Schulz dubbed a "biological" approach to both preventative and naturopathic therapeutic health care. Schulz also developed a close friendship with Paul Vogler's sister, Elisabeth Vogler, a Freideutsche Jugend pedagogue and dancer. In 1919–20 Elisabeth, who like Paul was a disciple of Gustav Wyneken,[10] one of the leaders in the Pädagogisches Reformbewegung, had spent time at Loheland, a newly established women's commune in the Rhön mountains. Elisabeth also formed a long-term partnership with Freideutsche Jugend pedagogical reformer Marie Buchhold. The latter was a member of the Wendekreis, a group of "revolutionary Hamburg teachers,"[11] which was also associated with Barkenhoff.[12]

Inspired inter alia by Heinrich Vogeler and Wyneken, Buchhold had been thinking hard about questions of communal living and educational reform. Evidently affected by Ludwig Klages's environmentalism and characterology, Buchhold focused on "teaching the body" in order to find a balance between the self and the world. A 1924 diary entry reads "By 'Körperlehre' (body instruction) … is meant the recognition of the human organism within the organism of the world."[13]

Let us now return to Berlin in 1920. Moholy-Nagy met Lucia Schulz in 1920 through his Freideutsche Jugend connections, and they were married early in 1921. This connection changed Moholy-Nagy's life in a number of ways, partly because Lucia Moholy, as she became known, did not sever her Freideutsche Jugend connections. In fact, during the summer of 1922 she and Moholy-Nagy spent their vacation near Loheland.[14] Meanwhile, the Rhön Mountains were rapidly becoming a focus for the German 1920s alternative movement. Paul and Paula Vogler bought a small summer house there. In the fall of 1923 Buchhold and Elisabeth Vogler founded a women's commune and school at Schwarzerden, 10.5 kilometers east of Loheland. The following summer, they began organizing Ferienkurse (holiday courses) there, encompassing a veritable smorgasbord of Lebensreform practices, with lectures, workshops, and demonstrations in gymnastics, massage, holistic health, breathing, pedagogy, music, literature, and psychology.[15] The Moholy-Nagys spent their 1924 and 1926 summer vacations at Paul and Paula Vogler's holiday home. Lucia certainly participated in the Ferienkurse, and László might have joined her on occasion, as Elisabeth Vogler remembers.[16]

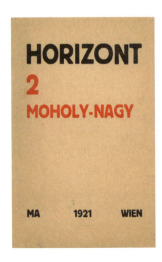

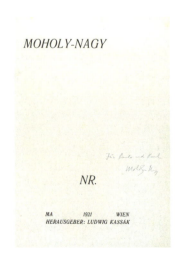

Sensory Training

Photographer unknown, Marie Buchhold (right) and Elisabeth Vogler, Schwarzerden, 1923.

Portrait of Lucia Moholy, ca. 1928. 43.6 × 31.8 cm.

Lucia Moholy, *Lucia Selbstporträt*, 1930, 23.9 × 17.9 cm.

The Voglers were closely associated with Schwarzerden and were involved in the evolution of its alternative healing practices. Paul Vogler developed a physiotherapeutic system of prophylaxis, deep massage, hydrotherapy, and other techniques, maintaining his alternative practices after he became a doctor in Berlin in 1927.[17] Paul and László became fast friends. Paul was his personal physician, and László designed Vogler's office. These were intimate, strong connections. Lucia once wrote to Elizabeth Vogler that, as time passed, "the agreement of our respective ways of thinking became clearer, the tone of our conversations more intense, the exchange of ideas more fruitful, our friendship became stronger, indeed more intimate."[18] After his death, Paul wrote of Moholy-Nagy that "drawing from the vital depths of his own views, he contributed substantially to posing our [mutual] questions."[19]

László's commitment to Schwarzerden is indicated by the fact that even in 1930, after his separation from Lucia, he took on the color design for the Gymnastics Hall, its most important structure.[20] Lucia, meanwhile, documented the commune school's activities in photographs.

This ongoing contact had a deep effect on Moholy-Nagy. In his 1929 pedagogical treatise *Von Material zu Architektur* (From Material to Architecture), Moholy-Nagy acknowledged his debt to the Reformschulbewegung, the Jugendbewegung, and the Wendekreis (that is, Marie Buchhold), as well as to Worpswede (Heinrich Vogeler and his circle) and, indirectly, to the Freideutsche Jugend and its communes.[21]

Let us return to the frontispiece. Comparing it with one of Lucia's photographs of a child receiving therapy (p. 16), one can well imagine that it was taken at Schwarzerden, with the woman (who remains unidentified) engaged in Körperlehre with Moholy-Nagy. The photographer is probably Lucia Moholy, the documentarist of Schwarzerden.

Moholy-Nagy absorbed reform-pedagogical notions from other sources as well. By early 1923 at the latest, in Berlin, Moholy-Nagy had come into contact with Heinrich Jacoby, an educator associated with the Bund Entschiedener Schulreformer (Association of Determined School Reformers), an outgrowth of the pedagogical reform movement within the Freideutsche Jugend. One of the central concepts in Moholy-Nagy's pedagogical approach, the notion that "everyone is talented," was adopted from Jacoby. The title of Jacoby's book *Jenseits von 'begabt' und 'unbegabt'*

Lucia Moholy, *Portrait of Heinrich Jacoby*, 1924. Modern gelatin silver print from original negative.

6. Kestnermappe – 6 Konstruktionen, 1923. Portfolio of thin green card with a textile structure and glued-on, printed paper title, 61 × 45 cm. Dedication to Heinrich Jacoby on title page, November 1, 1926.

Christoph Natter, *Künstlerische Erziehung aus eigengesetzlicher Kraft*, designed by László Moholy-Nagy (Stuttgart and Gotha: Verlag Friedrich Andreas Perthes, 1924).

F. T. Marinetti, "A Taktilizmus: Futurista kiáltvány" (Tactilism: A Futurist Manifesto), *MA* 7, no. 7 (June 1, 1921), p. 91.

(Beyond Talented and Untalented) expressed the author's insight that a teacher's job is to actualize the abilities inherent in each individual rather than "discovering" talent. Moholy-Nagy was hired by the Bauhaus in April 1923 to direct its metal workshop and to take charge of the Vorkurs (Introductory Course) as Johannes Itten's successor. Although Moholy-Nagy had never taught before, his pedagogy proved successful. We may certainly conclude that his experiences at Loheland the summer before and with Jacoby earlier that year had proved fruitful.

Everyone is talented.... *Everyone is equipped by nature to receive and assimilate sensory experiences. Everyone is sensitive to tones and colors, has sure touch and space relations, etc. This means that by nature everyone is able to participate in all the pleasures of sensory experiences, that any healthy person can also become a musician, painter, sculptor, architect, just as when he speaks, he is a 'speaker.' That is, he can give form to his reactions in any material.*...[22]

Moholy-Nagy invited Jacoby to give a lecture at the Bauhaus in 1924. At this time Lucia made a portrait series of Jacoby.[23] The lecture was such a success that László asked him back to give another talk in March 1925.[24] László also invited Jacoby to prepare a volume (unrealized) for the Bauhausbücher series on "creative music education." Moholy-Nagy referred to Jacoby's idea of "the common biological basis of all formation [education]" as "one of the most important intellectual achievements of our time" and as belonging "to the most valuable sources from which our present and future pedagogy can draw."[25]

While the phrase "everyone is talented" expresses the positive aspect of Moholy-Nagy's teaching, his critique was that traditional education leads people toward specialization, which in his view constitutes one of the principal obstacles to personal development.[26] However, Moholy-Nagy does not entirely dismiss specialized education. In a text with the subtitle "The Future Requires Integrated People," he writes that "the specialized person must again be based on a person organically integrated into society: strong, open, happy, as he was in his childhood."[27] As Alain Findeli points out, the Bauhaus had already developed a pedagogical model of integrated development of students' body, spirit, and intellect. Moholy-Nagy expanded this model to include science teaching, with a view to producing individuals able to build a new society.[28] However, he always privileged personal development over art: "not the object, rather man is the end in view."[29]

Jena art educator Christoph Natter was a further Bund Entschiedener Schulreformer member with links to Moholy-Nagy. Natter hired Moholy-Nagy to design the cover for his 1924 reform-pedagogical treatise *Künstlerische Erziehung* (Artistic Education), in which Natter calls for the education of our "crippled" sense and organs. This is such a strong statement that one wonders where this terminology came from.

Here is a passage from "Production–Reproduction," the article Moholy-Nagy wrote in 1922 with Lucia Moholy's assistance:[30]

The human construct is the synthesis of all its functional apparatuses, i.e., the human being will be most perfect in his own time if the functional apparatuses of which he is composed—the cells as well as the most complicated organs—are conscious and trained to the limit of their efficiency. Art effects such a training, and that is one of its most important tasks, since it is on the perfectibility of the sensory organs that the entire complex of effects depends....[31]

The tightly argued text links human beings, art, education, and the senses. Moholy-Nagy subsequently states that, "creative activities are useful only if they produce new, as-yet-unknown relations," since our sensory organs "are never sated, but rather crave ever new impressions following each new reception," and since art trains us to use these organs to their fullest capacity. The idea of the need for sensory stimulation is derived from the Empiriokritizismus of Ernst Mach and Richard Avenarius, who proposed subjectivity as the source of knowledge about the world, emphasizing that we can only know the world through our personal sense perceptions. They referred to indivisibility, that is, as Andreas Haus phrases it, the "monist merging into one another of perception and world" that eliminates the alienation between subject and environment through a reversal of the conventional perceptual model. "Rather than [material] bodies [in the real world] engendering perceptions," writes Mach, "perceptual complexes … construct these bodies." In other words, the perceiving subject continually reconstitutes

Sensory Training

itself through the selection and integration of sensory inputs. This is why perceptual training was highlighted: aesthetic experience trains the perceptual organs, and thereby allows subjects to strengthen and control the continuous (re)constitution of the self.[32] Aesthetic experience is not merely a supplementary activity, but has a crucial *biological* role to play. Haus points out that these ideas were promulgated among artists by Robert Müller-Freienfels, whose book *Psychologie der Kunst* (Psychology of Art) was published in 1922.[33] Müller-Freienfels's conception of Reizhunger, a hunger for stimulation of the perceptual organs, is reflected in Moholy-Nagy's article.

In addition to reading Müller-Freienfels (which seems likely), Moholy-Nagy will have absorbed empiriocritical concepts from other sources—they seem to have been all around him. In a later chapter of this book, "Immersion / Participation," we will see that in 1922 Moholy-Nagy teamed up with Hungarian art historian Alfréd Kemény, who had just returned from Moscow full of the ideas of Alexander Bogdanov and his Proletkult movement. As his student, Bogdanov had absorbed empiriocritical thinking directly from Avenarius in Zurich. Other empiriocritical sources for Moholy-Nagy were his friend Raoul Hausmann[34] and the Austro-Hungarian biologist and biocentric pop-philosopher Raoul Heinrich Francé.

It is as a consequence of empiriocritical thought that "sensory training," as Moholy-Nagy termed it in *The New Vision*,[35] became the cornerstone of his pedagogy. After an initial theoretical chapter, Moholy-Nagy continues his pedagogical treatise, *Von Material zu Architektur,* with an account of his sensory training practices. Bauhaus education did not begin with students learning how to make works of art or design products; instead, students first explored materials and their properties, working largely through what Moholy-Nagy termed "tactile exercises," reflecting the primacy of the sense of touch. Moholy-Nagy begins his account with Charles Scott Sherrington's sensorial taxonomy:

The physiologist divides the different impulses which reach the consciousness as sensations into exteroceptive (those set up by events in the outer world), proprioceptive (coming from the muscles and adjacent deep structures and from the inner ear) and interoceptive (arising from the internal organs and viscera). But the daily language remains at the traditional "five senses" as is the case with the … "four temperaments" … it is surely the sense of touch, more than any other,

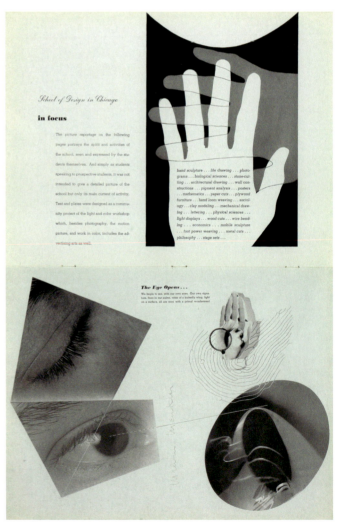

Untitled, 1925–26. Photogram on developing paper, 18.3 × 24.1 cm.

School of Design in Chicago, 1941. Two spreads, unpag. Edited by László Moholy-Nagy; design by György Kepes.

Qualität 9, nos. 1–2 (1931), special issue on photography, edited by Carl Ernst Hinkefuss. Design by László Moholy-Nagy, using his reversed photogram (based on an original of 1926), ca. 1926–31.

Film still, *Berlin Still Life*, Germany, 1932. 35 mm, black and white, silent, 8'5".

Film still, *Lightplay Black White Grey*, Germany, 1932, 35 mm, black and white, silent, ca. 5'30".

Sensory Training

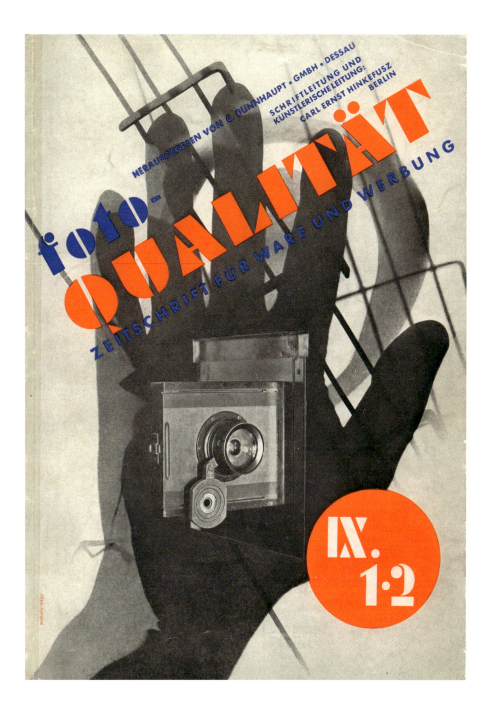

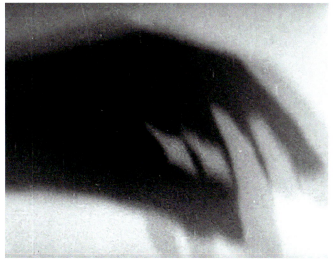

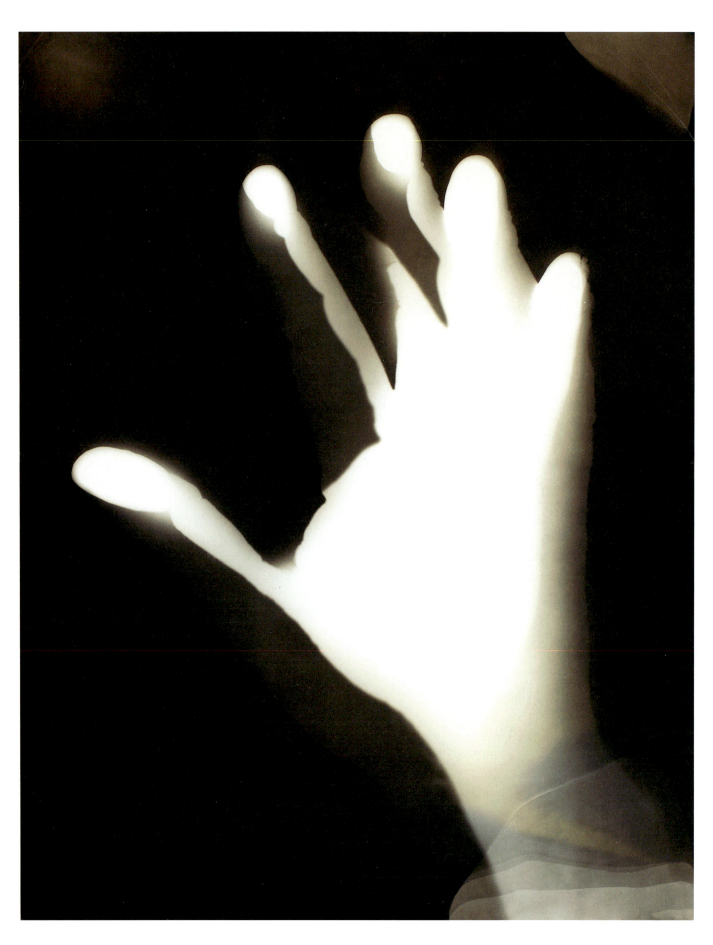

Untitled, 1939–41. Photograms on developing paper, 25.1 × 20.1 cm (*left*); 25.3 × 20.3 cm (*right*).

Sensory Training

that may be divided up into a greater number of separate qualities of sensations. The Bauhaus student in his initial exercises studies the material principally by means of his sense of touch.[36]

Moholy-Nagy's remark that "touch is a collective term for a number of different sensory faculties," echoes Marinetti's statement in his 1921 "Der Taktilismus. Futuristisches Manifest" (Tactilism. A Futurist Manifesto): "[t]he distinction between the five senses is obviously arbitrary, and it is certain that in time, many other senses will become discoverable and categorizable."[37] Nevertheless, images of the hand are the predominant symbol for the sense of touch.[38] Bauhaus students were instructed to explore differentiated aspects of tactility, as can be seen in Otti Berger's exquisite tactile chart, Rudolf Marwitz's "revolving tactile drum with contrasting tactile values," Werner Zimmermann's "tactile table for pressure and vibration," and Siegfried Giesenschlag's "tactile table for registering prickling sensations." From the New Bauhaus in Chicago, Moholy-Nagy cites Richard Pavlicek's "movable tactile chart," a "Luna Park [amusement park] for the fingers."[39]

Students would cover their eyes and try to identify the materials in one another's charts, in order to focus attention on the haptic sensation.[40] In Chicago this exercise was extended to the visually impaired, who were "asked to test some of the tactile exercises." "Their appreciation was most enlightening. It showed a possibility for tactile exercises in the education of the blind in the future" writes Moholy-Nagy.[41] This triggered research at the New Bauhaus on ways to serve people with more limited sensoria.[42] During World War II, the program to address the otherwise-abled intensified with the return of injured veterans.

Moholy-Nagy's focus in these exercises was not on art-making but aimed instead "to arouse and enrich the desire for sensation and expression."[43] However, he cited Marinetti, raising the possibility "of works of art resulting from the deepening of experience and the inspiration gained."[44] Indeed, Moholy-Nagy begins the section on sculpture with the exquisite "hand sculptures" the students created at the New Bauhaus. "The hand sculptures are nearest to timeless forms of all ages mainly because they express the pure functions of the hands."[45] They invoke the important symbolic value of the hand as a motif: hands are for making, and Moholy-Nagy incorporated the reform pedagogical principal of "learning by doing" into all his teaching.[46] These sculptures, just like the tactile charts, figured prominently in the films on their activities made by Moholy-Nagy and the students during the 1940s.

Echoes of these ideas can be found in Hausmann's 1921 text "PRÉsentismus," which, like Marinetti's "Tactilism," was published in *MA* (p. 21) thanks to Moholy-Nagy's efforts:

The Tactilism that Marinetti announced ... is a facsimile of the sadism of ancient Roman gladiator fights ... it presents nothing that is new. We call for the expansion and

Otti Berger, Tactile chart, from Moholy-Nagy's Vorkurs (Introductory Course), second semester 1928. Thread, wire mesh, paper, 14 × 57 cm.

Tactile charts, László Moholy-Nagy, 1932, pp. 22–23.

Film stills showing manipulation of hand sculptures, *Interview with Institute of Design students and display of student work*, Chicago, USA, 1942. 16 mm film transferred to DVD, color, silent.

Hand Sculptures by unidentified students of the School of Design, Chicago, n.d., wood.

Sensory Training

conquest of all of our senses. We want to explode their boundaries!! we're promoting haptism and odorism! ... Haptic art will expand people!

Hausmann could never resist outdoing a potential rival, and his introduction of the olfactory into the mix seems to have had an effect on Moholy-Nagy, whose 1925 "Partiturskizze zu einer mechanischen Exzentrik: Synthese von Form, Bewegung, Ton, Light (Farbe) und Geruch" (Score of a Mechanical Eccentric: Synthesis of Form, Movement, Sound, Light [Colour], Smell), a multisensory variety theater, included an olfactory dimension. Charles Niedringhaus's "Smell-o-Meter," produced at the New Bauhaus, indicates continued attention paid to the olfactory sense. "As the [olfactory] sensations play an important part in our experiences the idea of an odor organ arose. Its greatest advantage is to blend different odors in exactly given doses." Eduardo Kac has picked up on both Moholy-Nagy's and Hausmann's interest in his *Aromapoetry*, included in the final section of this book (p. 172).

In the theoretical introduction to *Von Material zu Architektur*, Moholy-Nagy writes:

The maxim lies accordingly not in working against [technology], but—if correctly understood—[working with it.] Through technology man can be freed, if he finally realizes—for what purpose.... Only if it is clear to someone that his life must come to crystallization within the community and in turn within the productive system, will he come closer to a true understanding of the meaning of technical progress. For not the form, not the amazing technical process of production, should be our real concern, but rather the sound planning of man's life.... We are faced today with nothing less than the reconquest of the biological foundations. Only when we go back to these can we reach the maximum utilization of technical progress in the fields of physical, nutritional, housing, and working culture—a thoroughgoing rearrangement of our whole scheme of life. Technical progress should never be the goal, but always the means.[47]

Lebensreform rather than technology is the goal. As Sibyl Moholy-Nagy memorably articulated it, "Constructivist hardware was medium, not end."[48] Moholy-Nagy is referring here to his encounter with the ideas of Raoul Heinrich Francé. The latter saw technology, and indeed all human culture, as an outgrowth of the same functional forces that result in natural forms. Having published a profusion of books and articles, Francé was at the height of his fame during the early 1920s.

Moholy-Nagy probably discovered his writings in January 1923, shortly after a crucial chapter from Francé's *Die Pflanze als Erfinder* (Plants as Inventors) was published in the popular Berlin art journal *Das Kunstblatt*. In this chapter Francé outlines his theory that all technology, both human and nonhuman, is comprised of seven basic forms, or Grundformen. Just as humanity was part of "nature," "human technology" was part of natural technology. Francé's naturalization of technology appealed to Moholy-Nagy

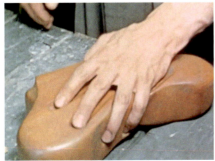

Geometrical and biotechnical elements

Until a short time ago geometrical elements such as the sphere, cone, cylinder, cube, prism, and pyramid were taken as the foundation of sculpture (Figs. 80, 129). But the biotechnical elements now have to be added as a new group available for application. In spite of this the *form concept* of sculpture, the *plastic form,* is understood in this book from the analysis of the stages of plastic development—and not from the application of geometric or biotechnical elements (solids).

The biotechnical elements previously entered more particularly into technical problems, where the functional conception called for the greatest possible economy (pages 60-61). The biologist Raoul Francé has distinguished seven biotechnical constructional elements: crystal, sphere, cone, plate, strip, rod, and spiral (screw), and says that these are the basic technical elements of the whole world. They suffice for all its processes and are sufficient to bring them to their optimum. The constructive application of these elements, in particular the spiral (screw), has led to solutions amazing in their relationship with earlier (baroque) æsthetic principles (Figs. 128, 110, 130, 131, 132, 155, 192).

Today we consciously utilize the whole stock of biotechnical elements, and the outcome is at once a new conception of beauty (Figs. 133-134).

Fig. 128. The seven biotechnical elements: crystal, sphere, cone, plate, strip, rod, and spiral (screw).

Fig. 129. Joost Schmidt, 1928. Some primary elements of sculptural creation.

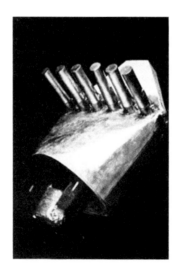

Fig. 16 a, b.
Charles Niedringhaus
(New Bauhaus, second semester, 1938)
"Smell-o-Meter." For mixing six different odors six tubes are used and an electric fan blows the smell into the opening for the nose.

Photo: Niedringhaus

Drawings of "the seven biotechnical elements" of Raoul H. Francé and Joost Schmidt's "primary elements of sculptural creation," in *The New Vision*, 2nd ed., 1938, p. 122.

Fig. 16, in Moholy-Nagy 1938, p. 34.

"Partiturskizze zu einer mechanischen Exzentrik," 1924–25. Bound into László Moholy-Nagy, Farkas Molnár, and Oskar Schlemmer 1925, p. 44.

Sensory Training

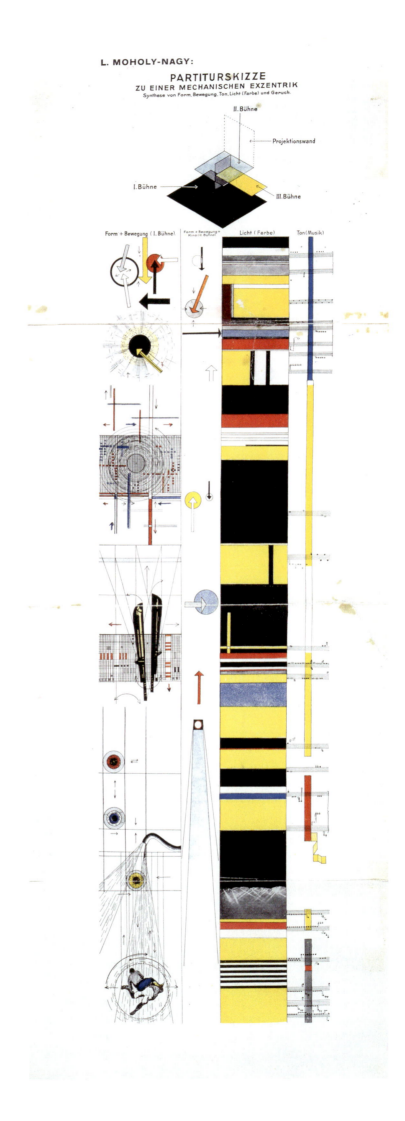

Zweite präsentistische Deklaration

Gerichtet an die internationalen Konstruktivisten

Im ersten präsentistischen Manifest erklärten wir den Aspekt einer Welt, die real ist, eine Synthese des Geistes und der Materie. Wir streben wieder nach der Konformität mit dem mechanischen Arbeitsprozeß. Wir fordern die Erweiterung und Eroberung aller unserer Sinne; wir werden in der Optik weiterschreiten bis zu den Grundphänomenen des Lichtes. Wir sprachen es unzweideutig aus: Unsere Aufgabe ist es, gegen die Allerweltsromantik in ihrer letzten und feinsten Form noch zu kämpfen, wir fordern ein Ende des kleinen Individualistischen und wir erklären, daß wir die Forderung nach einer Erweiterung und Erneuerung der menschlichen Sinnesemanationen nur erheben, weil ihr die Geburt eines unerschrockenen und unhistorischen Menschen in der Klasse der Werktätigen vorausgegangen ist! Und nun wenden wir uns gegen die Deklaration der ungarischen Konstruktivisten im „Egység" und rufen ihnen und den internationalen Konstruktivisten überhaupt zu: Unser Arbeitsgebiet ist weder der Proletkult der kommunistischen Partei, noch das Gebiet des l'art pour l'art! Der Konstruktivismus ist eine Angelegenheit der russischen Malerei und Plastik, die die ideoplastische (gehirnlich-nützliche) Einstellung des Ingenieurs als Spiel mit beliebigem Material nachahmt und damit weit unter der Ingenieursarbeit rangiert, die funktionell und erzieherisch ist. Versuchen wir auch keine intellektuelle Einwirkung auf das Proletariat, bevor wir uns über unsere Rolle als Deklassierte klar geworden sind. Unsere Aufgabe ist es, im Sinne einer universalen Verbindlichkeit an den physikalischen und physiologischen Problemen der Natur und des Menschen zu arbeiten und wir werden unsere Arbeit dort beginnen müssen, wo die moderne Wissenschaft aufhört, weil sie inobjektiv ist, weil sie nur das System der Ausbeutungsfähigkeit verfolgt und fortwährend Standpunkte einnimmt, die einer erledigten Zivilisationsform angehören. Wir haben voraussetzungslos und unvoreingenommen die ersten Schritte einer Naturbetrachtung zu unternehmen, die die Physik und Physiologie auf ihre eigentliche Wirkungsebene bringt, im Sinne einer kommenden klassenlosen Gesellschaft, ohne dabei in Utopismus zu verfallen, und völliger Klarheit über die noch innerhalb der bestehenden Gesellschaftswissenschaft und ihrer Methoden zu leistende Destruktionsarbeit. Wir haben die Zeit eines objektiven und positiven Aufbaues nur vorzubereiten, weil wir aus der Bedingtheit unserer Welt nicht hinaustreten können und wollen.

Unsere sinnesphysiologische und form-funktionell-physikalische Orientierung stellt uns im Gegensatz zu den bisherigen Techniken und Künsten vor die Einsicht, daß kein menschliches Erfahrungs- und Arbeitsgebiet um seiner selbst willen da ist, es ist in jedem ein analytisches Vorgehen im Unterbewußtsein über die Organmängel und Funktionshemmungen der menschlichen Psychophysis gebunden; dieses Tasten muß, in die Bewußtheit gerückt, eine unterste Annäherungs- und Ausgleichsgrenze zur Steigerung der somatischen Funktionalität ergeben. Von hier aus gesehen, ist die Maschine kein Apparat zur bloßen Ökonomisierung der Arbeitsleistung und die Kunst als einziges Produktionsgebiet, auf das das Kausalitätsgesetz keine Anwendung finden kann, trotzdem das Gesetz der Erhaltung der Energie auch dafür gilt, verliert ihren Charakter des Nutzlosen und Abstrakten. Die universale Funktionalität des Menschen verändert die Gesamteinstellung aller Arbeitsgebiete im Sinne erdatmosphärischer Bedingtheit und Notwendigkeit. Hieraus ergibt sich die dynamische Naturanschauung und die allgemeine Erweiterung aller menschlichen Funktionen, eine Anschauungsform wird geschaffen, die sich von der Dreidimensionalität als allzumenschlicher Hilfskonstruktion loslöst, ebenso wie sie die Vorstellung von der Trägheit aller Materie ablehnt. Der Generalnenner aller unserer Sinne ist der Zeit-Raum-Sinn. Die Sprache, der Tanz und die Musik waren Höchstleistungen der intuitiven Zeit-Raum-Funktionalität, und die Optik, Haptik etc. müssen auf einem neuen Wege nachfolgen, für den Ernst Marcus im Problem der exzentrischen Empfindung wichtige Vorarbeit geleistet hat. Das Zentralorgan Gehirn ergänzt gewissermaßen einen Sinn durch den andern, es vervollkommnet jeden durch gegenseitige Schwingungssteigerung unter Zeitübereinstimmung der Größe von Frequenz und Amplitude. Die dynamische Naturanschauung kennt hierfür nur ein Funktionalitätsprinzip der Zeit, die als kinetische Energie Raum und Materie bildet.

V. Eggeling   **R. Hausmann**

Viking Eggeling and Raoul Hausmann, "Second Presentist Declaration: Addressed to the International Constructivists," *MA* 8, nos. 5–6 (March 15, 1923), unpag.

Raoul Hausmann, "PRÉzentizmus. A fajnémet puffkeizmus ellen" (Presentism: Against German Racial Puffkeism), *MA* 7, no. 3 (February 1, 1922), p. 42.

Raoul Hausmann, "Egyetemes szervműködés" (Universal Organ Functioning), *MA* 8, nos. 7–8, (May 1, 1923), unpag.

because it legitimized his innate technophilia. Since human and nonhuman technology share seven basic forms, Francé also proposed that we stand to learn from nonhuman technologies. This concept—which we would now term "bionics"—was promoted by Francé as "Biotechnik" (biotechnology), a notion still in use, though in a slightly different sense. Moholy-Nagy referred to Biotechnik as "a method of creative activity," deployed by his students in making their works. As he writes in *Von Material zu Architektur*, "In all fields of creation workers are striving today to find purely functional solutions of a technical-biological kind: that is, to build up each piece of work solely from the elements which are required for its function."[49]

Sibyl Moholy-Nagy has suggested that Francé's conception of Bios, that is, the empiriocritical idea of the world as the sum total of our sensory perceptions, was a source for Moholy-Nagy's decision to devote himself to teaching: "He accepted the sharing of his life as biological law because it was bios—the interaction of vital impulses, that stimulated man to work for his emotional fulfillment."[50] At the same time, it also influenced Moholy-Nagy's propensity to think in terms of systems. And Francé's conception of Bios entailed a protosystems worldview, related to the Tektologiia (Tectology) of Alexander Bogdanov, who, as mentioned above, was a student of Avenarius. These were two key sources for Moholy-Nagy's fascination with systems.

As has already been suggested, Raoul Hausmann was a principal force in the development of Moholy-Nagy's sensorial views. Hausmann, like Hannah Höch, his girlfriend at the time (and also a close friend of Moholy-Nagy), participated in the birth of photomontage, and the couple theorized and practiced dance, fashion, sound poetry, photography, and music as well as science. They were early adherents of interdisciplinary artistic practices and, after meeting Moholy-Nagy in 1920, became crucial to the expansion of his conception of what might interest an artist, and how an artist might pursue such interests. Hausmann's enthusiasm for outré natural scientific theories, such as Ernst Marcus's empiriocritical-based theory of "eccentric perception" (which holds that rather than "experiencing" nature through our senses, we actually constitute nature through our sensorium), merely throws Hausmann's remarkable achievements into high relief.

As early as 1921 Moholy-Nagy, along with Hans Arp, Ivan Puni, and Hausmann, signed the "Aufruf zur Elementaren Kunst" (Call to Elementary Art), drafted by Hausmann.[51] When Moholy-Nagy became the Berlin correspondent for Lajos Kassák's Hungarian avant-garde journal *MA* (Today) in 1921, he began forwarding Kassák articles by Hausmann that dealt with the senses and their expansion. Particularly when considered

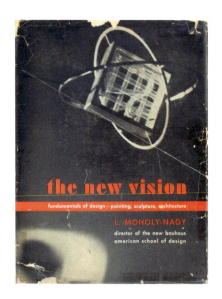

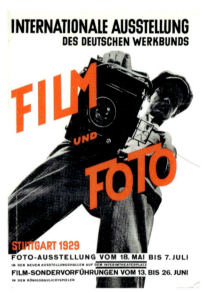

in conjunction with Marinetti's "Tactilist" manifesto (*MA*, June 1, 1921), this series of texts—"PRÉzentizmus" (Presentism, *MA*, February 1, 1922),[52] "Optofonetika" (Optophonetics, *MA*, October, 15, 1922), "Zweite präsentistische Deklaration. Gerichtet an die internationalen Konstruktivisten" (Second presentist declaration, addressed to the International Constructivists, *MA*, March 15, 1923) and "Egyetemes szervműködés" (Universal organ functioning, *MA*, May 1, 1923)—constitutes one of the most remarkable corpuses of writing on sensory education and sensory expansion in 1920s' avant-garde literature.

Hausmann's optophonetics and his life-long engagement with the expansion of perception signified more than its usual definition of the translatability of light into sound energy, expressing instead a general concern with perception. Indeed, Hausmann wrote of an "optophonetische Weltanschauung" (optophonetic worldview) in 1922, viewing this as a basic component in a new way of experiencing the world.[53] In his article "Universal Organ Functioning" he even called for a "recalibration and expansion of the human *physis*," as Arndt Niebisch phrased it: a complete renewal of the human body on the basis of this Weltanschauung. In later chapters we shall consider in more detail the ways in which Hausmann's ideas seeded Moholy-Nagy's imagination.

While we have focused here on the tactile (with an excursion into the olfactory), it was visuality that dominated Moholy-Nagy's thinking and artistic production, with photography and film playing a crucial role in this context. Moholy-Nagy was highly critical of the way in which art photography was practiced when he began taking pictures in the mid-1920s. His book *Painting, Photography, Film* contained only one reproduction by a recognized art photographer in the entire volume: a 1911 streetscape of Paris by the German-American Alfred Stieglitz. The caption for this photograph reads "The Triumph of Impressionism or photography misunderstood. The photographer has become a painter instead of using his camera **photographically**." There is irony, rather than sarcasm, in this critique, for it was Stieglitz who pioneered the new style of post-Pictorialist, sharp-focused photography, and it was he who, a few years later, championed the work of Paul Strand, the first practitioner of the photographic style Moholy-Nagy later pursued. In *Vision in Motion* Moholy-Nagy tried to atone for his faux-pas by reproducing Stieglitz's proto-Modernist masterpiece *The Steerage* (1907), captioning it: "Alfred Stieglitz is the great pioneer of contemporary photography. His work and his integrity are already a matter of history."[54]

As indicated above, Moholy-Nagy's main critique in respect of contemporary art photography was that the camera's technical capabilities were not being used to the full by photographers eager to emulate painting. Rather than looking to art photographers, Moholy-Nagy therefore examined, as a model for artists, the ways in which scientists, criminologists, documentary photographers, X-ray technicians—anyone but "photographers"—deployed the camera. "The photographic apparatus has provided us with surprising possibilities which we are only now beginning to evaluate. These optical surprises latent in photographic procedure become available to us very often through objective 'nonartistic' pictures taken by scientists, ethnographers, etc."[55]

Moholy-Nagy did not stop at suggesting that the technical capabilities of the still and film camera should be exploited to the full. He proposed that any and all imaging equipment be enlisted in this quest. Though his suggestion that scientific imaging equipment be used for aesthetic ends[56] was grounded in a long amateur photography tradition, he was the first interwar artist to suggest using such equipment to make art—a notion that contributed significantly to the emergence of photomicrography, telescopy, and radiography as art in the 1920s.[57] These ideas were articulated as part of a proposal to reconfigure contemporary photographic and cinematic practice, which came to be known as Neues Sehen (New Vision) and comprised Europe's contribution to the New Photography and Film, in conjunction with the related photography and film of Neue Sachlichkeit (New Objectivity).[58] More than anyone else, it was Moholy-Nagy who established the stylistic and theoretical parameters for New Vision in Weimar Germany. He achieved this by describing the trend and through both his publications and his influence on leading New Vision journals of the day, such as the Dutch *i10* and the German photography annual *Das deutsche Lichtbild*, as well as by his involvement with influential New Vision exhibitions, such as *Neue Wege der Photografie* at the Kunstverein Jena in 1928 and the 1929 *Film und Foto* exhibition in Stuttgart.[59]

the new vision, 1938. Cover design by Moholy-Nagy employing a photograph with a detail of his mobile sculpture *Gyros* from 1936.

Poster for the exhibition *Film und Foto*, Stuttgart, 1929. Designer unknown.

Invitation to the opening of the exhibition *Neue Wege der Photographie* (New Paths of Photography), Kunstverein, Jena, 1928. Design by Walter Dexel.

Masthead for *i10*, vol. 1, no. 1 (1927).

Sensory Training

Photographers and filmmakers, in Moholy-Nagy's view, must play with the apparatus, varying focal length, sharpness, tonality, point of view, and so on, yet must do so without any preconceived aesthetic notions, such as emulating painting, prints, or theatrical productions. "The enemy of photography is the convention, the fixed rules of the 'how to do.' The salvation of photography comes from the experiment. The experimenter has no preconceived notions about photography."[60] In his introduction to *telehor*, Sigfried Giedion remembers Moholy-Nagy lying on the ground and pointing his camera upward from the ground and straight downward from a balcony during a joint vacation at Belle-Île-en-Mer in 1925, shortly after Moholy-Nagy began to use a camera.[61] Moholy-Nagy's obsession with novel viewpoints and visual qualities was part of his effort to "educate" vision. When people encountered these images or film sequences depicting the world from new points of view, their vision could literally be altered. Andreas Haus argues that "Moholy's creative procedures contain a critique of traditional ways of perception which cannot any longer cope with the bourgeois environment or which, defeated by its misleading logic, freeze the perceiver into passivity and a creative impotence."[62] Herbert Molderings takes a similar position, employing the example of Moholy-Nagy's photograph from the Berlin Radio Tower (p. 37), which was printed as a reverse (negative) image, to argue that "The combination of the pseudo-X-ray effect with the steep view from above results in the tower's structure becoming unrecognizable at first glance. Instead of perceiving what the photograph reproduces in a passive fashion, the image incites the viewer to mentally alter the shapes into recognizable forms. Thus, seeing becomes a more difficult, a slower and thereby a more conscious process."[63]

In this regard Moholy-Nagy's major inspiration was again Hausmann and his psychobiological attempt, inspired by Ernst Marcus, to bring about a radical reform of sensory experience. As Hausmann wrote in an unpublished text from 1921: "The dead mechanism of our Newton-determined vision, is neither vision nor perception—it is

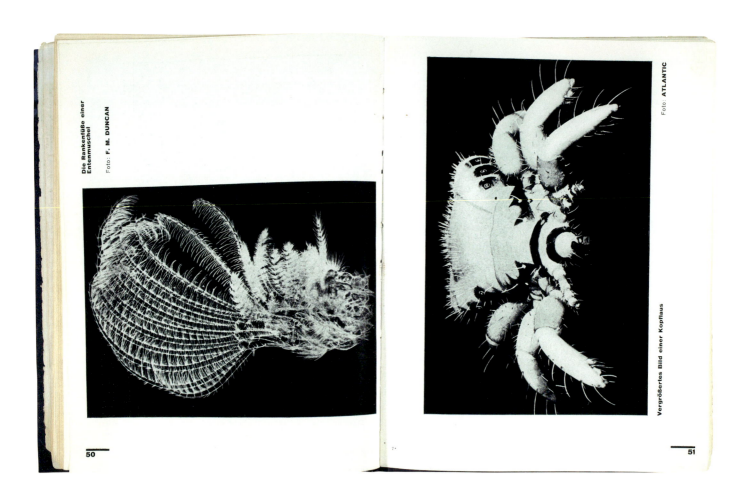

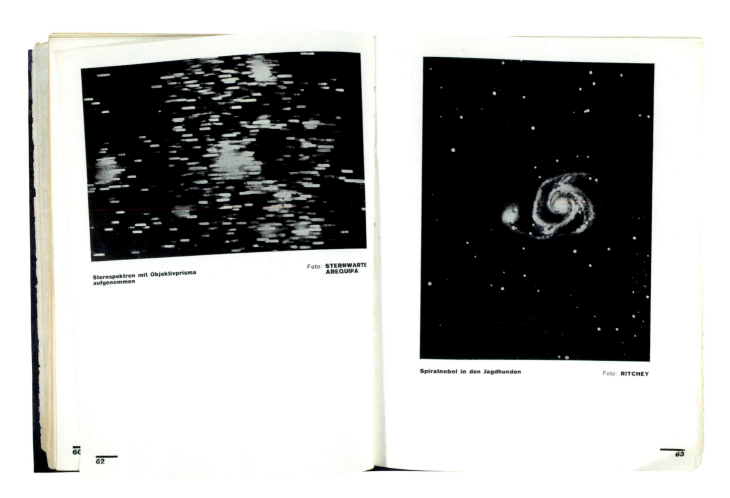

Spreads from Moholy-Nagy 1925, demonstrating the capabilities of the camera. Cirrus feet of a barnacle, and enlarged photograph of a head louse, pp. 50–51; star spectra photographed with prismatic lens, p. 62. X-ray photographs of hands and X-ray photographs of a frog, pp. 66–67; Charlotte Rudolf, Palucca and Racing Tempo Immobilized, pp. 52–53.

AUFNAHMEPROBEN Röntgenfoto: **AGFA**

Aus dem Buch:
Einführung in die Röntgenfotografie
von Dr. phil. John Eggert.

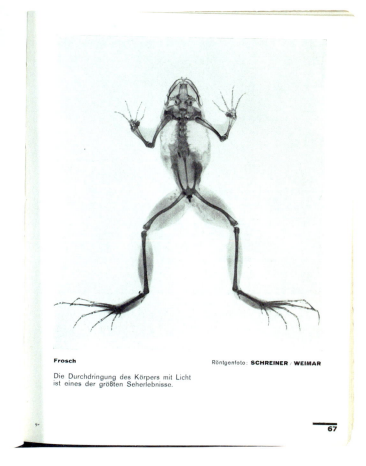

Frosch Röntgenfoto: **SCHREINER / WEIMAR**

Die Durchdringung des Körpers mit Licht
ist eines der größten Seherlebnisse.

Palucca Foto: **CHARLOTTE RUDOLF, DRESDEN**

Foto: **ATLANTIC**

Renntempo gebannt

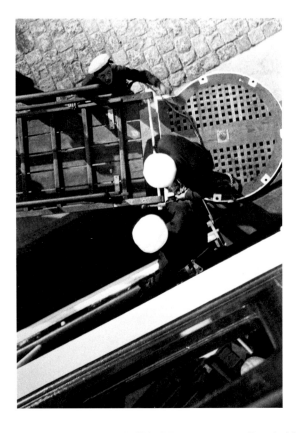

Untitled (Eiffel Tower), 1924–27. 23.3 × 17.5 cm.

Radio Tower Berlin, ca. 1928. 24.5 × 18.5 cm.

Gangplank from above, 1930. 25.2 × 20.2 cm.

Bauhaus balconies in Dessau (Lou Scheper on an Atelierhaus balcony, Bauhaus, Dessau), 1927. 38.3 × 29 cm.

View from the Berlin Radio Tower, ca. 1928. Reversed and positive gelatin silver prints, 28 × 20.5 cm.

Footprints, n.d., vintage gelatin silver print, 25.3 × 20.6 cm.

a simple division of living-dynamic appearance into mere rubricated classes, categories, and concepts." Hausmann's conclusion—"No, we are not and we do not want to be: the photographers!"—was based on an outmoded view of photography as mere Wahrnehmung (perception); in contrast, Moholy-Nagy decided to employ photography— and film—precisely as the principal means to bring about a revolution of vision.[64] Hausmann would eventually come around to this position as well and indeed produced a remarkable corpus of New Vision photography. In this instance, it was he who followed in Moholy-Nagy's footsteps.[65]

Standing at Schwarzerden, then, what was Moholy-Nagy thinking about when the frontispiece photograph (p. 1) was taken? Perhaps he was musing that, when he raised his eyes after the Körperlehre session, he might see the world in an entirely new way.

Film stills from *Impressions from the Old Port of Marseilles (Vieux Port), Metropolitan Gypsies* and *Berlin Still Life*, Germany, 1932–33. 35 mm, black and white, silent.

DE STIJL

MAANDBLAD VOOR NIEUWE KUNST, WETENSCHAP EN KULTUUR. REDACTIE: THEO VAN DOESBURG. ABONNEMENT BINNENLAND F 6.-, BUITENLAND F 7.50 PER JAARGANG. ADRES VAN REDACTIE EN ADMINISTR. KLIMOPSTRAAT 18 'SGRAVENHAGE (HOLLAND).

5e JAARGANG No. 7.   JULI 1922

PERI (HONGARIJE)   RUIMTECONSTRUCTIE 2

L. MOHOLY-NAGY
PRODUKTION – REPRODUKTION

Wenn wir die menschliche Ausdrucks- und Formungsweise in der Kunst und den ihr naheliegenden anderen (Gestaltungs-) Gebieten richtig verstehen und zu einem Weiterbau kommen wollen, müssen wir die erfüllenden Faktoren: den Menschen selbst und die in seiner gestaltenden Tätigkeit von ihm angewandten Mittel untersuchen.

Der Aufbau des Menschen ist die Synthese aller seiner Funktionsapparate, d. h. daß der Mensch in seiner Periode dann der vollkommenste ist, wenn die ihn ausmachenden Funktionsapparate — die Zellen ebenso wie die kompliziertesten Organe — bis zur Grenze ihrer Leistungsfähigkeit bewußt bezw. ausgebildet sind.

Die Kunst bewirkt diese Ausbildung — und das ist eine ihrer wichtigsten Aufgaben, da von der Vollkommenheit des Aufnahmeorgans der ganze Wirkungskomplex abhängt — in dem sie zwischen den bekannten und den noch unbekannten optischen, akustischen und anderen funktionellen Erscheinungen weitgehendste neue Beziehungen herzustellen versucht und deren Aufnahme von den Funktionsapparaten erzwingt. Es liegt in der menschlichen Eigenart, daß die Funktionsapparate nie zu sättigen sind, sondern nach jeder neuen Aufnahme zu weiteren neuen Eindrücken drängen. Das ist die Ursache der immer bleibenden Notwendigkeit neuer Gestaltungsversuche. Unter diesem Aspekt sind die Gestaltungen nur dann zunutze, wenn sie neue, bisher unbekannte Relationen produzieren. Damit ist gesagt, daß die Reproduktion (Wiederholung bereits existierender Relationen) aus dem besonderen Gesichtspunkt der Gestaltung im besten Falle nur als virtuose Angelegenheit zu betrachten ist.

Da vor allem die Produktion (produktive Gestaltung) dem menschlichen Aufbau dient, müssen wir versuchen, die bisher nur für Reproduktionszwecke angewandten

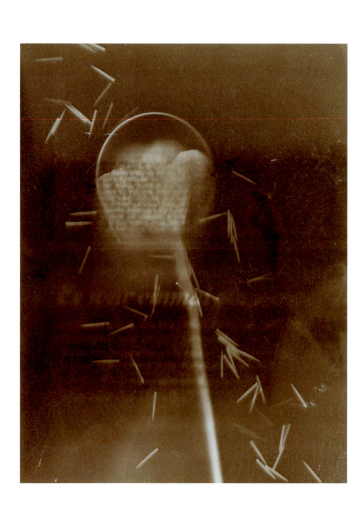

Production–Reproduction

In July 1922 a remarkable article was published in the Dutch journal *De Stijl* under the – at the time – provocatively unartistic title "Production–Reproduction." At first glance reminiscent of a text concerning industrial output or the technical requirements of the printing industry, the article was unusual, even for an art journal as eclectic and avant-garde as *De Stijl*. Its contents, as Andreas Haus has pointed out, reflected an awareness of a tradition of thinking about art from a biologistic standpoint: the empiriocritical tradition of Richard Avenarius, Ernst Mach, and Robert Müller-Freienfels.[1] As is evident from the chapter "Sensory Training," it is this tradition that Moholy-Nagy absorbed through the work of Alexander Bogdanov, Raoul Francé, and Raoul Hausmann. Rather than art per se, the article seemed more concerned with human sensory capabilities and their biological requirements, and reflected the empiriocritical theory of the body constituted as a perceiving system. "Production–Reproduction" goes on to suggest deploying equipment normally used in *re*production, such as wax gramophone plates and light-sensitive photographic paper, for original artistic *pro*duction. The article was heavily edited, if not partly written, by Moholy-Nagy's first wife, Lucia Moholy, and represented the first of many texts in which Moholy-Nagy called for sensory training in artistic education.

The gist of the argument in "Production–Reproduction" is that since our sensory organs "are never sated, but rather crave ever new impressions following each new reception," and since art trains us to use our sensory organs to their fullest capacity, "creative activities are useful only if they produce new, as-yet-unknown relations." This is where the argument takes an interesting twist: since "it is primarily productive creation that serves human [physical and sensory] development, we must seek to expand the use of apparatuses (means) used so far only for reproductive purposes to productive purposes as well." Innovation, aesthetic originality, Moholy-Nagy says, is a biological necessity in order to train the sensory organs to their utmost capacity; it is artists' responsibility to find ways to sate our biological need for ever-new sensory inputs by using whatever technology is available to bring about ever-new relations. He suggests that we examine various apparatuses and technical tools and ask ourselves, "What

"Produktion – Reproduktion," and László Péri, *Raumkonstruktion III* (mistakenly indicated as *Ruimteconstructie 2*), *De Stijl* 5, no. 7 (July 1922).

Untitled, 1923–24. Photogram on gaslight paper (?), 23.8 × 17.9 cm.

Photograph of Enrico Caruso's high "C" as recorded on a record, in Moholy-Nagy 1929, p. 46. Microphotography by Lettehaus.

Untitled, 1923–25. Photogram on developing paper, 12.1 × 12.8 cm. National Gallery of Canada, Ottawa. Purchased from the Phyllis Lambert Fund, 1982. Photo © NGC © Estate of Laszlo Moholy-Nagy / SODRAC (2014).

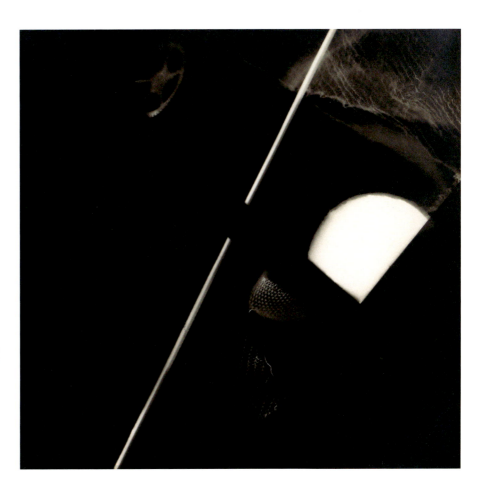

is it used for? What is the nature of its function? Is it amenable to expanding [the use of] the apparatus so that it can also be employed productively, and is it worth doing this?" His proposal is to submit two "reproductive" technologies to interrogation: the phonograph and the photograph—both still photography and film. This sounds like a decidedly unusual media pairing, though Moholy-Nagy manages to capture it in an intriguing photogram that seems to have been made by sprinkling a rose with gramophone needles (see p. 40).²

Starkly biologistic and functionalist, based on a certain understanding of positivistic scientific theory, proposing laboratory research and tinkering rather than artistic inspiration and creation, "Production-Reproduction" was self-consciously anti-Expressionistic and anti-Romantic. Its cool and rational focus was particularly unexpected because it was the combined brainchild of a former Expressionist artist and a member of the Jugendbewegung. Though it was not meant to be Dadaistic, the alliterative pairings of "production/reproduction" and "gramophone/photograph," only emphasized the antipoetic and therefore provocative nature of the text.

For the record player, the proposition is that artists (composers) should use experimental laboratory research to develop a "groove script" to systematize the types of sounds that could be produced. Varying the length, width, depth, etc., of the incisions into the wax (master) disks would produce "new, hitherto nonexistent sounds and tonal relationships" that might then be used in musical composition. Moholy-Nagy's proposal in the realm of still photography is that the bromide silver plates used to capture scenes in the world, mediated by a camera lens, should be exposed to light directly using mirror or lens devices that produce Lichtspielen. Capturing such "moments of light play" on the plate is the goal. Finally, in the field of film, Moholy-Nagy proposes finding the technical means to record the Lichtspiel directly onto light-sensitive film, presumably without the use of a lens. His goal here is an abstract film that in effect "records" the play of light, and when he did make a film employing this strategy, it was conceived in connection with the idea of the photogram. In the early 1930s he wrote that his film *Lichtspiel Schwarz Weiss Grau* (Lightplay Black White Grey) "was made to demonstrate two things: the surprising black-white tonalities of the photogram … in continuous movement and the resulting possibilities with movement and light…."³ The question of how this is to be done without deploying a camera lens is not addressed. However, his proposal for the "productive" use of the camera's "reproductive" capacities falls flat if a camera is used, for example to record the light play of an artist such as Thomas Wilfred or of his own Light Prop for an Electric Stage (1930). On closer examination, this difficulty also applies to the photogram, where he is, after all, suggesting the recording, that is, the reproduction of moments of light play. As Gabriele Jutz points out in her article on this manifesto, Moholy-Nagy seems to have been unaware of the tradition of painting directly onto film (dating back to the early 1910s), which would have been more analogous to incising directly into the wax plate of a record than to recording light projections using a camera.⁴ Of course Moholy-Nagy's mind was not, at this point, on painting onto film, but rather on employing the play of light in creating art. The idea of light play, particularly aerial light shows, derived from Raoul Hausmann's writings of the time, though Moholy-Nagy translated Hausmann's Dadaistic bombast into the cool language of the technician-artist.⁵

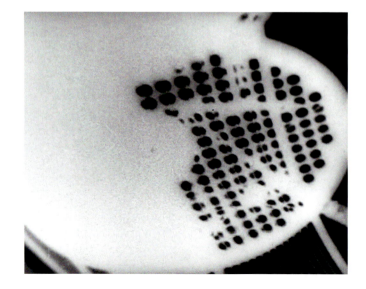

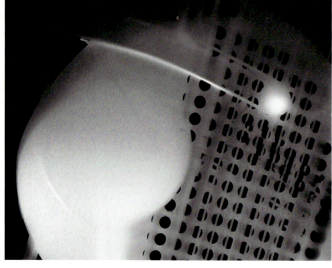

Production–Reproduction

Theoretical problems aside, these suggestions launched initiatives on Moholy-Nagy's part that resulted in his enormous corpus of photograms, now considered one of the most important aspects of his artistic production. It also stimulated the development of a device that could produce light effects mechanically (rather than, for example, by the artist working with light-sensitive paper in a darkroom), as well as a process of experimentation with sound production using both wax plates and subsequently sound film, and, finally, the production of his film *Lightplay Black White Grey*, now considered a classic of experimental cinema. In the 2000s Floris Neusüss and Renate Heyne set out to test Moholy-Nagy's idea and to use the Light Prop (or rather, a replica of it) to make photograms that would capture a moment of light play. This was not easy to achieve. The results, both in black-and-white and in color, are, however, stunning (p. 176).

We have seen in "Sensory Training" that the source of the physiological pedagogy behind "Production-Reproduction" lay in Moholy-Nagy and Lucia Moholy's experiences with the Freideutsche Jugend (Free German Youth) and the Lebensreformbewegung (Life Reform Movement). Their understanding of this cause evolved in particular from the pedagogical concepts applied in women's communes that the couple frequented during vacations in central Germany's Rhön Mountains. In July–August 1922, the Moholy-Nagys spent their summer break near the Loheland women's commune, and it turned out to be an important learning experience for both of them. As Lucia recalled, "During a stroll in the Rhön Mountains in the summer of 1922 we discussed the problems arising from the antithesis Production versus Reproduction. This gradually led us to implement our conclusions by making photograms, having had no previous knowledge of any steps taken by Schad, Man Ray and Lissitzky."[6] Moholy-Nagy alludes to a Loheländerin (a woman from Loheland) who introduced him to the technique.[7] This would have been Bertha Günther, an early member of the Loheland group, who made photograms of petals, leaves, flowers, and other organic material between 1920 and 1922.[8] Günther's delicate photograms are beautiful examples of this medium, reflecting a long tradition of amateur production.[9] Moholy-Nagy was impressed by the seemingly infinite range of tones that resulted from the simple process of light falling onto light-sensitive paper modulated by organic material. His own oeuvre in this medium, which he began in Berlin after the aforementioned 1922 holiday, gave rise to luminous works of art, which initially repeated the formal geometric strategies he articulated in his paintings and linocuts. Very soon Moholy-Nagy realized that the photogram's black ground, which resulted from placing translucent objects, materials, and fluids onto the light-sensitive paper, succeeded in conveying, much more than his paintings ever could, a more powerful sense of limitlessness, and therefore of the impression that the "constructions," as he described lighter-toned assemblages, were floating in this space. Indeed, it is possible that the paintings thematizing transparent planes of color on dark grounds, which his student Franciska Clausen observed him working on late in 1922, were inspired by these experiments with the photogram process. In any case, the resulting photograms became less "composed"

Bertha Günther, untitled (leaves and blossoms), n.d. (ca. 1920–22). Photogram on printing-out paper; paper: 17 × 12.3 cm, image: 14 × 9.5 cm.

Untitled, n.d. (ca. 1923–25). Photogram on gaslight paper (?), 23.8 × 17.9 cm.

Frame from a shadow sequence (reversed tonality), *Lightplay Black White Grey*, Germany, 1932. 35 mm, black and white, silent, ca. 5'30" (left). Floris Neusüss and Renate Heyne, Untitled, 2005. Photogram made with László Moholy-Nagy's Light Prop at Bauhaus Archiv, 50 × 50 cm (right).

Untitled, 1922. Photogram on daylight printing-out paper, 14 × 8.9 cm.

Untitled, 1925–28. Photogram on developing paper, 23.2 × 17.9 cm.

than his paintings and linocuts, more free-flowing. Following Günther's example, Moholy-Nagy experimented with laying flowers on the light-sensitive paper, resulting in beautiful photograms, probably made (judging by the size of the paper) after he was hired by the Bauhaus the following March.[10]

In 1935 Moholy-Nagy recalled that "In the autumn of 1922 Harold Loeb and Matthew Josephson, the editors ... of *Broom* came to visit me to ask for the right to publish my photographs and they told me that an American photographer Man Ray, of whom I had not heard until then, was also producing photograms.... I presented them both with an article about light as a creative element of manipulation and in the March 1923 issue of *Broom* they published four of my photograms and four by Man Ray together with my article."[11] Moholy-Nagy was also asked to produce a cover design for this issue of *Broom* but, although he made a series of these designs, none were used. The resulting article, "Light: A Medium of Plastic Expression," addressed both photography and photograms, and this publication, his first in English, launched Moholy-Nagy's career as a master of the new medium of the photogram and as a photographic theorist.

The article begins with what is in effect a sweeping dismissal of all artistic photography up to that point. This is followed by a witty argument for abstract photography in which the common justification for abstract art, one he himself would soon adopt (namely the notion that the camera's ability to reproduce the visible world with perfect perspective renders the painter's task of doing so obsolete) is deftly turned on its head:

Since the discovery of photography virtually nothing has been found as far as the principles and technique of the process are concerned. All innovations are based on the esthetic representative conceptions existing in Daguerre's time (about 1830), although these conceptions, i.e., the copying of nature by means of the photographic camera and the mechanical reproduction of perspective, have been rendered obsolete by the work of modern artists.[12]

He goes on to make the point that "optical phenomena perceived by the eye" are converted "into a comprehensible whole" by the intellect. The mind is not a mere screen onto which the lens of the eye projects the world, but rather a creative organ that structures our sight. The photographic camera, on the other hand, "reproduces only the purely optical picture (distortion, bad drawing, foreshortening)," and can therefore perform a useful function, for example in scientific research and other applied fields. These are kernels of the thinking that would comprise his theory of "New Vision" when his first book *Malerei, Photographie, Film* (Painting, Photography, Film) appeared in 1925.

Moholy-Nagy does go beyond discussing camera photography. His assertion of the photogram's legitimacy elaborates on the (questionable) argument made previously in "Production-Reproduction":

Despite the obvious fact that the sensitivity to light of a chemically prepared surface ... was the most important element in the photographic process ... the sensitized surface was always subjected to the demands of a camera obscura adjusted to the

Documentary photograph of László Moholy-Nagy's exhibition at the Galerie Neue Kunst Fides, Dresden, 1926.

Untitled, 1923–25. Photogram on gaslight paper (?), 17 × 12.3 cm.

Construction, 1924. Oil on canvas, 78 × 66 cm.

"Light: A Medium of Plastic Expression," in *Broom* 4, no. 4 (March 1923), pp. 283–84.

Cover design for *Broom* 4, no. 4 (March 1923), n.d. (late 1922). Photogram on daylight printing-out paper, mounted on cardboard, 18 × 13 cm.

L. Moholy-Nagy

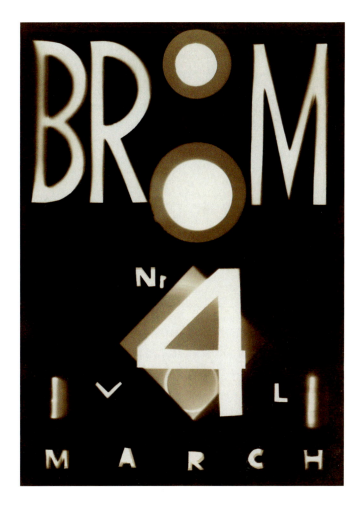

air. Afterwards we emerged to the glare of the logical arclights of the Boulevard de Strasbourg. . . .

I almost forgot. *Locus Solus* had a finale which swept me off my feet. Under the sea, the sea being represented by a gauze curtain dropped across the stage. Everything was quite unrelated: fishes moved back and forth, two sea monsters drew a chariot which was symbolic of nothing, a mermaid sang on a sort of throne, a young man in a bathing suit performed an obscene dance and, somewhere in a corner, a little girl in conventional beach costume was playing, oblivious of the mermaid, the fishes, the sea monsters, the obscene dance. There was something magnificent in the pointlessness of the scene; something daily, familiar, unobserved: it was a little world, our world perhaps, existing over the footlights, under the sea. The curtain fell.

MALCOLM COWLEY

LIGHT: A MEDIUM OF PLASTIC EXPRESSION.

Since the discovery of photography virtually nothing new has been found as far as the principles and technique of the process are concerned. All innovations are based on the aesthetic representative conceptions existing in Daguerre's time (about 1830), although these conceptions, i. e. the copying of nature by means of the photographic camera and the mechanical reproduction of perspective, have been rendered obsolete by the work of modern artists.

Despite the obvious fact that the *sensitivity to light* of a chemically prepared surface (of glass, metal, paper, etc.) was the most important element in the photographic process, i. e., containing its own laws, the sensitized surface was always subjected to the demands of a *camera obscura* adjusted to the traditional laws of perspective while the full possibilities of this combination were never sufficiently tested.

The proper utilization of the plate itself would have brought to light phenomena imperceptible to the human eye and made visible only by means of the photographic apparatus thus perfecting the eye by means of photography. True, this principle has already been applied in certain scientific experiments, as in the study of motion (walking, leaping, galloping) and zoological and mineral forms, but these have always been isolated efforts whose results could not be compared or related.

It must be noted here that our intellectual experience complements spatially and formally the optical phenomena perceived by the eye and renders them into a comprehensible whole, whereas the photographic apparatus reproduces the purely optical picture (distortion, bad drawing, foreshortening).

One way of exploring this field is to investigate and apply various chemical mixtures which produce light effects, imperceptible to the eye, (such as electro-magnetic rays, x-rays).

Another way is by the construction of new apparatus, first by the use of the *camera obscura*, second, by the elimination of perspective. In the first case using apparatus with lenses and mirror-arrangements which can cover their environment from all sides; in the second case, using an apparatus which is based on new optical laws. This last leads to the possibility of "light-composition," whereby light would be controlled as a new plastic medium, just as color in painting and tone in music.

This signifies a perfectly new medium of expression whose novelty offers an undreamed of scope. The possibilities of this medium of composition become greater as we proceed from static representation to the motion-pictures of the cinematograph.

I have made a few primitive attempts in this direction, whose initial results, however, point to the most positive discoveries (and as soon as these attempts can be tested experimentally in a laboratory especially devised for the purpose, the results are certain to be far more impressive).

Instead of having a plate which is sensitive to light react mechanically to its environment through the reflection or absorption of light, I have attempted to *control* its action by means of lenses and mirrors, by light passed through fluids like water, oil, acids, and crystal, metal, glass, tissue, etc. This means that the filtered, reflected or refracted light is directed upon a screen and then photographed. Or again, the light-effect can be thrown directly on the sensitive plate itself, instead of upon a screen. (Photography without apparatus.) Since these light effects almost always show themselves in motion, it is clear that the process reaches its highest development in the film.

L. MOHOLY-NAGY

Printed by Rich. Labisch & Co., Graphische Kunstanstalt G. m. b. H., Berlin (Germany)

traditional laws of perspective while the full possibilities of this combination were never sufficiently tested.[13]

In order to exploit these technical capabilities, he revisits his proposal for the construction of apparatuses that produce light effects, employing, for the first time, his expression *Lichtgestaltung* (light-composition). This, he says, "signifies a perfectly new medium of expression whose novelty offers an undreamed of [sic] scope."[14] He invokes film again, continuing:

The possibilities of this medium of composition become greater as we proceed from static representation to … the cinematograph. I have made a few primitive attempts in this direction.… Instead of [making photograms], I have attempted to control [the] action [of light] by means of lenses and mirrors, by light passed through fluids like water, oil, acids, crystal, metal, glass, tissue, etc. This means that the filtered, reflected or refracted light is directed upon a screen and then photographed.… Since these light effects almost always show themselves in motion, it is clear that the process reaches its highest development in the film.

The results of these experiments seem not to have survived, and, in any case, he underlines the necessity for more "laboratory" research.

Shortly after the appearance of the *Broom* article, *Der Sturm* published "Neue Gestaltung in der Musik. Möglichkeiten des Grammophons" (New Composition in Music: Potentialities of the Phonograph); this was the essay Moholy-Nagy wrote during summer of 1922, delineating his ideas about direct manipulation of wax recording plates to produce sound.[15] A still life by Clausen from late 1922 of a corner of Moholy-Nagy's studio documents the presence of an 78 rpm record. Her decision to feature the record disk is an indication of its salience to Moholy-Nagy's concerns at the time. These articles, and his other theoretical writings of 1922–1924 (including "Production-Reproduction" and "From Painting with Pigment to Design Achieved with Projected Coloured Light")[16] would culminate in the publication of *Painting, Photography, Film*, which was "assembled"–according to a note on page four–during summer of 1924, and therefore in Neuwart, near the Schwarzerden and Loheland communes. The book – as he added in the note, its publication was delayed because of unspecified "technical difficulties"–appeared in 1925 as the eighth in the Bauhausbücher series, and would consolidate Moholy-Nagy's reputation as a media theorist.

Just as he expanded on the themes of photography and film in "Light: A New Medium of Plastic Expression," Moholy-Nagy expanded on the ideas of sound production previously expressed in "Production-Reproduction" in yet another article, "New Composition in Music," published in the July 7, 1923, issue of *Der Sturm*. He begins the article by acknowledging the pioneering importance of Futurist experiments in Bruitist (noise) music, and Piet Mondrian's call (in a *De Stijl* article) for a new kind of music that balances natural energies. Once again, he makes outrageous claims: "1. By establishing a groove-script alphabet a comprehensive instrument is created that renders all instruments used so far superfluous." He calls for a new "mechanical harmonic scale" recorded using a new system of graphic symbols. He points out

Franz Roh, *60 Fotos* Design by Jan Tschichold, Berlin: Klinkhard and Biermann, 1930. Using a photogram by László Moholy-Nagy, of 1923–25 (Edwynn Houk Gallery, New York).

vision in motion, 1947. Design by Moholy-Nagy, using a photogram of 1939–43 (present location unknown).

Will Grohmann, *Die Sammlung Ida Bienert*, Potsdam: Müller & Kiepenheuer, 1932/33. Design by László Moholy-Nagy.

"Neue Gestaltung in der Musik. Möglichkeiten des Grammophons," in *Der Sturm* 14, no. 7 (July 1923), p. 102.

Franciska Clausen, *Grammofonplatte* (Gramophone Record, scene in Moholy-Nagy's Berlin studio), January–March 1923. Oil on cardboard, 38 × 48.5 cm.

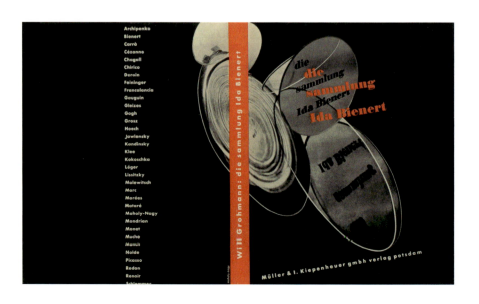

Production–Reproduction

Neue Gestaltung in der Musik
Möglichkeiten des Grammophons
L. Moholy-Nagy

Unter den heutigen musikalischen Versuchen spielen die Untersuchungen mit den Verstärkeröhren, welche einen neuen Weg in der Herstellung aller akustischen Erscheinungen ermöglichen, eine grosse Rolle. Die Bestrebungen der italienischen Bruitisten, neue Instrumente mit neuer Tonbildung zu konstruieren, sind durch die Versuche mit der Verstärkeröhre als Einheitsinstrument, mit dem alle Arten akustischer Phänomene erzeugbar sind, im weitesten Masse erfüllt. Aber mit dieser Möglichkeit allein ist nicht alles erschöpft, was für die Umgestaltung der Musik zu erwarten wäre. Ich weise auf den ausgezeichneten Artikel von P. Mondrian: Die neue Gestaltung in der Musik und die italienischen Bruitisten (De Stijl) hin, worin er die Grundlagen zur Erneuerung der Tongestaltung analysiert.

that this is advantageous as the "composer can create his composition playback-ready" and is thus not "dependent on the complete knowledge of the interpretive artist," and finally states that "the introduction of this system of musical performance will also facilitate ... independence from large orchestral enterprises and the wide distribution of the creative original...." His wide-ranging suggestions for practical introduction and creative use of the technique include the notion that photomechanical processes could reduce to playback size the large-scale wax plate needed to manipulate the grooves, along with proposals to investigate "mechanical, metallic, and mineral" sounds, explore "improvisation on the wax plate" in place of composition, and use projectors and film.

Moholy-Nagy was eager to begin experimentation and, as he later recalled, early in 1923 "I won George Antheil and H. H. Stuckenschmidt over to my ideas. The Vox-Gesellschaft ... even agreed to make their Experimental Laboratory available to me. Unfortunately, however, it did not come to this. At the time I was called to the Bauhaus to teach and Antheil moved to Paris [June 1923]...."[17] Stuckenschmidt gives an intriguing account of their experimentation at the studios of the Vox-Gesellschaft in Berlin:

We experimented together, played [the records] backwards, which ... produced astonishing effects. We scratched them side-ways, so that the needle no longer traced regularly, but rather made strange noises and produced grotesque glissandi. We even scratched into the grooves with fine needles, and in doing so, produced rhythmic patterns and sounds, which changed the meaning of music radically. Moholy-Nagy felt that one could bore into the blank grooves directly with needles, and in doing so, realize authentic record music.[18] In an article in *MA*, Stuckenschmidt restates some of the ideas first expressed by Moholy-Nagy in "New Composition in Music: Potentialities of the Phonograph."[19] In particular, he focuses on the superfluity of performance once composers start working directly onto the "recording" medium, a development Stuckenschmidt sees as relegating musical instruments to the "display cases of museums of antiquities" in the "foreseeable future." In a clear reference to Moholy-Nagy he adds, "today, a number of important modern artists are concerned with investigating the possibility of incising authentic tones into the phonographic disk."[20] In turn, when Stuckenschmidt edited a special themed "Music and Machine" issue of the Viennese modern music journal *Musikblätter des Anbruch,* he not only included what may be the first dissemination of Moholy-Nagy's essay "Geradlinigkeits des Geistes–Umwege der Technik" (Directness of the Mind–Detours of Technology), but also republished "New Composition in Music: Potentialities of the Phonograph" (p. 52).

However, these artistic experiments did not work out: it proved too difficult to incise into a regular-sized record, or to incise a larger master before reducing this to the size of a regular disk.[21] One of Moholy-Nagy's early photographs, published in

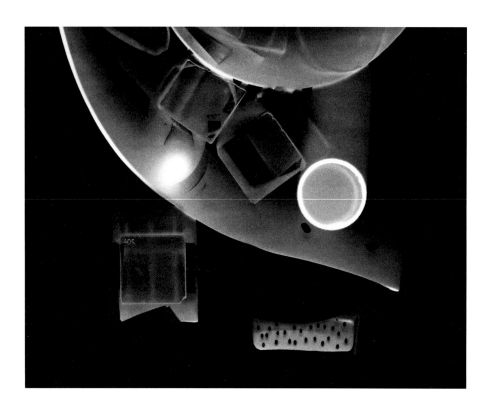

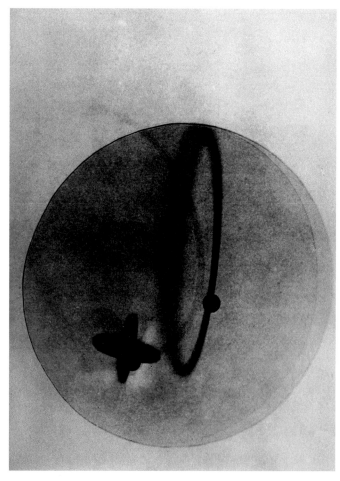

Untitled, 1943. Photogram on gelatin silver paper, 20.4 × 25.6 cm.

Untitled, 1929. Photographic enlargement of a photogram, 40 × 30 cm, produced as part of the "Giedion Portfolio." Original photogram from 1925, ca. 24 × 18 cm, lost.

Untitled ("fotogramm"), 1929. Photographic enlargement of a reversed photogram (contact print from the original), 38.5 × 28 cm. Probably produced as part of the "Giedion Portfolio." Original reversed photogram from 1925, 23.1 × 17.2 cm, lost.

Untitled, 1929. Photographic enlargement of a photogram, 40 × 30 cm, produced as part of the "Giedion Portfolio." Original photogram, ca. 1926–28, ca. 24 × 18 cm, lost.

Production–Reproduction

Coursely Woven Ribbon, 1939–41. Photogram on developing paper, 25.3 × 20 cm.

Untitled ("Confetti"), 1939–43. Photogram on developing paper, 48.5 × 38.8 cm.

Untitled, 1940. Photogram on developing paper, 40.3 × 50.4 cm.

Production−Reproduction

MUSICO-MECHANICO, MECHANICO-OPTICO
Geradlinigkeit des Geistes — Umwege der Technik
Von L. Moholy-Nagy

Mechanismen in der Kunst? Gestern noch mit dem Bumerang der „persönlichen Handschrift" totgeschlagen, heute im Kampf durchgesetzt, morgen triumphierend, übermorgen eine selbstverständliche Leistung, worüber kein Wort zu verlieren sein wird.

Gewiß! Heraus mit den Beweisrequisiten!

Zwei Wege der Überzeugung: Ich habe satt die Geige, das Klavier, das Cymbal und die Harfe; ich habe satt Staffelei und Pinsel samt graphischen Techniken; ich bin es satt, als Steinmetz zu arbeiten; ich habe satt die Rezitation, satt mein Tintenfaß und meinen Gänsekiel.

Alle sind viel zu unexakt, als daß man sich bei ihrer Benützung nicht dauernd schämen müßte, wenn man einmal im Leben eine Autotour gemacht hat: Bosch und Zeiß, lackiertes Blech und Spiegelglas — das „handwerkliche"! (Mit Maschine gemacht!) — Es sitzt.

Die Erklärung ist einfach: Glaubt jemand, daß die Begabung eines Musikers, Malers davon abhängt, ob er sich mit Maschinen oder mit Handwerkzeug ausdrückt? Wichtig ist nur für jeden, seine Ausdrucksintensität zu erlangen. Das Werk ist eben nicht allein von der Begabung abhängig, sondern auch von der Intensität des Kampfes, der mit den materiellen Mitteln: Werkzeug und Stoff ausgefochten wird.

Aber unser vieltausendjähriges Handwerk ist so bekannt, so langweilig, mit seinem wohlbekannten Leisten — ich bin es satt.

Wir versuchen es mit der Maschine. Ja, sie läßt sich nicht ohne Kampf in Besitz nehmen — aber vorwärts! Anstrengend, gewiß — es wird doch etwas daraus!

Aha! Die Langeweile, der Reiz des Unbekannten, das ist die treibende Kraft, welch Unernst!

Für diese nun der zweite Weg: (Ernst und logisch aufgebaut; die Langeweile oder Kurzweile ausgeschaltet.)

Der Mensch ist der Mikrokosmos. Über ihm und in ihm walten universelle Gesetze. Sein ganzes Wesen und Schaffen ist ein einziger Versuch, diese Gesetze auszudrücken, ihnen eine Form zu verleihen. Es ist heute unser Wunsch: Allgemein gültige (Harmonie- und Gleichgewichts-) Gesetze allgemein gültig zu formulieren. Diese Formulierung vermengt sich aber noch — überall und im überwiegenden Maße — mit der Art des persönlichen Ausdruckes. Einer exakten Notation widerstreben unsere vorsintflutlichen Instrumente und Werkzeuge, oft aber auch unser unvollkommener (natürlich nur in technisch-mechanischen Relationen unvollkommener) Körperaufbau.

So müßte es mit der Maschine versucht werden.

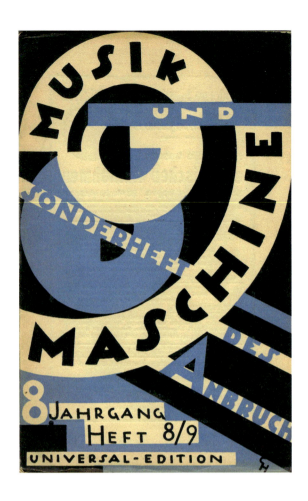

P. Picasso: Der erste Manager aus „La parade", Ballett von Jean Cocteau (Klischee Stavba)

Mechanisierung der Musik
Die Interpretation bedeutet die Zerstörung der Musik

Aus der Unmöglichkeit, eine Komposition bezüglich des Tempos und der Dynamik präzis zu notieren, ergibt sich notwendig das Bestreben, gleichzeitig mit der Niederschrift die Aufführung definitiv festzulegen. Das ist nur durch mechanische Instrumente möglich. Unter den bisher bekannten haben sich nur das Grammophon, das elektromechanische Klavier (Hupfeld-Phonola, Werke-Mignon usw.) sowie das Orchestrion und die verwandte Drehorgel behauptet. Bei all diesen Apparaten ist die Wiedergabe ein für allemal geregelt und nur durch Eingriffe (Veränderung der Drehgeschwindigkeit) zu variieren. Die durch private Affekte des lebendigen Interpreten möglichen Differenzen der Aufführungen sind ausgeschaltet. Das trügerische Gedächtnis, die begrenzte Technik und jegliche Indisposition des Spielers können nicht mehr den Eindruck durch Fälschung der Werte zerstören.

Leider hat man, irregeführt durch den traditionellen Respekt vor „individueller Leistung", einen gänzlich verkehrten Weg eingeschlagen, um die Musik auf die Maschine zu übertragen. Man ließ nämlich, um zum Beispiel ein Klavierstück zu mechanisieren, das betreffende Stück regelrecht durch einen Interpreten spielen und übertrug dieses Stück völlig adäquat auf eine Rolle, so zwar, daß jedes Niederdrücken einer Taste, jede Pedalbewegung in einer sehr differenzierten Reliefschrift auf mechanischem Wege präzis registriert wurde.

Nur beim Orchestrion wurde meines Wissens stets das einfachere und einzig gute System angewandt, die Reliefschrift ohne Vermittlung einer Aufführung direkt und authentisch, genau den Notenwerten entsprechend, aufzuzeichnen. Dieses System hat ganz natürlich den Vorteil, daß die Registrierung nicht von der individuellen Leistungsfähigkeit eines Einzelnen abhängig ist. Mithin, auf das Klavier angewandt: man kann mit dieser Methode beliebige Tonmassen gleichzeitig anschlagen lassen, man kann die Stärke und Geschwindigkeit einer Musik über die natürlichen Grenzen der menschlichen Technik hinweg steigern. Man wird, mit einem Wort, in der Lage sein, völlig neue und bisher unbekannte Klangphänomena zu realisieren, deren Wirkung vom Komponisten selbst aufs genaueste geprüft und festgelegt werden kann.

Das Studium der Möglichkeit, auf die Grammophonplatte authentisch Töne zu gravieren, beschäftigt heute eine Reihe bedeutender moderner Künstler. Die Lösung dieses Problems würde einen völligen Umsturz in der Musik zur Folge haben. Denn während heute nur der Pianist durch das viel bessere und künstlerischere mechanische Klavier eine Luxuserscheinung geworden ist, wird das authentische Grammophon das Orchester entbehrlich machen. Dieses wird sogar lächerlich primitiv klingen neben einem Instrument, dessen Klangfarben unbegrenzt, dessen Skalen unendlich differenziert und dessen Töne absolut temperiert sind. Man hat das Grammophon schon heute so vervollkommnet, daß Nebengeräusche ganz wegfallen, daß der Klang die größten Räume füllt.

Es wird also in absehbarer Zeit DER MUSIKALISCHE INSTRUMENTALIST NUR NOCH LEGENDÄRES INTERESSE haben. Die heute üblichen Musikinstrumente werden die Schränke der Antiquitätensammler füllen.

Für die zeitgenössische Musik sind diese Tatsachen von eminenter Wichtigkeit. Die zunehmenden Schwierigkeiten in den Werken moderner Musiker stellen an die Ausführenden immer höhere, fast nicht mehr zu bewältigende Anforderungen. Die Zeit, wo die Idee des Komponisten die Ausführbarkeit durch lebende Interpreten endgültig überschreitet, ist bedenklich nahe. Durch die Mechanisierung sämtlicher Instrumente ist jede Schwierigkeit beseitigt.

Auch die Intonation mathematisch reiner (temperierter) Intervalle, wie sie das heutige Zwölfton-System erfordert, ist auf mechanischen Instrumenten leicht zu erreichen.

Auf diese Weise wird man die Musik, die heute unter den Händen der Dirigenten und Virtuosen zu sterben droht, retten können.

Stuckenschmidt
Wien, August 1924.

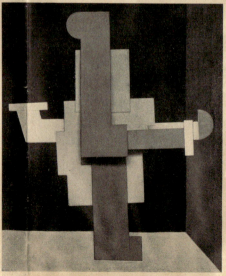

K. Schmidt u. G. Teltscher — Figurine des Mechanischen Balletts
(Mit Genehmigung des Bauhausverlages, München-Weimar)

Production—Reproduction

Painting, Photography, Film focuses on the fine-grained texture of record grooves, demonstrating how impossibly difficult such work would have been (p. 55). The microscopic photograph of "Caruso's High C" (p. 41) that appeared in Moholy-Nagy's second book *Von Material zu Architektur* (From Painting to Architecture) makes this all the more apparent. He abandoned his experiments on this front at some point during the mid-1920s, but it was no great loss for Moholy-Nagy, for a new opportunity to realize his idea was by then on the horizon: sound film. It should be noted however that other artists were more successful with similar endeavors and by 1930 composers such as Paul Hindemith and Ernst Toch were performing their compositions for gramophone in public.[22]

Moholy-Nagy's interest in sound, its notation, and the translation from notation into tones had its origins in Raoul Hausmann's "optophonetics," in which the light we see and the sound we hear (when conveyed electrically) are but different manifestations of the same electromagnetic energy. Color could thus be modulated to change the sound and vice versa. Hausmann's Optophone was in development by the fall of 1921 and, thanks to Moholy-Nagy, a short article on it appeared in *MA*.[23]

In the first 1925 edition of *Painting, Photography, Film* Moholy-Nagy reproduced a musical score by his compatriot Alexander László. With his *Präludien für Klavier und Farblicht* (Prelude for Piano and Colored Light),[24] the latter had developed a system of projecting colored lights that Moholy-Nagy initially saw as a realization of his own idea of light play.[25] This was an exciting discovery for Moholy-Nagy, and he and László formed a life-long friendship. However, László's score was removed from the second, 1927, edition of the book, while a text contrasting László's sound-light procedure with Walter Brinkmann's Hausmann-inspired optophonetic process was introduced.[26] Moholy-Nagy criticized László's color-sound equivalences for being intuitive, rather than grounded in physics as Hausmann's and Brinkmann's proposals were.[27] Moholy-Nagy inscribed his own copy of László's book (p. 55) with the phrase "Optophonetic wird die Lösung sein" (Optophonetics will be the solution).

Moholy-Nagy's detailed description of Brinkmann's optophonetic process ends with the claim that "…the exploitation and perfection of the [optophonetic] principle… advance[s] in closest association towards the 'musical film,' a system which makes the film image itself sonorous and 'music-generating.'"[28] This statement was made in 1927. Abandoning his experiments using the wax recording disk in 1928,[29] Moholy-Nagy continued to turn his attention to the emerging technology of sound film:

[S]ince every mark on the sound track is translated into some note of noise in projection, my experiments with drawn profiles, letter sequences, fingerprints, geometrical signs printed on the track also produced surprising acoustic effects.… It will not be possible to develop the creative possibilities of the talking film to the full until the acoustic alphabet of sound writings will have been mastered.… Once this is achieved the sound film composer will be able to create music from a counterpoint of unheard… sound values, merely by means of opto-acoustic notation.[30]

Musikblätter des Anbruch 8, nos. 8–9 (1926), special issue on "Music and Machine," edited by Hans Heinz Stuckenschmidt. Cover design by "CH."

Hans-Heinz Stuckenschmidt, "Mechanization of Music," with illustrations of works by Pablo Picasso (above left) and Kurt Schmidt and Georg Teltscher (below right), in *MA* (Today), edited by Lajos Kassák, "Music and theater issue," vol. 9 (September 15, 1924), unpag.

Film still from *Berlin Still Life*, Germany, 1932. 35 mm, black and white, silent, 8'5".

In 1933 Moholy-Nagy succeeded in making a film based on these ideas, aptly entitled *Tönendes ABC* (Sounding Alphabet), a short sequence of which appeared in the June 1933 issue of Dutch journal *De 8 in Opbouw* (p. 56). Sibyl Moholy-Nagy remembers that "he worked on a sound film engraving linear shapes on film negative. When he played it back on a sound projector he achieved a coincidence of tone and line that had never been demonstrated before. 'I can play your profile,' he would say to a friend, sketching the outline of the face in his notebook. 'I wonder how your nose will sound.'"[31] It was in this film that Moholy-Nagy finally realized Hausmann's dream of optophonetics. Both men remained fascinated by this topic until the end of their lives. Moholy-Nagy's posthumously published *Vision in Motion* contains the following words, "All endeavors will point—as Raoul Hausmann previsioned—in one direction, to an optophonetic art."[32]

In his lecture and presentation on "Die neuen Film-Experimente," ("The New Film Experiments"), held in Frankfurt on 4 December 1932, Moholy-Nagy showed films which put this thinking about film and sound into practice: by Munich engineer Rudolf Pfenninger (the first to transpose these notions onto the screen) and by German abstract filmmaker Oskar Fischinger. These ideas spread, most notably to the UK, where in 1935 the pioneering Scottish documentary filmmaker John Grierson (the first to apply the term *documentary* to film) hired a young Glasgow School of Art student to the General Post Office Film Board. Grierson knew Moholy-Nagy and would also have known *Sounding Alphabet*, which had been shown in London.[33] The art student in question, Norman McLaren, learned of the "drawn sound" technique, and brought it to New York when he traveled to the United States in 1939 with a Solomon Guggenheim Foundation grant. Meanwhile Grierson had been hired by the Canadian government in 1938 to found the National Film Board of Canada, and in 1941 invited McLaren to work at the NFB (pp. 56–57).

By 1943 McLaren was head of Studio A, the NFB's animation division, and it is there that he developed this "drawn sound" into a high art form, becoming perhaps the greatest master of the medium.[34] McLaren was just one of many artists who have pursued suggestions first made by Moholy-Nagy in "Production-Reproduction."[35] Despite its contradictions, this article turned out to be one of Moholy-Nagy's most influential theoretical texts.

Production–Reproduction

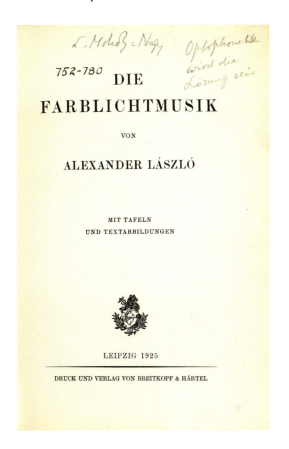

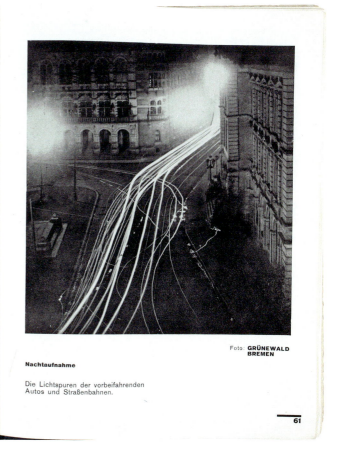

Raoul Hausmann, "Optofonetika" (Optophonetics), with three ink drawings by Fernand Léger, in *MA* (Today) 8, no. 1 (October 15, 1922), p. 4.

Alexander László, *Die Farblichtmusik* (Leipzig: Breitkopf und Hartel, 1925). This copy, which belonged to Moholy-Nagy, includes his inscription: "Optophonetik wird die Lösung sein" (Optophonetics will be the solution).

Photograph by Moholy-Nagy of a record made "bei von Löbbecke" [Graphische Kunstanstalt Dr. von Löbbecke u. Co., Erfurt], and by "Grünewald, Bremen," in: Moholy-Nagy 1925, pp. 60–61.

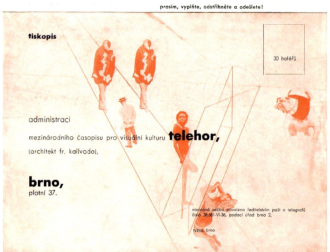

Flyer for *telehor* 1, nos. 1–2 (1936). Including reproductions of a photoplastic by László Moholy-Nagy and two photographs of Rudolf Pfenninger working on his 1932 optophonetic film *Das Wunder des gezeichneten Tones*. Design by František Kalivoda.

Invitation to "The New Film Experiments," a lecture and film presentation given by Moholy-Nagy for the Bund Das Neue Frankfurt, e.V., December 4, 1932. Printed card, 7 × 10.3 cm.

Article by Jan Duiker discussing Moholy-Nagy's films, including frames from *Tönendes ABC*, *De 8 en Opbouw* no. 12 (June 10, 1933).

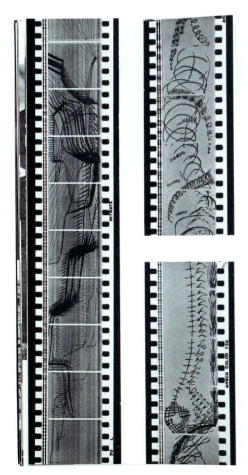

Oskar Fischinger, Film still from *Tönende Ornamente* (Sounding Ornaments), ca. 1932. 35 mm film, black and white, sound. Centre for Visual Music, Los Angeles. Photo courtesy of CVM © Center for Visual Music.

"L'audible et le visible: Les experiences de Norman McLaren sur les sons dessinés," in *Art d'aujourd'hui* no. 5 (November 1955), pp. 44–45.

Copy of a photomontage projected as the background for Erwin Piscator's production of Walter Mehring's *The Merchant of Berlin*, Piscator-Bühne, Berlin, 1929. Copy photograph by Lotte Jacobi, silver bromide print, 25.8 × 38 cm.

Gesamtwerk

[In addition to l'art pour l'art individualism and subjectivity] the second way [art of the previous generation operated] consisted of an attempt to bring together into one entity separate works or fields of design that were isolated from one another. This entity was to be the "Gesamtkunstwerk," architecture, the sum of all the arts.... Yesterday, during the period when specialization was at its height, the concept of a "total work of art" was readily comprehensible. With its ramifications and its fragmenting action in every field, specialization had destroyed belief in the possibility of embracing the totality of all fields, the wholeness of life. Since, however, the Gesamtkunstwerk is only a summing up, albeit an organized one, it cannot satisfy us today. What we need is not the "Gesamtkunstwerk," alongside and separated from which life flows by, but rather the self-organizing synthesis of all vital impulses towards the all-embracing Gesamtwerk (life) that counteracts isolation, in which all individual accomplishments arise from universal necessity.[1]

This is how Moholy-Nagy viewed Richard Wagner's conception of Gesamtkunstwerk: an outmoded attempt to mitigate the fragmentation of a bygone era. Contrasting with Wagner's notion, Moholy-Nagy drew on Walter Gropius's 1923 revised program for the Bauhaus, the Central European Lebensreformbewegung (Life Reform Movement), Lajos Kassák's concept of the "collective individual," the international Communist movement, and Germanic *Biophilosophie* (biocentrism) in order to promote a new way of being in the world, a modus operandi of which art was only a part.[2] In doing this, he was engaging in an activity pursued by almost all avant-garde artists of the day, aiming to "pull art back into practical life."[3] In typical International Constructivist fashion, employing terminology derived from Lebensphilosophie (life philosophy), and often using lists as a kind of literary trope, he promoted a way of moving beyond what he saw as the individualism of "art," and progressing toward a collective attitude that integrated art, as well as all other aspects of life (science, philosophy, the city, economics, politics, life reform, etc.), into a utopian project of personal fulfillment and common progress. In doing so, he would combat education that entailed overspecialization, which, as we have seen in the chapter "Sensory Training," was a negative aspect of modern life that prevented people from adapting organically to modernity. To the best of my knowledge, he never again addressed the question of the Gesamtkunstwerk.

Moholy-Nagy's synthetic approach derives from his experience of Budapest's rich intellectual scene in the early twentieth century, which saw the launch of the careers of figures such as philosopher George Lukács, film theorist Béla Balázs, sociologist Karl Mannheim, art historian Arnold Hauser, psychoanalyst Sándor Ferenczi, composer Béla Bartók, and mathematician John von Neumann.[4] As a law student, Moholy-Nagy had open access to the meetings and lectures of the Galileo Circle, founded by radical students at Budapest University in 1908. The Galileo Circle organized regular lectures, seminars, and debates on social, economic, political, and cultural issues of the day from Marxist, scientific, atheist—and after the outbreak of World War I—pacifist perspectives. It also engaged in a remarkable publication program, "Galilei Füzetek," the Galileo Brochures, producing translations of intellectual classics as well as the latest philosophical, ideological, and scientific literature.[5] By the time the Hungarian Soviet Republic was declared on March 21, 1919, a solid foundation had been laid for leftist Budapest intellectuals' rethinking of the world.

While the Galileo Circle was important, it was his experience of the short-lived Hungarian "Republic of Councils" of 1919—a "revolutionary" government that came to power without a revolution—that left the deepest impression on Moholy-Nagy. An uneasy coalition between the Social Democrats and the Communists forged by the collapse of the Austro-Hungarian Empire, the "Soviet" was characterized by a confusion of political, ideological, and nationalist sentiments. It was a failure in economic, political, and military terms but was at the same time a fascinating experiment in social engineering and the application of intellectual approaches to political control. Whatever one's political orientation, one cannot but be amazed by the goals this government set out to achieve in a very short time.[6] Its hasty reforms ranged from bans on prostitution and alcohol, the codification of full civil rights for women, and public nutrition programs to a chaotic attempt to redistribute what was deemed to be surplus living space and even furniture! The surreal atmosphere was heightened by the daily fairy tale readings in public parks for up to 120,000 proletarian children. Though Marxism was of course paramount, these ambitious undertakings were also suffused with the ideas of the Hungarian variant of the Lebensreformbewegung, which had enjoyed considerable popularity among Hungarian intellectuals during the first two decades of the century. Since some of these intellectuals were now part of the state apparatus, Lebensreform principles were actually put into practice.

Like their counterparts in Soviet Russia, the Hungarian Soviet's leadership recognized culture and the media as means to social change. The "Department of State Propaganda for Socialism," a division of George Lukács's "People's Commissariat for Public Education," envisaged a mass-educational role for film while undertaking an ambitious publication program with a universal scope. Estimates put the total figure for books, brochures, posters, flyers, handbills, and other material printed during the 133-day regime at 23 million![7] Many modern artists rose to leading positions in the artists' association and the Fine Arts Directorate, including the cultural workers in Lajos Kassák's avant-garde circle, centered on his journal *MA* (Today). Dubbed the "Activists" by Kassák in his eponymous 1919 manifesto, the members of this circle produced publications and organized exhibitions, matinées, and performances. Such activities demonstrated to Moholy-Nagy—a minor player in the Activist circle—that artists could participate in the fundamental transformation of society. Moholy-Nagy's specific emphasis on education (that is, as personal fulfillment) was indebted to Kassák. In his "Activism" manifesto, read on the eve of the declaration of the Soviet, Kassák insisted that "since we need to build a new human being for a new society, we must keep in mind that this ultimate objective of socialism is not going to be achieved overnight.... For us the meaning of life lies therefore beyond the speculative revolution of political parties ... [in] humankind's struggle to find its own identity." The "New Human Being," the "collective individual," as he memorably phrased it, was the goal, not socialism or communism.[8]

Established in March 1919, the Hungarian Soviet Republic came to a sudden end in August that same year. Along with many other leftist intellectuals, Moholy-Nagy left the country. Once he had arrived in Berlin during March 1920, Moholy-Nagy naturally oriented himself toward the left wing of the German Lebensreformbewegung. He had collaborated on the Budapest-based cultural journal *Jelenkor* (The Present Age) in 1917–18 with his university friend, art historian and photography/film theorist Iván Hevesy, but it was Moholy-Nagy's ongoing contact with Kassák that made it possible for him to experiment with a new type of publishing.

Kassák had escaped to Vienna after the collapse of the Soviet and had relaunched *MA*. His most important achievements in exile (1920–26) were probably the Viennese editions of *MA* and the anthology *Új művészek könyve / Buch neuer Künstler* (Book of New Artists). The anthology and the issues of *MA* from March 1921 to July 1922 (p. 155) stemmed from his collaboration with Moholy-Nagy; without him, Kassák could not have internationalized *MA* to the extent he did. As Kassák recalled in 1966: "We produced the *Buch neuer Künstler* according to a shared plan, but I wrote the foreword and solved its typographical organization. I was in Vienna and he in Berlin."[9] His position as correspondent gave Moholy-Nagy an entrée into Berlin's avant-garde circles. "As the representative of *MA* (1921) ... I felt free and mature enough to take a leading part in the discussions based upon the Hungarian political and artistic experiences [of the Soviet]. Also, *MA* published the works of the most advanced European artists [and] had an excellent reputation."[10]

Images from *1919 A vörös május* (1919 Red May) (Budapest: Közoktatásügyi Népbiztosság, 1919). Left to right: Sale of Party Tracts; Procession at the corner of Bath Street; Procession of the staffs of the Cinematographs. Photographers not identified.

Brücken (Bridges), 1920 [1921]. Oil on canvas. 95 × 71 cm.

Gesamtwerk

It was evidently this collaboration on *MA* that gave rise to the idea of "an anthology from Futurism to Constructivism," which was well received among Moholy-Nagy's new friends in Berlin, whose support was crucial to the project.[11] Kassák had always called for the integration of life and art. His conception of the "collective individual" envisaged a new kind of human, who would attempt self-perfection while contributing to the commonweal. In his introduction to the anthology, Kassák wrote:

The scientific way of thinking has not only removed humanity from god, it has also shown humanity's way to itself. Humanity has recognized its place in the world. The way we set our lives up is determined by social consciousness, and the most beautiful moments are those, when we approach things with practical awareness.

He expressed the unity of life and art by declaring that "there isn't a separate society and a separate art any more … our age is the age of the constructive … art, science, technology all meet at a single point." This single point, he implies, is "real art." Furthermore, "real art is the most complete reality. Thus real art has no romantic goals. As the synthesis of life today, real art is itself the goal." This "real art" is what Moholy-Nagy, adopting Walter Gropius's terminology after Gropius hired him to the Bauhaus in 1923, would refer to as the *Gesamtwerk*.

In *Book of New Artists*, Kassák and Moholy-Nagy attempted to convey the "synthesis of life today" through their selection of images. In his paintings of 1920–21, Moholy-Nagy had already developed a Dada-inspired iconography of industrial and technological motifs, such as transmission towers, power lines, disembodied flywheels and railway motifs (signal signs, semaphores, bridges, tracks).[12] He and Kassák had taken note of the architectural and technological images in Le Corbusier's and Amadée Ozenfant's journal *L'Esprit Nouveau* and by late 1921 would have been acquainted to some degree with Russian Constructivism. This experience and awareness sensitized them to the power of industrial imagery. Thus, alongside reproductions of avant-garde artworks, Kassák and Moholy-Nagy included photographs of a transmission tower, a film projector, a racing car, a dynamo, grain silos, a massive steel spiral staircase, a glazed railway station shed, an industrial hole punch machine, a ventilator, an electric clock, a power station, a steel bridge, and an airplane hangar, as well as aircraft. Inclusion of these images, along with two musical scores, photographs of modern architecture, and a film script left no doubt that they were also thinking of "art" beyond traditional media, invoking more than just the visual sense.

Dosti Wolkera!

Sotva umřel, stal se »největším básníkem generace«, aby po něm nemohlo přijíti nic většího. Všichni, kdož nevěří v možnost nového, a všichni, kdož cítí svou vlastní nemohoucnost, velebí jej jako ztracenou spásu. Zdálo by se, že s Wolkerem je už i poesie mrtva. Ex kathedra se hlásá, že Wolker byl začátkem i koncem poesie. Ano, byl aliou a omegou, ale toliko úseku, a poesie dnes proudí jinudy. S mrtvými žijí jen ti, kdož nemají dosti životnosti.

DOSTI WOLKERA! Tento výkřik diktován jest poctivostí k básníkovu dílu. Moha se ozvati, vykřikl by takto sám proti kupení sentimentálních a vzlykavých výkřiků a superlativů: »Evangelium mládeže, zjevení, lyrický genus, největší básník generace atd.«, neboť jeho snem a hrdostí bylo poctivé dělnictví. Pánové, existuje i zdvořilost k mrtvým! Básník třídního boje byl povýšen za básníka národního, jeho proletářství buřičství se mu odpustí za jeho uměleckou nevýbojnost. A tak se zvedají Wolkerovi opony divadel, měšťák tone v sentimentalitě, vždyť mrtvého básníka může dokonce i milovat — jako mrtvou již revoluci. Povýšen byv na básníka národního — proti této profanaci, za niž by se byl styděl nejvíce Wolker sám, nikdo se neozval — dostal se do čítanek. Dává se u maturit. Dohořela jeho buřičská oževavost.

DOSTI WOLKERA! Byl prý posledním velkým špatným básníkem — ideologickým. Jeho smrt mu zabránila, aby se stál dobrým. Měšťák cucá dnes z této nemilé příhody ctnost. Vytvářel prostě a se vší tvůrčí naivností nové lidství, proto jsme ho milovali, nevytvořil však nového tvaru. Těsně za ním počíná opravdu nové a velké umění.

Richtlinien für eine Synthetische Zeitschrift.

Wir haben Forderungen, welche unausgesprochen, oft auch unbewußt, schon Forderungen vieler Menschen sind. Eine synthetische Zeitschrift hat die Aufgabe die Forderungen bewußt zu machen und die Quellen der intuitiven Kraft, welche sich dauernd aus dem Gesamtbau des Menschen nährt, zu vermehren.

Ihr Inhalt ist **die neue in vielem schon heute realisierbare Form des Lebens**. Diese neue Form des Lebens bedingt eine vollkommene Neuwertung und Weiterführung aller Forschungen und Ergebnisse auf a l l e n Arbeitsgebieten des Menschen. Alle verfügbare Kräfte sind in deren Dienst zu stellen. Das muß aus doppelter Notwendigkeit entstehen; die eine ist: daß wir unseren in uns individuell aufgeklärten Arbeitswillen in den Dienst der Kollektivität des Lebens stellen wollen. Die andere: daß die heutigen Aufgaben des heutigen Lebens solcher Natur sind, daß ein Mensch oder wenige Menschen sie nicht einmal zu ihrer individuellen Befriedigung bewältigen können. Die Konzentration dieser Kräfte aber kann unser Leben und das Leben aller am ökonomischsten, am gesteigersten und am konstruktivsten aufbauen; d. h. wir brauchen nicht mehr dem Zwang aller möglichen Vorgänge zu folgen: wir müssen sie **gestalten**.

Alle Gestaltung und Produktion ist zeitlich bestimmt. Unsere Periode ist die des **Klarlegens und Reinigens**.

Unter diesem Aspekt gibt es keine getrennten Rangklassen für Kunst, Wissenschaft, Technik, Handwerk usw. sondern nur gleichwertige und einander beigeordnete Kräfte.

Eine Zeitschrift, welche an der wirklichen Gestaltung des Lebens arbeiten will, darf also nicht ihre Kraft auf einzelne Komponenten, z. B. Kunst beschränken, sondern sie soll die Arbeiten möglichst aller heute tätigen **produktiven** Kräfte (Wissenschaftler, Künstler, Ingenieure, Handwerker usw.) in sich summieren.

Wir nennen **produktiv** nur jene Arbeit, welche die im Augenblick ihres Entstehens maximalen Forderungen des Lebens erfüllt.

II.

Um nicht nur grundlegende theoretische Arbeiten zu schaffen, deren sofortige Anwendung in der Praxis nicht immer durchführbar ist, müssen wir parallel mit diesen Arbeiten die heutigen praktischen Gestaltungsmöglichkeiten, insofern sie Teil unseres Weltbildes sind, stark im Auge behalten. Insbesondere:

Pädagogik: von der Elementarausbildung bis zu den höchsten Stufen der Erziehung.

Architektur. Film.
Prinzipielle Fragen des Städtebaues.
Privat- und Kollektivbau.
Erledigung aller Romantizismen (Biedermeier und Wolkenkratzer; die Verwendung des horizontalen Liftes macht den Verkehr in horizontalen Anlagen ebenso rasch und rentabel wie der vertikale Lift in Hochhäusern).
Verhältnis der malerischen, plastischen und anderen Gestaltungen untereinander und zur Architektur.
Hygienische Fragen: Beleuchtung, Kanalisation usw.
Neue Filmmanuskripte (welche heute wegen der Kurzsichtigkeit der Filmgesellschaften noch nicht zur Durchführung gelangen).
Neue Methoden des Nachrichtendienstes.
Die Mittel zu dem Aufbau einer 1600 millionigen Gedankengemeinschaft: Radio; Flugwesen; internationale Sprache; Austauschmöglichkeiten usw.
Der neue Arzt soll erst das Wesentliche der Funktionen finden, nicht nur das Ordnungswidrige feststellen.
Soziale, wirtschaftliche Probleme. Der neue Staat.
Die Maschine.
Kurze technische Umschau.
Reflexionen. Wertung. Produktive Einfälle. Kritik.

Neue Gestaltung in der { Malerei / Musik / Plastik / Literatur / Philosophie / Psychologie } u. ihre Werkarbeit.

Theater, Varieté, Zirkus.
Materialfragen: Glas, Metall usw. Neue Chemie.
Typographie.
Amerikanertum und die europäischen Fragen.
In der Form der Mitteilungen ist strengste Präzisität zu fordern, **ohne eine persönliche Oktroy**. Voraussetzung für die Bewertung der Beiträge: die objektive Arbeit an der Schaffung des **neuen** Weltbildes. **Die Moral der zukünftigen Ordnung ist mathematische Sicherheit, keine blosse Gefühlsangelegenheit.** —

Kontakt mit allen Gebieten des Schaffens.
»Je sais tout« (ohne lächerlich zu werden!).

III.

Redaktion: Komitee, dessen Mitglieder Spezialaufgaben haben können; jedoch wird alles gemeinsam durchgesprochen.
Mitarbeiter: alle schöpferischen Menschen, die mit ihren produktiven Werken beteiligen (und nicht solche, die nur ihre persönlichen Meinungen gedruckt zu sehen wünschen).

Sprache: Nationalsprache; mit fremdsprachigen kurzen Zusammenfassungen einzelner Aufsätze. Nach drei bis vier Nummern event. eine internationale Ausgabe in verschiedenen Sprachen.

IV.

Projekt der ersten Nummern:
1. Welche sind die Forderungen des heutigen Menschen? Das Antizipieren einer neuen Lebenskonstruktion.
2. Architektur.
3. Film.
4. Werkstatt.
  Laboratorium.
    Praktisches.
    Spekulatives.

Überall eingestreut kurze Leitsätze über wesentliche Probleme. Innerer Kontakt mit den Lesern und Anregung zur Mitarbeit. Besondere Berücksichtigung des jungen Menschen.

E. PRAMPOLINI:
STUDIE PROSTOROVÉ KONSTRUKCE

5. Politisch-geistige Einstellung zu universalen Fragen.
6. Neue Erfindungen und Experimente.
   Musik. Grammophon. Mechanische Sprechmaschine. Reines Sprechen. Photographie.
   Konstruktiv-kinetisches Kraftsystem.
7. Kritik (als ständige Rubrik) über Kunst-
      Technische   } Werke
      Wissenschaftliche
   Produktive Reflexionen über Medizin.
      Mathematik
      Geometrie: Bòlyai.
      Euklides, Geometrie
8. Neue Phänomene und Typen.
   Neues Wort.   Dichter-
   Neue Typographie.   Künstler- } Photographien
   Drahtlose Photographie. Techniker-
   Drahtlose Filmzeitung. Reklame. Plakat.
      Ihre Werke.
   Neue Ausstellungen usw.
9. Neue Filmmanuskripte.
   Bewegungskunst.
   Theater.
   Elektrisches Varieté.
10. Optophonetik.
    Die Einheit der Organfunktionen. Tasten — riechen.
11. Organisationsfragen.
    Propagandagestaltung.
    Unaufhörliche Kräftekonzentration.
12. Kunst.
    Filmstreifen.
    Röntgenaufnahmen.
    Gymnastik.
    Glashäuser.
    Projekte für Versenkung der Zimmer.
    Projekte für Hebung der Zimmer.
    Arbeits-, Schlaf-, Baderaum.
    Typhäuser.
    usw., usw.

Überall viele Bilder im Text oder mit kurzer Erläuterung, darunter, weil dies eine der wirksamsten Mitteilungen ist.
1922.

V.

Wir haben in Europa schon eine Reihe von sehr schönen Zeitschriften, welche in ihren Einzelheiten oft hervorragend sind. Was wir aber bei den Meisten vermissen, das ist: Lebendigkeit, Frische und Unbeengtheit. Die Neigung der Redakteure, Richtungen (»Ismen«) und daraus Akademien aufzurichten, ist viel zu groß.

Es muß eine synthetische Zeitung kommen, welche — ohne d a u e r n d das Redakteur-Gesicht zu zeigen —, in ihrer Gestaltung von den Elementen einer Zeitschrift ausgeht, welche das Bindende nicht in einem Ismusgesetzbuch, sondern nur in ihrer lebendigen Funktion sieht.
1924.   L. Moholy-Nagy.

O aranžovaných obrazech.

Fotografie Eiffelovy věže, pohled na Crystal Palace jsou jistě krásné, ale oč více je proti tomu pohlednice poslaná z nejvyššího patra pařížské věže s francouzskou červenou známkou, datem a razítky, které věrohodně ověřují správnost všech těchto přátelských pozdravů. A právě tak psaní od milenky je výmluvnější, účet od krejčího přesvědčivější, lístek do biografu či šeku k spinění a bankovka je vždycky nějaké bohatství«. Objektivnost těchto originálů je nesporná, v okamžiku poví absolutně všechno a nevynechá se ani hodina na tramwayovém lístku, třeba momentálně fakty pro nás zdánlivě docela zbytečné; tyto bezprostřední svědci a všechny ostatní skutečnosti, když ne př-mo, alespoň fotograficky doloženě jsou nejčistšími výrazovým materiálem pro aranžované básnické obrazy, které v okamžiku vypoví nejvýpravnější příběhy, kde suma slov je vyjádřena jasným určitým integrálním výrazem. Básně, pohádky a prósy těto výtvarné koncentrované řeči nezdržují, nikdy neunaví a plně odpovídají poetické potřebě v přímočaré rychlém moderním životě.

Heythum

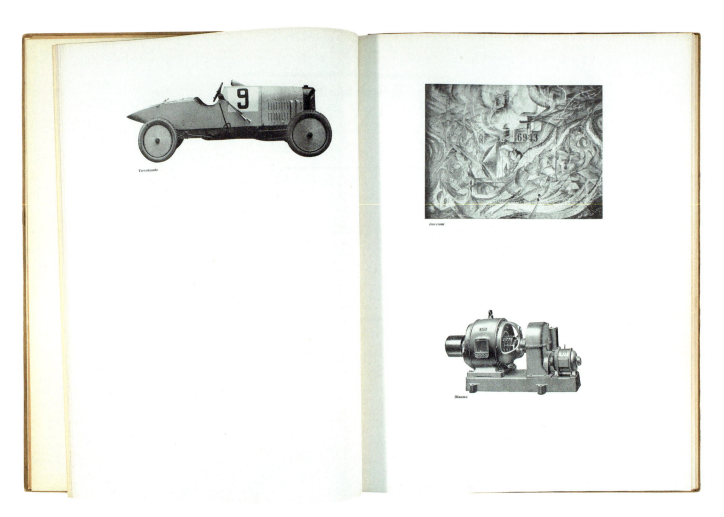

Four spreads from Kassák and Moholy-Nagy, *Book of New Artists*, 1922. Layout by Lajos Kassák include reproductions of works by Umberto Boccioni, Alfred Kreymborg, Julian Freedman, Kasimir Malevich, and El Lissitzky.

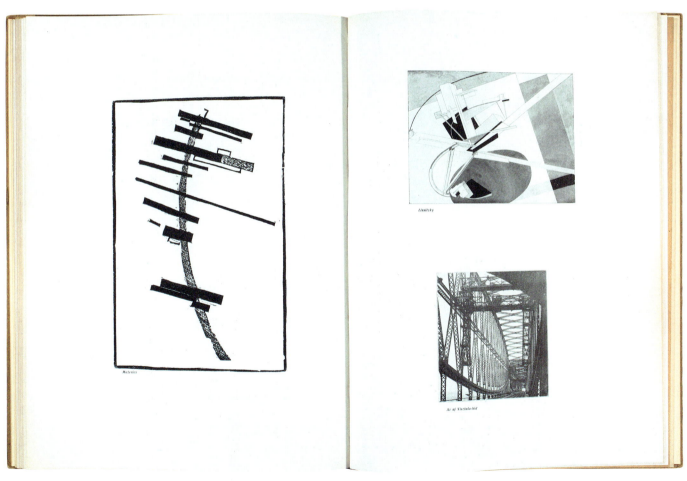

Book of New Artists is regarded as the first significant anthology of the international avant-garde after World War I. It differed from earlier anthologies, such as the almanac *Der Blaue Reiter*, which focused on fine and folk art.[13] This difference lay, as Kai-Uwe Hemken notes, in the way that *Book of New Artists* functioned as both art history and a manifesto, a chronicle of Cubism, Futurism, Expressionism, and Dada culminating in a new, as-yet-unnamed style of art, or rather, in an emergent cultural attitude.[14] As such, the *Book of New Artists* might be regarded as an early document of International Constructivism and Neue Sachlichkeit (New Objectivity). Most importantly, Moholy-Nagy and Kassák's collaboration on *MA* and *Book of New Artists* constituted a trial run for what would develop into Moholy-Nagy's notion of the Gesamtwerk.

In 1922 Moholy-Nagy drafted a program for a "synthetic," that is, interdisciplinary, journal (p. 63), which would go beyond what he and Kassák had recently achieved. Although this plan was not published until 1924, in the Czech avant-garde journal *Pásmo* (Zone), Moholy-Nagy was already clear before this date about his intention, echoing the aims of the Lebensreformbewegung, of combining different branches of knowledge, research, and human activity with a view to furthering the cause of total reform of life.

"The content," he wrote in the proposal, "is the new, in many aspects, already realizable form of life. This new form of life requires a complete reassessment and continuation of all research and outcomes in all fields of human endeavor. All available energies are to be placed at its service. There are two reasons for this urgency: one is that we wish to place our individually arrived-at will-to-work [Arbeitswillen] at the service of the collectivity of life [Kollektivität des Lebens]. The other is that the contemporary obligations of contemporary life are such that one person or a few people cannot accomplish them to their own individual satisfaction."[15] The topics he proposed to cover were substantially broader than in *Book of New Artists*, and Moholy-Nagy's list, like the positioning of movements and machines in the anthology, implied an evolutionary development that suggested a gradient of importance.[16] He started with pedagogy, moving on to architecture (for Kassák, the highest form of all art), and subsequently (also in a privileged position) to film. This is followed by urban planning, which would become an important theme in Moholy-Nagy's late writings. Only after these topics have been addressed is

art's relationship to architecture broached, along with the crucial questions (again, in Kassák's view) of the private vs. the collective, and "the supplanting of all Romanticisms." At this point, Moholy-Nagy moves beyond the themes Kassák cited in his foreword to the anthology, and addresses his own enthusiasms, such as promoting the "horizontal elevator" (that is, moving sidewalk), hygiene ("lighting, sewers"), alternative news media–"the means of developing a 1600-million-strong intellectual community through radio, flight, an international language, exchanges, etc.,"–and alternative medicine (influenced here, as explored in the chapter "Sensory Training," by his first wife, Lucia Moholy, and their mutual friends Paul and Paula Vogler). Interestingly enough, it is only at this point that "social and economic problems" enter the equation, followed by the machine, new technology, "new achievements in painting, music, sculpture, literature, philosophy, and psychology," theater, variety theater, the circus, "questions of materials such as glass, metal, etc., the new chemistry," typography, and finally, "Americanism and the European question." It is noteworthy that painting and sculpture appear toward the end of the list (separated by music and followed by literature, philosophy, and psychology), and it is striking too that photography is not even mentioned. Art is just another form of knowledge, he implies, and indeed not a privileged one, as Kassák still held. Moholy-Nagy goes on in this piece to propose twelve headings outlining the content to be covered in the first issues. Some of these elaborated on topics previously listed, while others introduced "new experiments and inventions" such as the record player, the "Kinetic-Constructive System of Energies," "productive reflections on medicine, mathematics and geometry," "wireless photography," the "wireless film journal," optophonetics, the "unity of the senses. Touching–smelling," X-ray photography, gymnastics, glass architecture, etc. The lists both echo and transcend the concerns brought to *Book of New Artists*, bringing Moholy-Nagy's own enthusiasms into the mix.

On March 31, 1923, Moholy-Nagy was hired by the Bauhaus Meisterrat (masters' council) to teach the second semester of the Vorkurs (introductory course) and to act as Formmeister (master of form) in the Metal Workshop.[17] Why did Walter Gropius and his peers hire a twenty-eight-year-old immigrant with a heavy Hungarian accent, practically no formal art education, barely five years of artistic practice, no real teaching experience, and an elementary grasp of metalworking to replace the recently departed Johannes Itten? Gropius was the principal advocate of the appointment. As early as summer 1922 he must have realized that Moholy-Nagy, in conjunction with Alfréd Kemény and Lucia Moholy,[18] proposed a kind of synthesis, a program of action that went beyond art and embodied many of the concerns Gropius wished to pursue in the Bauhaus. To borrow Moholy-Nagy's own words, this program was both "constructive" (in that it was syncretic) and "dynamic" (in that it was also in a constant state of development). He articulated it in six theoretical texts written during 1922: "Dynamisch-Konstruktiven Kraftsystem"; "Produktion–Reproduktion"; a contribution in a Hungarian émigré journal to "Vita az új tartalom és az új forma problémájáról" (Debate on the Problem of the New Content and the New Form); "Neue Gestaltung in der Musik. Möglichkeiten des Grammophons"; "Light: A Medium of Plastic Expression"; and "Richtlinien für eine Synthetische Zeitschrift" (Guidelines for a Synthetic Periodical).[19] The salient points of their content can be summarized in the following terms: 1. A utopian striving for a more just society rooted in Hungarian Activism and the Communist movement; 2. A Bogdanovian "tectological" (that is, Ostwaldian "energeticist") understanding of the universe as a systemic interplay of energies rather than of matter,[20] and an emphasis on the centrality of sensory input and the senses; 3. A commitment to "elementarist" abstract painting and sculpture; 4. An empiriocritical/biocentric pedagogical approach that regarded human beings as the sum of their sensory experiences and in turn, as part of the organic whole of life, viewing a conjunction of art and technology as the means to fully realize everyone's innate potential, particularly their ability to fully employ–indeed expand–their sensory capacities; 5. A positive but critical attitude toward technology: we should control technology rather than allowing technological developments to control us; 6. An openness to working in both old and new media and with old and new materials; 7. A program of abandoning pigment with a view to working directly with light instead as the primary medium of visual expression; 8. An attempt to formulate in print the totalizing impulse toward what he would term the Gesamtwerk in order to further his goal of designing a more harmonious and fulfilling lifestyle for everyone.

Gropius's recognition that Moholy-Nagy had arrived at an inspiring program of aesthetic and reform ideas, which was au fond pedagogical, proved to be spot-on and Moholy-Nagy more than fulfilled Gropius's expectations. As late as 1965 Gropius wrote: "What the Bauhaus has achieved cannot be thought of without bringing back into one's mind the fiery spirit of Moholy, the Great Stimulator."[21]

Gesamtwerk

Brochure for Bauhausbücher, ca. 1925. Design by László Moholy-Nagy.

Once Moholy-Nagy took up his post at the Bauhaus in late March 1923, Gropius became his champion and mentor in a way that Kassák, due to his temperament, would never have been. Gropius had recently introduced a new slogan for a reformed Bauhaus, "Art and technology: A new unity." It is therefore no surprise that Moholy-Nagy abandoned Kassák's formulation of the synthesis of art and life, and adopted Gropius's Gesamtwerk terminology. For his part, Gropius recognized in Moholy-Nagy not only someone who had demonstrated a kindred spirit in this regard, for example in his work on *Book of New Artists*, but also someone with an ambition and talent for editing and publicity, for synthesis and communication. He invited Moholy-Nagy to be his co-editor on the Bauhaus's new book series, which came to be known as the "Bauhausbücher."

Moholy-Nagy's conception for the series went some way toward achieving the goal of a "synthetic" publication project that he had articulated in 1922. In a letter to the Russian Constructivist Alexander Rodchenko on 18 December 1923, Moholy-Nagy attached a list of thirty topics in many fields for these "brochures," as he referred to them. Extensive as the publication program and its implementation was, this list was far more ambitious than what he was able to realize by 1929, when the fourteenth and last of the Bauhausbücher was published: his own *Von Material zu Architektur* (From Material to Architecture). Topping Moholy-Nagy's 1923 enumeration was the "Debate on Constructivism," with "Die neue Lebenskonstruktion" (The New Life-construction) in second place.[22] In *From Material to Architecture* he elaborates on the notion of the Gesamtwerk, the "new life-construction," and the relation of individual fulfillment to the collective good, this time employing the terminology of the biocentric/empiriocritical worldview he had adopted:[23]

Each person's every action and expression is made up of various components rooted in our biological structure. Each utterance comprises an engagement with the world and the self and explains one's condition at that moment. Such an expression is fruitful only – if apart from personal satisfaction – it possesses objective relevance for the collective. That is why our efforts today, especially those in the field of pedagogy, are directed toward the recovery of this foundation. That is why we are today far less interested in the intensity and quality of "artistic" utterances than we are in the

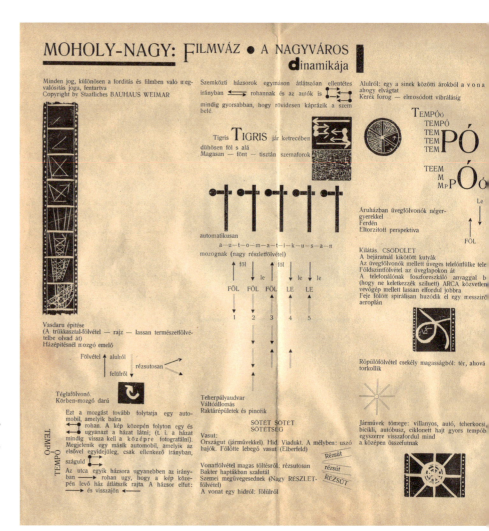

MA (Today) 9 (September 15, 1924), "Music and Theater" issue, edited by Lajos Kassák. This issue was timed to coincide with Friedrich Kiesler's *International Theater Exhibition* in Vienna, 1924. Showing László Moholy-Nagy's storyboard for "A nagyváros dinamikája" (Dynamic of the Metropolis), dated "Berlin 1921–22," unpag.

Gesamtwerk

elements of our humanness that—with the force of law—determine our function and the form of our existence. This does not mean that ... the great individual values of the arts are to be placed in question. Quite the contrary—it is precisely those values that are firmly anchored in the elements under discussion. In fact, those values are obscured for the great majority by the uniqueness of, and tendency to idolize, individual interpretations.... It is only that which crystallizes out of the Gesamtkomplex [sum total] of one's own experiences that truly comprises a person.[24]

Moholy-Nagy's project was part of a larger undertaking characteristic of vanguard artists in Weimar Germany (not to mention the rest of Europe, and Soviet Russia in particular), namely an attempt to overcome what were seen as the negative effects of exaggerated individualism in the past, which led to the atomization of society and ultimately to the horrors of World War I. As Matthew Wilson-Smith has put it: "The only radical solution was a total one, one in which sundered parts were integrated again—not, as völkisch Romantics would have it, through appeal to primordial sentiment, but through appeal to objective organization and technological power. Not so much a recovery as a total reengineering of the real."[25] This statement underlines the utopian biological determinism—typical of biocentric thinking—that underlies Moholy-Nagy's totalizing position. This biological determinism, coupled with Moholy-Nagy's utopian pedagogical project, resulted in a series of proposals during the 1920s that sought to immerse and involve participants, as well as inform and even expand their sensory capacities.

Moholy-Nagy, following Gropius, claimed to have removed the "art" from the "total work of art," translating it into a "total work," the Gesamtwerk. Still, we often think of Moholy-Nagy—along with Alexander Rodchenko, Lazar el Lissitzky, and Theo van Doesburg—as the paradigmatic interdisciplinary practitioner of Modernism, viewing him as an artist who, combining his strategies within projects, might be considered an exemplary early-twentieth-century exponent of the "total work of art." As I suggest in the chapter "Art as Information / Information as Art" his publication projects can be regarded as a form of Gesamtkunstwerk in and of themselves. Moholy-Nagy's de facto proposal of an end to the traditional hierarchy of media was, however, pioneered by Wagner in his

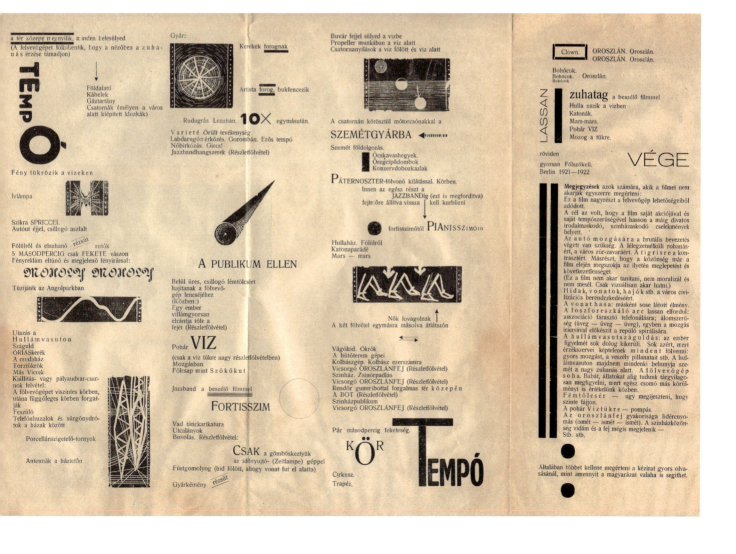

L. Moholy-Nagy:
Dynamik der Gross-Stadt.

Die Manuskriptskizze Dynamik der Gross-Stadt entstand im Jahre 1921. Ich wollte sie zusammen mit meinem Freunde Karl Koch von dem »Institut für Kulturforschung«, der mir zu dieser Arbeit viele Anregungen gegeben hat, durchführen. Wir sind leider bis heute nicht dazu gekommen; das Institut hatte kein Geld dafür. Grössere Gesellschaften, wie die UFA, wagten damals das Risiko des bizarr Erscheinenden nicht; andere Filmleute haben »trotz der guten Idee die Handlung darin nicht gefunden« und darum die Verfilmung abgelehnt.

Vier Jahre sind seitdem vergangen und unter der ursprünglich revolutionär wirkenden These von dem FILMMÄSSIGEN, d. h. unter dem aus den Möglichkeiten des Aufnahmeapparates und der Bewegungsdynamik entstehenden Film kann sich heute ein jeder wenigstens etwas vorstellen. 1924 wurden solche Filme in Wien auf dem Internationalen Theater- und Musikfest von Fernand Léger in Paris — als Zwischenakt im schwedischen Balett — von Francis Picabia aufgeführt. Amerikanische Lustspielfilme enthalten zum Teil ähnliche filmmässige Momente und man kann sagen, dass jetzt schon alle guten Filmregisseure sich um die Ergründung der und dem Film eigenen optischen Wirksamkeit bemühen und dass die heutigen Filme viel mehr auf Bewegungstempo und Kontraste des Hell-Dunkels und der verschiedenen optischen Sichten aufgebaut sind, als auf eine theatralische Handlung.

Wir sind aber noch ganz am Anfang. Theoretische Erwägungen, einige in der Intuition verwurzelte Versuche von Malern und Schriftstellern. Gutglück des Zufalls während der Atelierarbeit: das ist alles. Wir brauchen dagegen eine systematisch funktionierende Filmversuchsstelle mit der weitgehendsten Förderung der Filmindustrie. Heute machen einige Maler allein Versuche. Diese Arbeit wird mit Misstrauen begegnet und dieses Misstrauen kann man nicht einmal übel nehmen. Die Technik der Filmherstellung, die ganze Apparatur erlauben keine Privatarbeit mehr; und die »besten« Ideen nützen nichts, wenn sie nicht durch ihre Umsetzung in die Praxis die Basis einer Weiterentwickelung bilden können. Darum wird das Schaffen einer zentralen Filmversuchsstelle zur Ausführung von Manuskripten, welche neue Ideen enthalten, bald auch unter privatkapitalistischem Aspekt eine selbstverständliche Forderung sein, der man stattgeben wird.

Der Film »Dynamik der Gross-Stadt« will aber weder lehren, noch moralisieren, noch erzählen; er möchte visuell, nur visuell wirken. Die Elemente des Visuellen stehen hier nicht unbedingt in logischer Bindung miteinander; trotzdem schliessen sie sich zu einem lebendigen Zusammenhang raumzeitlicher Ereignisse zusammen und schalten den Zuschauer aktiv in die Stadtdynamik ein.

Kein (Kunst-) Werk ist durch die Nebeneinanderreihung seiner Elemente erklärbar. Das unfehlbar Totale der Nebeneinanderreihung, die unfassbar sichere Bezogenheit der kleinsten Teile untereinander und zu dem Ganzen sind die Imponderabilien der Wirkung. So kann ich nur einige Elemente dieses Films erläutern, damit man wenigstens nicht über — uns heutigen Gestaltern — selbstverständliche Begebenheiten stolpert.

Das Ziel des Filmes war: Ausnützung der Apparatur; eigene optische Aktion; optische Tempohaftigkeit; — statt literarischer, theatralischer Handlung: Dynamik des Optischen. Viel Bewegung, mitunter bis zur Brutalität gesteigert. Dazu Kontrast: Ruhe-Aufspritzen, Brodeln. Gegenüber stechenden erdrückenden Momenten — traumhafte, schwebende Stellen; usw.

Die Verbindung der einzelnen, logisch nicht zusammengehörenden Teile erfolgt entweder optisch, z. B. durch horizontale oder vertikale Streifung der Einzelbilder (um sie einander ähnlich zu machen), durch Blende (indem man z. B. ein Bild mit einer Irisblende schliesst und das Nächste aus einer Irisblende hervortreten lässt), oder durch gemeinsame Bewegung sonst verschiedener Objekte, auch durch assoziative Bindungen, z. B. Zitrone-Italien. (Einige eingehender erläuternde Bemerkungen finden sich rechts neben dem Texte.)

Dynamik der Gross-Stadt.
(Skizze zu einem Filmmanuskript.)

Alle Rechte, insbesondere das Recht der Verfilmung und Übersetzung behält der Autor sich vor.
(Copyright by Bauhaus/Dessau.)

Das Entstehen einer Eisenkonstruktion.

Kran bei Hausbau in Bewegung.
Aufnahmen: von unten
von oben
von schräg

Tricktischaufnahme von sich bewegenden Punkten, Linien, welche in ihrer Gesamtheit in einen Kran (Naturaufnahme) übergehen.

Ziegelaufzug.
Wieder Kran: in Kreisbewegung.
Grossaufnahme.
Die Bewegung setzt sich in einem Auto fort, das nach links saust. Man sieht ein und dasselbe Haus dem Auto gegenüber in der Bildmitte; (das Haus wird immer von rechts in die Mitte zurückgezogen; dies ergibt eine starre, ruckartige Bewegung). Ein anderes Auto erscheint. Dieses fährt gleichzeitig entgegengesetzt, nach rechts.
— Tempo, Tempo, Tempo.
Häuserreihe auf der einen Seite der Strasse, durchscheinend, rast rechts durch das erste Haus. Häuserreihe läuft rechts weg und kommt von rechts nach links wieder. Einander gegenüber liegende Häuserreihen, durchscheinend, in entgegengesetzter Richtung rasend, und die Autos immer rascher, sodass bald ein FLIMMERN entsteht.
— Tempo, Tempo, Tempo.
Ein Tiger kreist wütend in seinem Käfig. Ganz klar — oben hoch — Bahnzeichen:

● ▬ ● ▬ ● ▬ ● ▬ ●

(Grossaufnahme).

Diese Stelle als brutale Einführung in das atemlose Rennen des Tohuwabohu der Stadt.

Der hier starre Rhytmus lockert sich langsam im Laufe des Spiels.

Der Tiger:
Kontrast des offenen unbehinderten Rennens zu Bedrängung, Beengtheit. Um das Publikum schon anfangs an die Überraschungen und Alogik zu gewöhnen.

Alle automatisch, au-to-ma-tisch in Bewegung

△ auf △ auf △
△ △ ab ▽ ab ▽
AUF Auf △ AB Ab ab
1   2   3   4   5
△
△
△
△
▽
△

Rangierbahnhof.
Ausweichestellen.
Lagerräume und Keller.
Finsternis. FINSTERNIS.
Eisenbahn.
Landstrasse (mit Fuhrwerken), Brücken.
Viadukt. Unten Wasser, Schiffe in Wellen.
Darüber der schwebende Zug.
Zugaufnahme von einer Brücke aus: von oben; von unten. (Der Bauch des Zuges, wie er dahin fährt; aus einem Graben zwischen den Schienen aufgenommen.)
Ein Wächter salutiert. Glasige Augen.
Grossaufnahme.
Der Zug von einem Damm aus.
Der Tiger wütend.

Die Steigerung der zivilisatorischen Einrichtungen in der Überschneidung und Durchdringung unzähliger Niveaus.
Der Zug von unten: sonst nie Erlebtes.

schräg schräg

Die Räder. Sie drehen sich bis zum verwaschenen Vibrieren.
Tempo —o
Tempo —o —o
Tem
Tem   PO—po—o—O
Tem

Glasaufzug in einem Warenhaus mit

Negergroom. Schief.
Perspektive verzerrt.   aufabauf

Gesamtwerk

Hell-dunkel.
Ausblick. Tumult. Die am Eingang angebundenen Hunde.
Neben dem Glasaufzug eine Glastelefonzelle mit Telefonierendem.
DURCHblick. Aufnahme des Erdgeschosses durch die Glasplatten.
Das GESICHT des Telefonierenden (Grossaufnahme) — eingetrieben mit phosphoreszierendem Material, damit keine Silhuette entsteht — dreht sich GANZ DICHT an dem Aufnahmeapparat vorüber, rechts;
über seinem Kopf (durchscheinend) zieht ein von weitem kommender Flieger in einer Spirale
Tiefe Fliegeraufnahme über einem Platz mit 8 Strassenöffnungen

Tempo, Tempo, Tempo.

Die Fahrzeuge: Elektrische Strassenbahn, Autos, Lastwagen, Fahrräder, Droschken, Autobus, Cyklonette, Motorräder fahren in raschem Tempo vom Mittelpunkt auswärts
dann plötzlich alle umgekehrt; in der Mitte treffen sie sich
die Mitte öffnet sich, ALLES sinkt
tief, tief, tief
(Der Apparat wird rasch umgekippt; das Gefühl eines Tiefstürzens entsteht.)
TEMP—o—O
Untergrundbahn.
Kabel. Kanäle.
Unter den Strassenzügen die ausgebauten Kloaken.
Lichtglanz auf dem Wasserspiegel.
BOGENLAMPE. Funken spritzen
Autostrasse spiegelglatt
Lichtpfützen von oben und
              schräg
                     mit weghuschenden Autos.
Parabelspiegel eines Wagens vergrössert.
5 Sekunden lang schwarze Leinwand.
Lichtreklame mit verschwindender und neuerscheinender Lichtschrift

MOHOLY   MOHOLY   MOHOLY

Feuerwerk aus dem Lunapark
MITrasen mit der Achterbahn.

Assiziation für mühsames Telefonieren. Traumhaft (Glas—Glas—Glas); gleichzeitig wird man durch die langsame Drehung auf die Bewegung des erscheinenden Flugzeugs vorbereitet.

Der Mensch kann im Leben auf vieles nicht achten. Manchmal deswegen, weil seine Organe nicht rasch genug funktionieren, manchmal, weil ihn die Momente der Gefahr etc. zu stark in Anspruch nehmen. Auf der Schleifenbahn schliesst fast ein jeder die Augen während des grossen Stürzens. Der Filmapparat nicht. Im Allgemeinen können wir z. B. kleine Babys, wilde Tiere kaum objektiv beobachten, da wir während der Beobachtung eine Reihe von andern Dingen beobachten müssen. Im Film ist es anders. Auch eine neue Sicht.

Teufelsrad. Sehr schnell.
Die heruntergeschleuderten Menschen stehen schwankend auf und steigen in einen Zug. Polizeiauto (durchscheinend) rast nach.
In der Bahnhofshalle wird der Apparat erst in **horizontalem** Kreis, dann in **vertikalem** gedreht.
Telegrafendrähte auf den Dächern. Antennen. Porzellanisolatortürme.
Der TIGER.
Grossfabrik.
Rotation eines Rades.
Durchscheinende Rotation eines Artisten.
Salto mortale.
Hochspringen mit Stab. Fallen. 10mal hintereinander.
Publikum, wie Wellen des Meeres.
VaRIETö, fiebrige Tätigkeit.
Fussballmatch. Grob. Starkes TEMPO.
Frauenringkampf. Kitsch.
Jazzbandinstrumente (Grossaufnahme)
Metallkegel — innen leer, glänzend — wird gegen das Objektiv geschleudert, (inzwischen) ein Mann zieht seinen Kopf blitzschnell zurück.
Grossaufnahme.
Ein Glas Wasser (NUR der Wasserspiegel in Grossaufnahme) in Bewegung, wie Springbrunnen, spritzt auf
JazzBAND mit dem SPRECHENDEN FILM FortiSSimO
Wilde Tanzkarrikatur. Strassenmädchen. Boxen. Grossaufnahme. NUR die HAEnde mit den Kugelhandschuhen. Zeitlupe. ZEITLUPE. Rauch qualmt wie Blumenkohl über eine Brücke; photographiert, wenn ein Zug darunter vorbeifährt.
  hr   r Schornstein qualmt; daraus ein
 c ä e
S   g
TAUCHER; sinkt kopfabwärts ins Wasser. Propeller im Wasser in Tätigkeit. Kloakenöffnungen unter und über dem Wasserspiegel. Durch die Kanäle mit Motorboot zur
Schmutz- und Müllsammelstelle. Verarbeitung des Mülls in Fabrikbetrieb.
Berge von verrosteten Schrauben, Büchsen, Schuhen usw.
PATERNOSTER-Aufzug mit Aussicht bis ans Ende und zurück, im Kreis.
Der ganze Film wird von hier (verkürzt) RÜCKWÄRTS gedreht bis zu der JaZZBAND (auch diese umgekehrt) von FORTIssIMO zu pianissim-o-o —
Glas Wasser.
Leichenschau (Morgue) von oben.
Militärparade.
Marsch-marsch-rechts.
REITDAMEN — links.
Die beiden Aufnahmen übereinander kopiert, druchscheinend
Schlachtviehhof. Tiere.
Ochsen tobend.
Die Maschinen des Kälteraums.
Löwe.
Wurstmaschine. Tausende von Würsten.
Fletschender Löwenkopf. (Grossaufnahme.)
Theater. Schnürboden.
Der Löwenkopf. TEMPO' o -O!
Polizist mit Gummiknüppel auf dem Potsdamerplatz.
Der KNÜPPEL. (Grossaufnahme.)
Das Theaterpublikum.
Der Löwenkopf immer grösser werdend bis zuletzt der riesige Rachen die Leinwand füllt.

Einige Sekunden lang dunkel.
Grosser Kreis.
         TEMP-o-O
Cirkus von oben, fast Grundriss.
Trapez. Mädchen.
Beine.
Löwen. CLOWN. Dressur.
LÖWEN. LÖWEN!
Clowns.
Wasserfall dröhnt. DER SPRECHENDE FILM.

Unser Kopf kann es nicht.

Um das Publikum zu erschrecken (auch ein dynamisches Moment).

Die häufige und unerwartete Erscheinung des Löwenkopfes soll Unbehagen und Bedrückung hervorrufen (wieder — wieder — wieder).
Das Theaterpublikum ist heiter — und der KOPF kommt DOCH! usw.

L. MOHOLY-NAGY:

DYNAMIC OF THE METROPOLIS

SKETCH FOR A FILM
ALSO TYPOPHOTO

The manuscript sketch Dynamic of the Metropolis was written in the year 1921–22. I hoped to carry it out with my friend Carl Koch, who gave me many ideas for this work. So far, unfortunately, we have not managed to do so; his Film Institute had no money for it. The larger companies like UFA were at that time unwilling to risk enterprises which appeared bizarre; other film-people could 'find no **action** in it despite the good idea' and so declined to film it.

Some years have passed since then and everyone today has some idea of what is meant by the proposition – revolutionary in its effect in the early days – of the FILMIC, that is, of the film which proceeds from the potentialities of the camera and the dynamics of motion. Such films have been shown in 1924 in Vienna by Fernand **Léger** at the **International Festival of Theatre and Music** and in Paris – as an entr'acte in the **Swedish Ballet** – by Francis **Picabia**. Some American comedy films contain similar filmic moments and we may say that by now all good film-directors are concerned to establish the optical effect proper to the film **alone** and that the films of today are constructed to a much greater extent upon tempo of movement and the contrast of light and shade and the various optical views than on theatrical action. This type of film is not concerned with the actor's star-performance, nor indeed with the actor's performance at all.

We are still, however, at the very beginning. Theoretical deliberations, a few experiments by painters and writers which have been based upon their intuitions, chance good fortune during studio work: that is all. What we need, however, is an experimental film centre that will work systematically, with the most intensive promotion by public authorities. Yesterday a few painters were still experimenting on their own. This work was received with suspicion, for the technique of film-production, the whole paraphernalia no longer admits of private effort. The 'best' ideas are useless if they cannot be transposed into practice and thus form the basis of further development. The setting up of a central **film experimental centre** to execute scripts which contain new ideas, even under private, capitalist auspices, will therefore soon be an obvious and recognised necessity.

The intention of the film 'Dynamic of the Metropolis' is not to teach, nor to moralise, nor to tell a story; its effect is meant to be visual, **purely** visual. The elements of the visual have not in this film an absolute logical connection with one another; their photographic, visual relationships, nevertheless, make them knit together into a vital association of events in space and time and bring the viewer actively into the dynamic of the city.

122

No work (of art) can be explained by the sequence of its elements. The totality of the sequence, the sure interaction of the smallest parts upon one another and upon the whole are the imponderables of the effect. Thus I can explain only some of the elements of this film, so that at least people will not stumble over cinematically obvious happenings.

Aim of the film: to take advantage of the camera, to give it its own optical action, optical arrangement of tempo – instead of literary, theatrical action: dynamic of the optical. Much movement, some heightened to the point of brutality.

Individual parts which do not 'logically' belong together are combined either optically; e.g., by interpenetration or by placing the individual images in horizontal or vertical strips (so as to make them similar to one another), by a diaphragm (e.g., by shutting off one image with an iris-diaphragm and bringing on the next from a similar iris-diaphragm) or by making otherwise different objects move in unison, or by associative connections.

As I was reading the corrections for the second edition, I heard reports of two new films which seek to realise the same aspirations as those proposed in this chapter and the one on Simultaneous Cinema (p. 41), Ruttmann's film 'Symphony of the Metropolis' shows the rhythm of the movement of a town and dispenses with normal 'action'. – In his film 'Napoleon' Abel Glance uses three film-strips running simultaneously side by side.

%

123

Warehouses and cellars

Darkness

DARKNESS

Becoming gradually lighter

Railway.
Highway (with vehicles).
Bridges. Viaduct. Water below, boats in waves. Cable railway above.
Shot of a train taken from a bridge: from above; from below. **(The belly of the train,** as it passes; taken from a trench between the rails.)
A watchman salutes. Glassy eyes.
Close-up: an eye.

126

The appurtenances of civilisation heightened by making countless levels intersect and interpenetrate.
The train from below: something never experienced before.

Glass lift in a warehouse with a negro attendant.
Oblique.
Perspective distorted.
Chiaroscuro.
View out. Tumult.
The dogs tethered at the entrance. Next to the glass lift a glass telephone box with a man telephoning.

View THROUGH. Shot of the ground-floor through the glass panes.

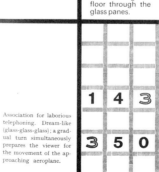

Association for laborious telephoning. Dream-like (glass-glass-glass); a gradual turn simultaneously prepares the viewer for the movement of the approaching aeroplane.

AN ANGRY LYNX.

The wheels. They turn to the point when the vibration fades.

up   down   up

The face of the man telephoning (close up) — smeared with phosphorescent material to avoid producing a silhouette —turns VERY CLOSE to the camera; above his head to the right (translucent) the aeroplane is seen approaching in a spiral from far off.

127

László Moholy-Nagy, "Dynamic of the Metropolis" (1925), in Moholy-Nagy 1969, pp. 122–37.

L. MOHOLY-NAGY: DYNAMIC OF THE METROPOLIS

SKETCH OF A MANU-SCRIPT FOR A FILM
Written in the year 1921/22

Author and publishers reserve all rights, especially those of filming and translation.

Close-up.
The movement continues with a car dashing towards the left. A house, always the same one, is seen opposite the car in the centre of the picture (the house is continually being brought back to the centre from the right; this produces a stiff jerky motion). Another car appears. This one travels simultaneously in the opposite direction, towards the right.

This passage as a brutal introduction to the breathless race, the hubbub of the city.

The rhythm, which is strong now, gradually slackens during the course of the film.

A metal construction in the making

First, animated cartoon of moving dots, lines, which, seen as a whole, change into the building of a zeppelin (photograph from life).

A tiger paces furiously round and round its cage

TEMPO   TEMPO   TEMPO

Row of houses on one side of the street, translucent, races right towards the first house. Row of houses runs off right and reappears from right to left. Rows of houses facing one another, translucent, rushing in opposite directions, and the cars moving ever more swiftly, soon giving rise to FLICKERING

TEMPO
TEMPO
TEMPO
TEMPO

The tiger:
Contrast between the open unimpeded rushing and the oppression, constriction. So as to accustom the public from the outset to surprises and lack of logic.

Crane in motion during the building of a house
Photographs:
from below
from above

Hoisting bricks
Crane again: in circular motion

Quite clear – up at the top – signals:

(Close-up.)

All automatic, au-to-ma-tic in movement

↑up   ↑up
↑   ↓   ↑   ↓
↑   ↓down ↓down
UP ↑up ↑DOWN ↓down ↓down

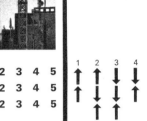

1 2 3 4 5
1 2 3 4 5
1 2 3 4 5

Shunting yard
Sidings

1 2 3 4 5
↑ ↑ ↓ ↑ ↓
↑ ↓ ↓ ↓ ↓
↑   ↑
      ↑

124

Low aerial photograph over a square with

8

streets opening into it.

ARC-LAMP, sparks playing. Street smooth as a mirror.
Pools of light. From above and

oblique

with cars whisking past.

Reflector of a car enlarged.

TEMPO-o-

The vehicles: electric trams, cars, lorries, bicycles, cabs, bus, cyklonette, motor-cycles travel in quick time from the central point outwards, then all at once they change direction; they meet at the centre. The centre opens, they ALL sink deep, deep, deep –

a wireless mast

SCREEN BLACK FOR 5 SECONDS

(The camera is swiftly tilted over; there is a sense of plunging downwards.)

Underground railway. Cables. Canals.

TEMPO

TEMPO-o-o

Under the tramways the sewers being extended.
Light reflected in the water.

Electric signs with luminous writing which vanishes and reappears.

YMOHOLY MOH

Fireworks from the Lunapark.
Speeding along WITH the scenic railway.

129

A man can remain oblivious of many things in life. Sometimes because his organs do not work quickly enough, sometimes because moments of danger, etc., demand too much of him. Almost everyone on the switchback shuts his eyes when it comes to the great descent. But not the film camera. As a rule we cannot regard small babies, for example, or wild beasts completely objectively because while we are observing them we have to take into account a number of other things. It is different in the film. A new range of vision too.

Devil's wheel. Very fast.
The people who have been slung down stand up unsteadily and climb into a train. A police car (translucent) races after it.
In the station hall the camera is first turned in a **horizontal,** then in a **vertical** circle.

Telegraph wires on the roofs.
Aerials.
The TIGER.
Large factory.
A wheel rotating.
A performer rotates (translucent).
Salto mortale.
High jump. High jump with pole.
Jumper falls. Ten times one after the other.

Punch and Judy show.
CHILDREN

Our head cannot do this.

Public, like waves in the sea.
Girls.
Legs.

VaRIETé,
feverish activity.
Women wrestling.
Kitsch.

Jazz-band instruments (Close-up).

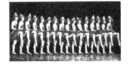

Metal cones — empty inside, glittering — are hurled towards the lens, (meanwhile) 2 women draw back their heads in a flash. Close-up.

(In order to scare the public. A dynamic moment too.)

TEMPO TEMPO TEMPO

Football match.
Rough.
Vigorous TEMPO.

Scrap is converted into factory work.
Mountains of rusty screws, tins, shoes etc.
PATERNOSTER lift with view to the end and back.
In the circle.

From here the whole film (shortened) is run BACKWARDS as far as the JaZZ-BAND (this backwards too).

from **FORTISSIMO-o-o**
to **PIA**NISSIMO

Military parade

WOMEN RIDERS—LEFT
The two shots printed one above the other, translucent.

Glass of water
Identification of corpses (morgue) from above.

RIGHT-RIGHT
RIGHT-RIGHT

MARCH-MARCH-
MARCH-MARCH-RIGHT

LEFT-LEFT-LEFT

Stockyards. Animals.
Oxen roaring.
The machines of the refrigerating room.
Lions.
Sausage-machine. Thousands of sausages.
Head of a lion showing its teeth (Close-up).
Theatre. Rigging-loft.
The lion's head. **TEMPO-o-O**
Police with rubber truncheons in the Potsdamer Platz.
The TRUNCHEON (close-up).
The theatre audience.
The lion's head gets bigger and bigger until at last the vast jaws fill the screen.

The frequent and unexpected appearance of the lion's head is meant to cause uneasiness and oppression (again and again and again). The theatre audience is cheerful – and STILL THE HEAD comes! etc.

A glass of water (expanse of water with glass rim in close-up) in motion like a fountain, spurts up
Jazz-BAND with the TALKING FILM
FortiSSimO
Wild dancing caricature. Street-girls.
THE TIGER

BOXING

Close-up.
ONLY
the HAnds with the boxing gloves.

Slow-motion. SLOW-MOTION.

Slanting chimney smokes; a DIVER emerges from it; sinks head first into the water.

THE DIVER

Smoke puffing like a cauli-flower, photographed over a bridge when a train is passing underneath.

Propeller in the water in action. Mouths of the sewers under and above the surface of the water. By motor-boat through the canals to the garbage and refuse collection depot.

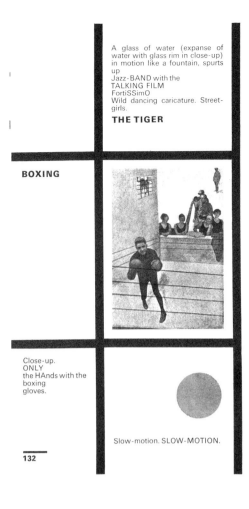
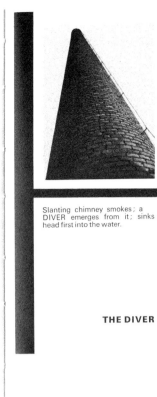

Dark for several seconds

DARK DARKNESS

Large circle

TEMPO-o-O
Circus from above, almost a ground-plan.

Lions. Acrobat on skis. Clowns.
CIRCUS
    CLOWN

Dressage

CIRCUS
Trapeze. Girls. Legs. Clowns.

LIONS.
LIONS!

CLOWNS.

DRESSAGE

Dressage.

Waterfall thunders. The TALKING FILM.
A cadaver swims in the water, very slowly.

Military. March-march.

Glass of water.

In motion.

SHORT-FAST

Spurts up –

THE WHOLE THING TO BE READ THROUGH AGAIN QUICKLY

END

"Section allemande," *Exposition de la Société des artistes décorateurs*, Grand Palais, May 14–July 13, 1930. Design by Herbert Bayer. Isometric rendering of "Raum 2," the gallery curated and designed by László Moholy-Nagy.

Installation photographs (with detail) of László Moholy-Nagy's design for "Raum 2," "Section allemande," *Exposition de la Société des artistes décorateurs*, Paris, 1930.

Documentary photograph of "Raum 1," *Film und Foto* exhibition, Stuttgart, 1929.

Gesamtkunstwerk conception. How are we to resolve these tensions? Wilson-Smith correctly disputes Manfredo Tafuri's position that Moholy-Nagy's theater "no longer has anything in common with Wagner's gesamtkunstwerk,"[26] characterizing the difference between their aesthetic conceptions as one of degree rather than of kind—because of the importance Wagner already accorded to media qua media. However, this argument leaves out of the equation the pedagogical, that is to say utopian reformist and therefore political, dimension of Moholy-Nagy's project, which is precisely the aspect that Tafuri emphasizes. In my view, this tension is not to be resolved, but should be seen as one of the creative factors in Moholy-Nagy's extraordinarily rich production.

While by no means the first Berlin avant-garde artist to make a film (Viking Eggeling and Hans Richter, and then Walther Ruttmann beat him to it), László Moholy-Nagy was among the first to write a film script. As Károly Kókai has demonstrated, the notion of the importance of film figured in the Viennese *MA*, and one cannot help but notice the prominence of film both in *Book of New Artists* and in Moholy-Nagy's 1922 plan for a "synthetic journal."[27] Indeed, *Book of New Artists*, as Hemken has pointed out, begins with a photograph of a movie camera and ends with Eggeling and Richter's sketches for an abstract film, suggesting that their kinetic, abstract artworks were the most advanced in the avant-garde at the time of publication (pp. 8, 190).[28] Moholy-Nagy claimed to have started writing "Dynamik der Gross-Stadt" / "A Nagyváros dinamikája" (Dynamic of the Metropolis) in 1921, and to have finished developing it during 1922, though it only appeared (in Hungarian) in *MA* in 1924, and was subsequently published (in German) in the Czech journal *Pásmo* and finally in its definitive version in *Painting, Photography, Film* in 1925. Moholy-Nagy was unable to shoot the film due to lack of funding and, as he did not finally make a film until the late 1920s, he became known during the 1920s not as a practitioner but as a theorist of cinema.

In the preamble to the screenplay's two German-language publications, he writes that the "manuscript sketch" (as he termed it) was inspired in part by his friend Carl Koch from the Institut für Kulturforschung (Institute for Cultural Research) in Berlin, making clear from the outset that his ambitions extended beyond formal innovation. The mission of this institute, founded by art historian and filmmaker Hans Cürlis in 1919, was the "scientific study of the culture of all peoples" and dissemination of the results through "word, image, and film." To this end, the founders—including Moholy-Nagy's art historian friend Karl With[29]—also set up a publications division and an "Archive for Educational and Reform Film." The Institute's avowed goal was a "new world cultural community in mutual awareness."[30] Cürlis described it as "the first German scientific institution that chose film consciously as the medium for the dissemination of its results."[31] This makes it clear that Moholy-Nagy conceived of "Dynamic of the Metropolis" within a pedagogical context which accorded with his synthetic, pan-epistemological ambitions at the time. He wrote in the preamble, however, that "the film … is not intended to teach, moralize, or tell stories: its effect is meant to be visual, purely visual. The elements of the visual are not necessarily bound logically to each other. Despite this, they connect with vital relationships of spatiotemporal events and actively draw viewers into the urban dynamic." Techniques such as sequencing, pairing of images, or fade-ins and fade-outs for shot transitions were deployed to establish connections between visual motifs and events. These links were underlined, so to speak, and emphasized through the use of typographic elements: lines, bars, circles, simplified semaphores, arrows, numbers,

Gesamtwerk

letters, zones of light and dark and grids. The intention was that all of these elements would be included—as in a Berlin university team's 2006 realization of the film—as animated sequences.[32] This operation on "purely visual" terms underscores the status of this film script as an early (for Moholy-Nagy), prephotographic New Vision project, using the full technical capabilities of the film camera and editing process. "Purely visual" is not to be conflated with "purely formal," however. As Moholy-Nagy makes clear in his description, the film concerns the big city, and the amusements clustered together there, such as soccer games, boxing matches, circuses, jazz bands, dancing and amusement parks, as well as urban-industrial motifs, such as construction cranes, power line towers, smokestacks, aerial views of streets, not to mention trains, streetcars, buses and cars, and indeed traffic signals, canal-barges, elevators, factories, or large-scale industrial constructions. It encompasses symbols of state power and repression, such as policemen wielding truncheons and rows of marching boots, but also includes images of modern society's problematic treatment of animals (slaughterhouses, caged lions). All of these reflected his emerging conception of the Gesamtwerk. Indeed, along with *Book of New Artists*, it can be regarded as the earliest manifestation of the Gesamtwerk. Although Moholy-Nagy was unable to realize "Dynamic of the Metropolis," he did make three films about cities between 1929 and 1933: *Marseilles Vieux Port* (Marseille: Old Port, 1929–32), *Berliner Stilleben* (Berlin Still Life, 1931–32) and *Grossstadt-Zigeuner* (Metropolitan Gypsies, 1932–33). I have suggested that these three films constitute a kind of trilogy on the contradictions of big-city life.[33] In them we witness the integration of New Vision aesthetics and scenes of everyday life, along with a political dimension, invoking the Gesamtwerk.

It was in a series of three exhibition designs of 1929–30 that Moholy-Nagy went furthest in realizing what were, in effect, representations of the Gesamtwerk. The German Werkbund's *Film und Foto* show, held in Stuttgart from May 18 to July 7, 1929, first afforded Moholy-Nagy an opportunity to curate and install a major exhibition, the introductory "Raum I," which was a New Vision manifesto. As I have discussed in detail elsewhere,[34] in this gallery Moholy-Nagy took his strategy (introduced in *Book of New Artists* and developed in "Dynamic of the Metropolis" as well as in *Painting, Photography, Film*) of integrating diverse photographic images—including applied photographs, such as scientific and criminological pictures; art photography, including avant-garde techniques such as photograms, photomontages, and typo-collages—and adapted it to a three-dimensional space. Deploying applied photographic images representing many aspects of life, ranging from transportation, sport, dance, medicine, and biology to astronomy and criminality, intermingled with New Vision aesthetic products, such as advertising, photograms, and photographs, he demonstrated how art could be integrated with life.

Moholy-Nagy's supreme realization of his representation of the Gesamtwerk is to be found in his design for "Raum 2" of the "Section allemande" at the Société des artistes décorateurs' twentieth annual exhibition in Paris, a project organized by the German Werkbund from May 14 to July 13, 1930.[35] Walter Gropius devised the concept and overall thrust of this German section, opting to divide the exhibition into a sequence of five galleries, although he only installed the first of these. The others were designed by Moholy-Nagy (#2), Marcel Breuer (#3) and Herbert Bayer (#4, #5). Although it was conceived for an exhibition of applied and decorative art, Moholy-Nagy's gallery also included a wide range of objects, along with images portraying a host of different subject matter.[36] A central area darkened with screens included an automatically operated slide projector, which showed photographs of design products, gymnastics, children, a water filtration plant, telescopes, public swimming pools, airplanes, and other images of everyday life, offering a "cross section through the totality of contemporary German culture,"[37] and, to cite Moholy-Nagy's art historian friend Sigfried Giedion's review, presenting an image of "the new Germany."[38]

Another of Moholy-Nagy's long-standing art historian friends, Alexander Dorner, director of the Provinzialmuseum in Hannover,[39] writes that he did not find Walter Gropius's contribution to be the most important element of this exhibition. He was more impressed by "the other rooms, which show our successful efforts to create a truly general culture: exemplary products in mass production. It is clearly shown that the goal of the German Werkbund's efforts is the redesign of our entire life organism, and so everything that supports this is shown in a slide show that runs automatically: from sheets of paper to chairs, from cups to upholstery, from the theater to the athletic center and from the newest Hanomag locomotive to an assembly line–produced automobile."[40] A special display entitled "Von Darmstadt bis Dessau" (From Darmstadt to Dessau) traced the development of the new German design. In Paris Moholy-Nagy again curated a space that integrated different types of objects from and representations of life. Although this was presented at a trade show for interior and product design, he also included examples of theater design and art photography. This was the whole panoply of life, a representation of the Gesamtwerk that he was working so hard to achieve.

At least one reviewer understood the exhibition as demonstrating "an organic connection between today's technical and social worlds."[41] In Dorner's formulation, "The most important thing, that which is demonstrated in all clarity, is the notion that new German design is not about a novel applied arts style, but rather about the conscious reformation of the great, functioning organism of our entire culture."[42] Dorner was so impressed by Moholy-Nagy's contribution to the Paris exhibition that he wrote to Moholy-Nagy while he was still in Paris, asking whether he would design a gallery, the Raum der Gegenwart (Room of the Present) for the Provinzialmuseum in Hannover, incorporating some of the architectural elements and displays from "Raum 2."

From the mid-1920s on, Dorner had reorganized the Provinzialmuseum in the light of an evolutionary conception of art history. As early as 1924, he had expressed his view that a museum was, above all else, an "Erziehungsinstitut" (a pedagogical institute).[43] In 1926 Dorner had hired Lazar El Lissitzky to design a Kabinett der Abstrakten (Cabinet of the Abstracts) to display examples of art from Cubism through Constructivism (including works by Moholy-Nagy), and to demonstrate how some of the formal ideas in this art were reflected in contemporary life by placing examples of contemporary product design on display as well. This project was realized in 1928.[44] However, Dorner did not see abstraction as the ultimate phase in the development of art. As the last in the series of forty-five galleries that he had (re)installed, Dorner conceived of a space that would demonstrate the principles that he saw as being at play in the contemporary world: the reproducibility of the artwork, the key role of photography, advertising, and film as new media permeating our environment, the dynamism of contemporary modes

Installation photographs of Jakob Gebert and Kai-Uwe Hemken's realization of László Moholy-Nagy's design for Raum der Gegenwart (Room of the Present), Kunsthalle Erfurt, 2009.

of transportation, and the integration of art and life through standardized industrial mass-production and participatory physical activity, such as dance and sport. He recognized "Raum 2" of the Paris show as a concrete basis on which to create a gallery in keeping with this vision, viewing it, and Moholy-Nagy's broader program, as encapsulating this new, collective spirit in German art, design, and society. This near-conjunction of Dorner's curatorial conception and Moholy-Nagy's theoretical ideas afforded the latter a further opportunity to develop his idea of a gallery reflecting his notion of the Gesamtwerk.[45] The resonance of Moholy-Nagy's artless Gesamtwerk and Dorner's thinking becomes particularly apparent in the title of Dorner's book *The Way beyond Art* and indeed in its content: "We have set 'art' in quotation marks to indicate that even our conception 'art' is but a temporary fact in human history."[46] He continues by asserting that "the traditional autonomy of the individual—once held in high esteem—strikes us today as obsolete, indeed as dangerous. We can no longer presume to capture the creative forces behind the individual in a self-enclosed biography. The value of the individual now … resides … in his participation in the general process of life…."[47] As Gebert and Hemken correctly point out, for both Dorner and Moholy-Nagy "… the Raum der Gegenwart was a pedagogical installation, one that was supposed to enlighten [visitors] concerning the new constellations and conditions of perception in highly industrialized times, one that trains our sense of sight."[48]

According to Ines Katenhusen, this gallery—which we might dub "Raum 3" in Moholy-Nagy's own series of installations—was to contain only reproductions of artworks, with the exception of the Lichtrequisit (Light Prop).[49] It is important to note that at the time neither Moholy-Nagy nor Dorner regarded the Light Prop itself as an artwork. It was seen to be, rather, as a "prop," a means for the production of the new art of designed kinetic colored light projections or reflections, an art of moving colored light.[50]

Initially, financial constraints hampered the construction of the Raum der Gegenwart, and, for obvious political reasons, after 1932 it became impossible to implement the project.[51] An exciting development is the realization of Moholy-Nagy's design in 2009 for the exhibition *Kunst Licht Spiele: Lichtästhetik der klassischen Avantgarde* (Art Light Plays: The Light Aesthetics of the Classic Avant-Garde) at the Kunsthalle, Erfurt, and the Schirn Kunsthalle in Frankfurt (Main).[52] Jakob Gebert and Kai-Uwe Hemken, the researchers and designers involved, have taken an intelligent approach in this undertaking, resulting in a credible, near-optimal achievement.

By the end of his career, in the United States, Moholy-Nagy's conception of the Gesamtwerk had taken on the form of "an international cultural working assembly" that would work toward "synthesis" of a long list of scientific, artistic, and other endeavors. Working "either for a long or a limited period together, in daily contact, in their studios and laboratories," members of a body of this kind "could represent a center of the highest aspirations. As the nucleus of a world-government it could prepare new, collective forms of cultural and social life for a coming generation."[53] The idea had evolved, yet the impulse essentially remained the same: the encyclopedic, totalizing, pan-epistemological Gesamtwerk that integrates all aspects of human endeavor.[54] Tensions can be identified between Moholy-Nagy's totalizing biological determinism and his rhetoric of "humanism," as well as between his biocentric tendencies and his insistence in his writings on the centrality of humanity, rather than "nature," and are also apparent if his rejection of the Gesamtkunstwerk is considered in the light of the aesthetic tendencies of the Gesamtwerk. However, it is more fruitful to accept these tensions rather than elide them.

kehr. Bei Heine und Werfel sind sie schwingendes Sentiment.

Wir sehen die ewige Zickzacklinie des Schwebens im Spiel der Kinder. Die Kerze des Vogellieds. Einfach. Ohne menschliche Einmischung. Wir sehen hinter Hüllen das Unvergängliche, das Allgespeiste. Wir sehen das Weibliche, das Männliche, den Hass, die Freude, den Schmerz.

Ihr nennt uns radikal. Es gibt keinen Radikalismus in der Kunst, die immer wurzelhaft ist. Ihr baut Systeme der Literatur. Ihr speichert Erd-Himmel-Flächen-Geistwerte. Wir achten jene Werte für die Erde. Aber wir wissen: Unter jenen Persönlichkeitswerten rauscht die Unendlichkeit der Schau. Wir kennen euch, kennen All, aber ihr kennt uns nicht, kennt euch, begrenzt. Wir schauen. Wir knieen. Wir sind in den Wirbel gerissen. Wir empfangen ehrfürchtig furchtlos die Gabe des Unbedingten. Wir sind Verwalter. Wir künden. Wir sind Schöpfer. Die Kunst lebt.

Kurt Liebmann

Dynamisch-konstruktives Kraftsystem

Die vitale Konstruktivität ist die Erscheinungsform des Lebens und das Prinzip aller menschlichen und kosmischen Entfaltungen.

In die Kunst umgesetzt bedeutet sie heute die Aktivmachung des Raumes mittels dynamisch-konstruktiver Kraftsysteme, d. h. die Ineinander-Konstruierung der in dem physischen Raume sich real gegeneinander spannenden Kräfte und ihre Hineinkonstruierung in den gleichfalls als Kraft (Spannung) wirkenden Raum.

Die Konstruktivität als Organisationsprinzip der menschlichen Bestrebungen führte in der Kunst der letzten Zeit von der Technik aus zu einer solchen statischen Gestaltungsform, welche entweder zu einem technischen Naturalismus ausartete, oder zu solchen Formvereinfachungen, die in der Beschränkung auf die Horizontale, Vertikale und Diagonale stecken geblieben sind. Der beste Fall war eine offene: excentrische (centrifugale) Konstruktion, die wohl auf die Spannungsverhältnisse der Formen und des Raumes hingewiesen hat, ohne aber die Lösung zu finden.

Deshalb müssen wir an die Stelle des **statischen Prinzips der klassischen Kunst** das **Dynamische** des universellen **Lebens** setzen. Praktisch: statt der statischen **Material-Konstruktion** (Material- und Form-Verhältnisse) muss die dynamische Konstruktion (vitale Konstruktivität, **Kräfteverhältnisse**) organisiert werden, wo das Material nur als **Kraftträger** verwendet wird.

Die dynamische Einzel-Konstruktion weitergeführt ergibt das DYNAMISCH-KONSTRUKTIVE KRAFTSYSTEM, wobei der in der Betrachtung bisheriger Kunstwerke rezeptive Mensch in allen seinen Potenzen mehr als je gesteigert, selbst zum aktiven Faktor der sich entfaltenden Kräfte wird.

Mit den Problemen dieses Kraftsystems hängt das Problem der im Raume frei schwebenden Plastik und des Filmes als projizierter Raumbewegung eng zusammen. Die ersten Entwürfe zu dem dynamischkonstruktiven Kraftsystem können nur experimentelle und Demonstrationsapparate sein zur Prüfung des Zusammenhangs zwischen Materie, Kraft, Raum. Danach folgt die Benutzung der experimentellen Resultate zur Gestaltung freier (von maschinen-technischer Bewegung freier) sich bewegenden Kunstwerke.

Kemény   Moholy-Nagy

Fröhliche Weihnachten

Es wird seit Jahren bemängelt, dass der Sturm seine Leser zu Weihnachten ohne literarischen Ratgeber lässt. Wir sind bekanntlich einseitig, und es gibt soviel Gutes, das nicht im Sturm erscheint. Auch unsere Leser haben schliesslich ein Recht auf Kultur, die sich nach Ansicht der halbgebildeten und der tiefgebildeten Menschheit in der Literatur für Männer ausspricht und für Frauen spiegelt. Auch unsere lieben Kleinen haben ein Recht auf Teilbildung. Und die reifere Jugend ist für Verleger ein wahres Fressen. Die werten Eltern sind mit Schiller und Felix Dahn eingedeckt, die moderne Mutter hat ausserdem ihren Frenssen und ihren Wedekind auf dem Nachttisch und das gesamte deutsche Volk

Immersion/Participation

"You know czardas?" "No. I've never danced it." "You will," he said, beaming. "Left and left–right and right." His voice was … intense.… "Hands on my shoulders. Left and left. Now jump." From a slow square-dance rhythm we changed to faster and faster tempi. My hair came undone, my belt fell to the floor. An earring followed, but we didn't stop. I had never felt such an obsession for dancing.… When we finally left the floor we were both drunk and we'd had no wine.[1]

This is how Sibyl Moholy-Nagy described her first dance with Moholy-Nagy, and it is the most vivid description of Moholy-Nagy's engagement with the kinaesthetic experience of bodily movement that I have encountered. Despite his reputation as a cool rationalist, he did not hesitate to incorporate his passion for the body and its capabilities into his aesthetic project.

During the 1950s a new type of art emerged within the Western paradigm. Building on European precedents from the 1920s (De Stijl interiors, Lazar el Lissitzy's *Proun Room* and "Abstract Cabinet," etc.), Latin American, North American, and European artists were developing concepts for artworks that posited full immersion of the "viewer" or art consumer within the artwork, or their active manipulation of the work. The "walk-in paintings," and most particularly the John Cage–inspired "Happenings" on the Eastern Seaboard of the United States, are clear examples of this tendency.[2] During the 1960s this trend was taken one step further. Art consumers (no longer mere "viewers") were called upon to participate, both bodily and mentally, in producing the art. It was their experience that became the "artwork." Salient examples include 1970s works by the Brazilian artist Lygia Clark that sought to hone participants' sensory/perceptual capabilities.

In Berlin during the 1920s László Moholy-Nagy was also thinking in terms of offering experiences that would enact sensory training for modernity.[3] As Sibyl Moholy-Nagy phrased it "everyone in possession of his senses could be a creative participant."[4] These ideas were first put forward in the manifesto "Dynamisch-Konstruktives Kraftsystem" (Dynamic-Constructive Energy System), written in conjunction with his compatriot, Communist art historian and critic Alfréd Kemény. In 1921 Kemény had attended the Third Comintern Congress in Moscow, where he encountered Alexander Bogdanov's ideas, which were popular with the Constructivists he met there.[5] I have argued elsewhere that Bogdanov had a strong effect on Kemény's thinking at this time, and that after his return to Berlin Kemény began a close collaboration with Moholy-Nagy, leading to the publication of "Dynamic-Constructive Energy System" in *Der Sturm* in 1922.[6] Moholy-Nagy brought to the manifesto Hausmann's conceptions of radiant energies and the dematerialization of art. Indeed, he had already signed Hausmann's manifesto "Aufruf zur Elementaren Kunst" (Call to Elementary Art), which had appeared in *Der Sturm* the year before. In it, the artist is seen as being "a mere carrier of energies that bring the elements of the world into being"–"tirelessly criss-crossing waves of energy that result in the form and spirit of an epoch."[7] In their joint manifesto, Kemény and Moholy-Nagy add Bogdanov's Wilhelm Ostwald–inspired notion that reality is composed of energy relationships. Understanding these relationships leads to the "science of building," or "architectonics" (Tektologiia), an early form of systems theory, though they translate it here as Konstruktivität (Constructivity): "Vital Constructivity is the form in which life appears, and the principle of all human and cosmic development. Translated into art, this today entails the activation of space by means of dynamic-constructive energy systems, that is, the construction into each other of energies that are actually at tension in physical space, a space (tension) that also functions as energy." After a critique of avant-garde sculpture and painting, the manifesto proclaims: "This is why we must replace the *static* principle of *classical art* with the *dynamic* principle of universal *life*. In practical terms: instead of static material constructions… dynamic construction (or vital Constructivity, i.e., the *relation* of energies) must be involved, in which the material is employed only as the *carrier of energies*…." The result, according to the authors, might be the "Dynamic-Constructive Energy System, whereby a person, up to that point merely receptive in his observation of works of art, experiences an intensification of his capabilities like never before, and himself becomes an active factor in the unfolding energies." They go on to relate this new paradigm

László Moholy-Nagy and Alfréd Kemény, "Dynamisch-konstruktives Kraftsystem" (Dynamic-constructive energy system), *Der Sturm* 13, no. 12 (December 1922), p. 186.

Dada-Constructivist Congress, Weimar, September 1922 (detail). Top row, left to right: Hans Vogel, Lucia Moholy, László Moholy-Nagy, Alfréd Kemény; Bottom row, left to right: Lazar El Lissitzky, Nelly van Doesburg, Theo van Doesburg.

13

Der Organismus Mensch steht in dem kubischen, abstrakten Raum der Bühne.
Mensch und Raum sind gesetzerfüllt. Wessen Gesetz soll gelten?
Entweder wird der abstrakte Raum in Rücksicht auf den natürlichen Menschen
diesem angepaßt und in Natur oder deren Illusion rückverwandelt. Dies geschieht auf der naturillusionistischen Bühne.
Oder der natürliche Mensch wird in Rücksicht auf den abstrakten Raum diesem
gemäß umgebildet. Dies geschieht auf der abstrakten Bühne.

Die Gesetze des kubischen Raums sind das unsichtbare Liniennetz der planimetrischen und stereometrischen Beziehungen.
Dieser Mathematik entspricht die dem menschlichen Körper innewohnende
Mathematik und schafft den Ausgleich durch Bewegungen, die ihrem Wesen nach
mechanisch und vom Verstand bestimmt sind. Es ist die Geometrie der
Leibesübungen, Rhythmik und Gymnastik. Es sind die körperlichen Effekte
(dazu die Stereotypie des Gesichts), die in dem exakten Equilibristen und in
den Massenriegen des Stadions, wiewohl hier ohne Bewußtsein der Raumbeziehungen, zum Ausdruck kommen. (Obenstehende Abbildung.)

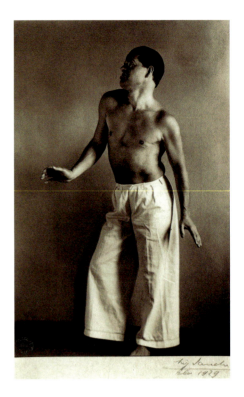

Die Absichten des Theaters „Pré"

Das Theater „Pré" hat die Aufgabe, den Menschen als Bewegungsteil einer räumlichen Spannung von wechselnder Beschaffenheit zu zeigen. Es fasst zunächst einen Tänzer auf als ein Wesen, das sich ganz als Zentrum und Peripherie des durch die Bühne gegebenen Raumes fühlt. Dieser Raum als Abstraktum, als kubische Kunstform, bedingt ein Bewusstwerden des Tänzers als Raumträger und Raumbewegter, der auch das Nichtsichtbare, die Logik der scheinbaren Leere, zu gestalten hat. Der Tänzer ist raumbewegend in dem Sinne, dass er alle Spannungsrelationen des Raumes in sich erlebt und ihnen eine offenbare Form durch seinen Körper verleiht. Der Tänzer des Theater „Pré" ist ausserstande, vor einem willkürlichen oder räumlich unkonstruktiven Raum Bewegungsrelationen zu erleben oder zu gestalten, stets muss der Kunstraum der Bühne derart räumlich konstruiert sein, dass die Emanation des Tanzes als einzig mögliche Bewegungslogik aus ihm entspringt. Aus dieser Notwendigkeit muss die Dekoration oder das Kostüm im alten Sinne fallen. Die Logik und Klarheit der Bühnenkonstruktion veranlasst und zwingt den Tänzer zu einer mit ihm organisch verbundenen Tanzform. Die bisherige Bewegungsromantik wird aufgehoben und analog dem Bühnenraumgebilde der Tanzende zum Ausdruck der Vertikalen, der Diagonale, des Quadrats. Gemäss den neuen Anschauungen vom Raum in der Malerei wird die Bühne behandelt und kubisch räumlich aufgebaut. Der sogenannte Hintergrund ist nunmehr lebendige Relation zum Mittelraum, in dem der Tänzer diese Relationen auffängt und in eine Bewegungssynthese seiner Körperglieder verwandelt, die aller nur menschlichen Mechanik entwöhnt sein müssen. Auf diese Weise wird die Tanzimprovisation unmöglich und der Tanz, die absolute Raumgebundenheit, ausgedrückt durch den menschlichen geistigen Bewegungswillen. Die Synthese des raumbewegten Menschen im Tanz bedingt die strengste Regel. Die scheinbare Freiheit der Grotesktänzerei wird als Anarchie empfunden und verworfen. In vollkommener Analogie zum Raum und zum Tanz muss die Musik das Tempo durch die akustischen Relationen gestalten. Das Theater „Pré" will die vollkommene Gesetzmässigkeit und Klarheit der raumzeitlichen Bewegung in der Einheitsform von Körper, Fläche und Ton verwirklichen: in einer neuen Form des Tanzes, der Bühne und der Musik.

Hausmann   Peri

Trennung
W. v. Z. zu Eigen

Der Eine: Wirr schreien Deine wunden
                Brüste
           Begehrend lachend
           Kreisend zuckend
           Das Wühlen unbewehrter
                Männerfäuste . . .
           In tiefen hohen Höhen
           besingen Vögel lieblich
                weiche Seen
           berieseln klange bange gelbe
                Wellen . . .
           Doch meines Blutes Schrei
                befiehlt
           Verrasen
           Schrei schreie Mutterschreie
           Deines Leibes

Der Andere: Bejage ungefügig Deine
                Schluchten
           Deines Wollens
           Und reite nie gesattelt durch
                die Wälder . .
           Verneine plumpes wildes
                Gellen
           bezeuge Deiner Armut karges
                Stöhnen
           Und rase durch die Bitte
                meiner Nacht
           Ich kralle rote gelbbezuckte
                Blumen
           Verlache altes grünbe-
                hauchtes Locken
           Und brause ungeschäumt das
                Sehnen
           meiner Hirne

Der Eine: Du hast die Lüste Deiner
                Nächte
           Das Rasen Deines unge-
                bäumten Blutes

Oskar Schlemmer, *Figure and Linear Space* (1924), in Moholy-Nagy, Molnár, and Schlemmer 1925, p. 13.

August Sander, *Hausmann as Dancer*, 1929. 25.5 × 15 cm.

Raoul Hausmann, *PRÉ*, 1920. Ink on paper, 34 × 34 cm. Acquisition number 7144/93. Berlinische Galerie, Berlin. Photo: Berlinische Galerie © ADAGP (Paris) / SODRAC (Montreal)

Raoul Hausmann and László Péri, "Die Absichten des Theaters 'Pré,'" *Der Sturm* (September 3, 1922), p. 138.

The U-Theater in Operation, ca. 1925. Mixed media, dimensions and present location unknown. In Moholy-Nagy, Molnár, and Schlemmer 1925.

Designs for the «Kinetic-Constructive System. A structure with paths of motion for sport and recreation," from 1922 and 1928. In Moholy-Nagy 1932, pp. 164–65.

Immersion/Participation

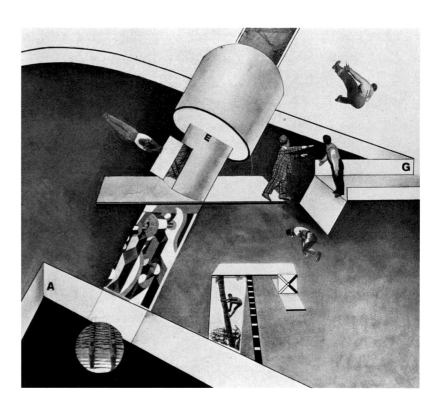

Fig. 145. Moholy-Nagy, 1922.
The first conception of the kinetic constructive system of Fig. 145 a (also see the sketch for the mechanical eccentric structure in Volume 4 of the Bauhaus books).

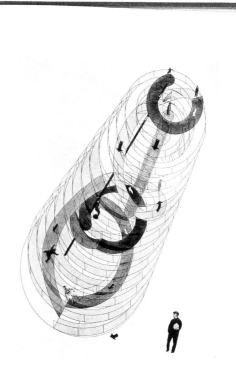

Fig. 145 a. Moholy-Nagy, 1922.
Kinetic constructive system. A structure with paths of motion for sport and recreation (executed by Stefan Sebök, Engineer, in 1928).

Sketch for Kinetic-Constructive System, 1922. Watercolor, ink, graphite, and collage on paper, 61 × 48 cm.

Untitled (conceptual sketch for Kinetic-Constructive System), 1921. Collage on paper, 34.2 × 44.5 cm.

Kinetic-Constructive System. A structure with paths of motion for sport and recreation, 1928. Ink, photomontage, and watercolor on card, 76 × 54.5 cm. Executed by István Sebök.

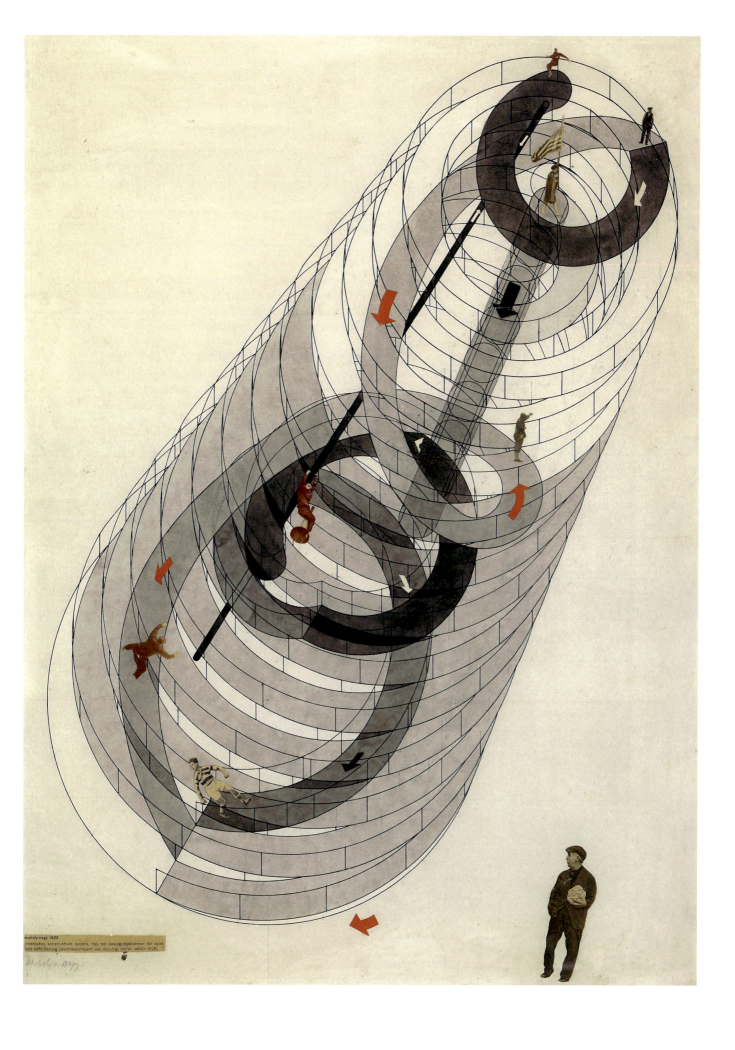

L. MOHOLY-NAGY Bühnenszene Lautsprecher

of art to "the problem of freely floating sculpture as well as of film as a projected spatial movement. The first attempts at dynamic-constructive energy systems can be only experimental demonstrations testing the connections between matter, energy, and space. [Only] then follows the use of these experimental results for the design of works of art free from mechanical-technical movement."[8]

This was quite an ambitious program. In particular it is important to note their call for the eventual dematerialization of the artwork into an unspecified form of pure energy, free, as they put it, from "mechanical-technical" movement, a free-floating art involving the active participation of (presumably) equally free-floating participants. This is the earliest articulation of this central aspect of Moholy-Nagy's aesthetic project, which he adopted from Hausmann's text "PRÉsentismus" (Presentism). Moholy-Nagy dates his conception of two key projects to the period in 1922 when he formulated this manifesto: the Lichtrequisit einer elektrischen Bühne (Light Prop for an Electric Stage) and the Kinetisches konstruktives System. Bau mit Bewegungsbahnen für Spiel und Beförderung (Kinetic-Constructive System. A structure with paths of motion for sport and recreation). The reference in the "Dynamic-Constructive Energy System" manifesto to "film as a projected spatial movement" also makes it clear that Moholy-Nagy began to formulate his ideas for what he later referred to as Polycinema in 1922. As discussed in the "Gesamtwerk" section of this book, the text also supports his claim that he began working on the film script "Dynamic of the Metropolis." by 1922.

In his first book, *Malerei, Photographie, Film* (Painting, Photography, Film) as well as in subsequent texts, Moholy-Nagy asked questions concerning film projection, the key new medium of the era. As a result of this process of inquiry, he proposed an environment, the "Simultaneous or Polycinema," within which multiple projectors, set behind moving mirrors or fastened to pivots, would project several moving films, simultaneously, onto large concave, textured, and convex surfaces, as well as geometrical solids. This would result in "new demands on our optical organ of perception, the eye, and our center of perception, the brain" in emulation of modern urban life, which has "increased the capacity of our perceptual organs for simultaneous acoustical and optical activity."[9] While he was never able to realize the Polycinema project, this is one of the first theoretical texts, and indeed specific proposals, relating to what would later be termed "expanded cinema."

Raoul Hausmann's experiments with bodily movement are also significant in this context. In 1922 Hausmann, together with Lászlo Péri, an International Constructivist artist and erstwhile actor who was one of Moholy-Nagy's Hungarian friends, proposed the "PRÉ" theater.[10] This must have been one of the first manifestos for an art of proprioception through dance. It was also evidently a source for Oskar Schlemmer's conception of bodily movement in space, first articulated in *Die Bühne im Bauhaus* (The Theater of the Bauhaus), Moholy-Nagy, Schlemmer, and Farkas Molnár's joint Bauhaus book.

Stage Scene: Loudspeker, ca. 1925, photomontage, dimensions and present location unknown, in Moholy-Nagy, Molnár, and Schlemmer 1925.

Stills from Peter Yeadon, *Kinetic Re-Constructive System*, 2006. CAD digital file. Based on the 1928 design for László Moholy-Nagy, Kinetic-Constructive System: A structure with paths of motion for sport and recreation.

Immersion/Participation

Many of Moholy-Nagy's photomontages, which he referred to as "photoplastics," involve images of bodily movement within or upon structures, some of which resemble elements in the Kinetic-Constructive System proposal. Examined in this light, and especially against the backdrop of the general 1920s' culture of physical activity, in particular at the Bauhaus, this body of work can be seen as evidence that Moholy-Nagy's concept of this system was evolving, in his thinking and artistic activities, between its first conception in 1922 and its most developed articulation in 1928. All of the relevant photomontages date from this period.

In "Theater, Zirkus, Varieté" (Theater, Circus, Variety theater), published in *Die Bühne im Bauhaus*, Moholy-Nagy states that he is building on the Futurists' "Theatre of Surprises." His discussion of the new theater's dynamism reveals that he was well aware of Fedele Azari's "Aero Teatro" 1918–19 performances in his plane over Busto Arsizio and later in the skies above Milan.[11] In this analysis Moholy-Nagy insists that mechanization of traditional theater will open it up, moving away from a horizontal to a more vertical orientation, which will incorporate devices such as film, cars, elevators, airplanes, mirrors, etc.[12] Teasing out the idea expressed in the "Dynamic-Constructive Energy System" manifesto Moholy-Nagy underscores the audience's active participation: "In today's theater the stage and audience are separated from each other too much and are too divided into activity and passivity to be able to achieve creative contacts and tensions between them. An activity must finally come to pass, which rather than leaving the masses to observe in silence, grabs them, draws them in, and at the highest level, allows for a liberating ecstasy to flow together with the action on the stage."[13]
In order to effect this integration, he proposes a new type of theatrical space, equipped with a proscenium extending deep into the audience, and also incorporating operable bridges and platforms at various levels, connected to each other by a cylindrical

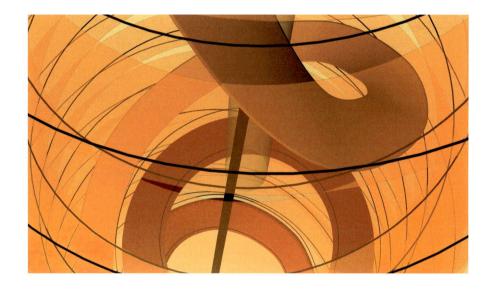

elevator shaft. He planned to heighten the immersive nature of this experience with an acoustic installation, a kind of early "surround sound," with speakers placed everywhere, including under the audience's seats.[14] Farkas Molnár illustrated Moholy-Nagy's ideas in his drawings for a U-Theater (p. 83). Molnár's drawing-photomontage of the U-Theater in action portrays figures jumping, diving, and climbing amid the architectural paraphernalia, creating the impression that these performers (and perhaps even audience members) were moving without or in spite of gravity.[15]

In his proposal for a Kinetic-Constructive System, Moholy-Nagy carried the participatory principles articulated in "Dynamic-Constructive Energy System" and "Theater, Circus, Variety theater" to their logical extreme. Rather than a theater, this Kinetic-Constructive System would be an environment in which the "audience" could become "actors," that is, could participate in ludic physical activity. As he phrased it in his 1925 article "Typo-Photo,"[16] this would facilitate "elements of human achievement" such as "the will to play, participation, [and] discovery…." Moreover this "play"—involving the proprioceptive, vestibular, tactile and visual senses—would constitute the "art," rather than the structure itself, which, after all, remained a "system" and a "structure," in other words, a mere site or scaffold for activity.

Though a couple of early schematic sketches exist for the Kinetic-Constructive System, the designs for these proposals were only finalized in 1928, with István Sebök's technical assistance (pp. 84–85). The photomontage elements depicting people moving within the structure on the beautiful planometric oblique projection of 1928 recall the collaged photographs in Gustav Klucis's *Dynamic City* and Molnár's rendering of the U-Theater in use. This underlines both the genealogy of Moholy-Nagy's conception of dynamic art, and his work with his compatriots Molnár and Sebök, collaborators who helped Moholy-Nagy resolve some of the proposal's practical and conceptual issues.

The 1922 and 1928 renderings seem to have been meant more as conceptual diagrams than as a basis for construction blueprints. However, if all the structural and mechanical details had been worked out and if the structure had been built, it would have stood about twelve stories high, with a fixed, tube-like elevator shaft at its core, akin to the one that Molnár had drawn for the U-Theater; this shaft would have run from near the structure's apex down to about its midpoint. The structure's principal component would have been a spiral ramp equipped with handrails, defining the edifice's (otherwise unclad) exterior. While it would have been the building's main structural support, this

L. MOHOLY-NAGY — Der wohlwollende Herr (Zirkusszene)

L. MOHOLY-NAGY — Menschmechanik (Varieté)

Immersion/Participation

T. Lux Feininger, *Sport at the bauhaus* (Xanti Schawinsky at left), ca. 1927. 23.7 × 17.9 cm.

The Well-Meaning Gentleman (Circus Scene) and *Human Mechanics (Variety Theater)*, ca. 1925. Photomontages, dimensions and present location unknown. In Moholy-Nagy, Molnár, and Schlemmer 1925. pp. 64–65.

Kinetic-Constructive System (details), 1928. Ink, photomontage and watercolor on card.

Still from Peter Yeadon, *Kinetic Re-Constructive System*, 2006, CAD digital file.

outer ramp would have itself rotated, corkscrew-like, thereby spinning the entire assembly around its axis. The sign of this axis, the fireman's pole, extending from the structure's highest platform to ground level, would have been fixed at its top but movable at its base, rendering the whole ensemble a dynamic, seemingly unstable dispositif, the very movability of the "axis" symbolizing its dynamism. This is especially striking, since, as Peter Yeadon determined in his digital modeling of the 1928 design, it was to have been a "frustum" that is, a "leaning" tower. In the interior, nested within the exterior ramp, there would have been another spiraling ramp "of the steepest practicable incline, for the use of more athletic visitors."[17] This latter component would have extended from the ground up to and beyond the outer ramp's apex, ending in a third platform at the structure's pinnacle (pp. 86–87).

Friedrich Kiesler's 1924 Raumbühne (Spatial Stage), constructed at the center of the Wiener Konzerthaus on the occasion of the International Exhibition of New Theater Techniques, also consisted of a spiral ramp with a circular stage platform at top. Kiesler had originally envisaged a lift on its central axis to move the actors to the various levels.[18] In all these ways, it is a kind of simpler precursor to the Kinetic-Constructive System and may have shaped Moholy-Nagy's conception to some extent, as it is likely that he saw the show. Conversely, there is also evidence that Kemény and Moholy-Nagy's manifesto impinged on Kiesler's thinking; in his text entitled "The City in Space" Kiesler calls for us to "liberate ourselves from the ground, [the] task of the static axis...."[19] Nevertheless, Kiesler's Raumbühne was, after all, a stage. There is a closer parallel in his Railway Theater project from the same year. This envisaged conveying the audience "electromechanically" around a spherical theater space on a rotating, spiral viewing ramp, much as the external ramp in the Kinetic-Constructive System would have spun participants around its interior elements.[20] Andor Weininger's proposal for a Spherical Theater (1926; p. 89) adopted a similar form; had it been built, the circus-style acrobatic action it presented, unfolding on the suspended spiral and on the other contraptions at the center of the building, could have been viewed either from below, from the sides, or from above, depending on where members of the audience chose to sit. Weininger emphasized the new theatrical space's sensory-educational function: "Situated along the inner wall of a sphere, the spectators experience a new relationship to space; due to the total view, due to the centripetal force, they experience a new mental, optical, acoustic situation: they face new possibilities of concentric, eccentric, polydirectional, mechanical space-stage events ... objective: to educate people to new modes of viewing by confronting them with new rhythms of movement...."[21]

Fig. 161. O. Firle, 1928.
Elevator shaft.
Photo: Krajewsky

182

Fig. 162. Smokestacks of a factory in Ohio.
Photo: Weltspiegel

183

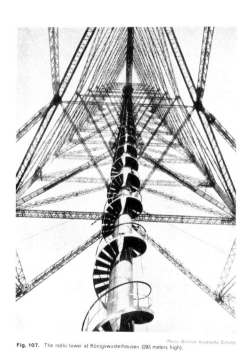

Fig. 107. The radio tower at Königswusterhausen (293 meters high).
Photo: Berliner Illustrierte Zeitung

122

elements, in particular the spiral (screw) has led to solutions amazing in their contrast with earlier (baroque) esthetic principles (Figs. 106, 107).
Thus we have reached a conscious utilization of the whole stock of biotechnical elements, and the outcome is at once a new conception of beauty.

Fig. 108. Korona Krause (Bauhaus, first semester 1924).
Equipoised sculpture (illusionistic).

An attempt at constructive application of the spiral, which carries the whole structure.

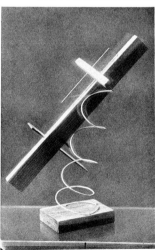

Photo: Eckner, Weimar

123

Top: Elevator shaft designed by Otto Firle (left) and smokestacks in Ohio (right), In Moholy-Nagy, 1932, pp. 182–83. Bottom: Radio tower at Königswusterhausen (left) and Korona Krause, *Equiposed Sculpture* (1924) (right). In Moholy-Nagy 1932, pp. 122–23.

Bexhill Seaside Pavilion, Bexhill on Sea, Sussex (1936). Gelatin silver print from original negative, estate edition, 1994.

Film still from *Impressions from the Old Port of Marseilles (Vieux Port)*, Germany, 1932. 35 mm, black and white, silent, 10'.

Immersion/Participation

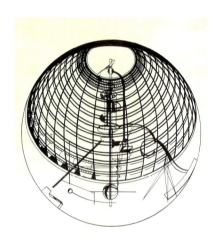

Although audience members here would have faced sensory challenges, these would have been tame when contrasted with those that the Kinetic-Constructive System would have presented to visitors. As in Weininger's proposed Spherical Theater, views upward, downward and laterally would have been incorporated within the Kinetic-Constructive System. However, the vistas in Moholy-Nagy's structure would have revealed a complex of interconnecting spiral ramps and flexible vertical elements, conjuring up a three-dimensional, labyrinthine, almost Piranesian impression, and further contributing to a sense of disorientation.[22] Meanwhile, more "athletic visitors," moving up and down the steeper nested spirals within the structure or sliding down its fireman's pole, would have been observed by those on the external ramp, like novice skateboarders watching their more experienced fellows from the edge of a skateboard park. Contrasting with Kiesler's and Weininger's closely related proposals, in the Kinetic-Constructive System visitors would have become "active factors" in coming to understand space, gravity, their own bodies and interoceptive organs. This calls to mind the line from "Production–Reproduction" in which Moholy-Nagy writes that "The human construct is the synthesis of all its functional apparatuses, that is, the human being will be most perfect in his own time if the functional apparatuses of which he is composed—the cells as well as the most complicated organs—are conscious and trained to the limit of their efficiency...."[23] Given the dangers and thrills of the Kinetic-Constructive System, its participants would have been pushing their bodies to precisely this kind of limit, and employing their vestibular-proprioceptive systems to sense these "cells" and "organs" in motion or imbalance. Rather than a towering artwork or an architectural structure, in the Kinetic-Constructive System Moholy-Nagy would have offered people opportunities to have visual, proprioceptive and vestibular experiences.

As has been pointed out by Klaus Weber and Barbara Lesák, and more recently by myself and Olivier Lugon,[24] the Kinetic-Constructive System resembles a fairground ride. Given that Moholy-Nagy's Berlin residences were located in the city's western districts, near Luna Park, the largest amusement park in Europe at the time,[24] it comes as no surprise that Moholy-Nagy includes an ecstatic description of its pleasures in the first, Hungarian-language version of his "Dynamic of the Metropolis" script (1922–24): "Fireworks in the Luna Park / Ride on the / Roller Coaster / Speeding / FERRIS wheel / Funhouse / Distorting mirrors / Other gimmicks...."[26] Moholy-Nagy's oeuvre contains further examples of his love of fairground rides, including photographs of a merry-go-round in England and a waterslide in Zurich.

Although Berlin's Luna Park boasted Expressionistic decorations of peep-show structures, executed in 1919–20 by Max Pechstein and Rudolf Belling, as well as the wildly Expressionistic exterior of the park's main roller coaster, also dating from the same period,[27] I have come across no evidence of artists actually designing amusement park rides. As Lesák has remarked, however, avant-garde artists were fascinated by such rides during the 1920s.[28] During an extended stay in Paris in 1911–12, Joseph Stella, an

Detail showing rollercoaster sequence, storyboard for "A nagyváros dinamikája" (Dynamic of the Metropolis), *MA* (Today) 9, edited by Lajos Kassák, (September 15, 1924).

Andor Weininger, Kugel-Theater (Spherical Theater) (1926), presentation drawing for an exhibition, ca. 1930, ink on cardboard, 56 × 46.3 cm.

Untitled (Aeroplane Swing, Brighton), 1935–37. 13.2 × 18.2 cm.

Rutschbahn (Slide), 1923. Mixed media on paper, 64.7 × 49.5 cm.

Poster design for the *Exhibition for Health Maintenance, Social Welfare and Body Exercises*, 1926. Gouache on paper, 31.3 × 24.2 cm.

Zurich, Waterslide, n. d. Vintage gelatin silver print, dimensions unknown.

Italian who had emigrated to the US, discovered the Parisian avant-garde's Cubist and Orphist paintings, as well as the Italian Futurists' work. After returning to New York in late 1912, he painted an astonishing series of works depicting the Coney Island amusement parks.[29] The "Futurist Opera" *Victory Over the Sun* by Alexander Kruchenykh, Mikhail Matiushin, and Kasimir Malevich had been performed at the Luna Park in St. Petersburg in 1913, taking "full advantage of the Luna Park's existing technological infrastructure" such as "large mobile spotlights."[30] In 1915 Giacomo Balla and Fortunato Depero proposed a kind of theme park in their "Futurist Reconstruction of the Universe," involving kinetic assemblages of various materials ("complexes"), "aerial concerts," the "roto-plastic noise fountain," etc. They wrote: "We will find abstract equivalents for all the forms and elements of the universe, and then we will combine them according to the caprice of our inspiration, to shape plastic complexes (rotating on one axis) which we will set in motion."[31]

Moholy-Nagy's fellow Bauhausler Max Burchartz called in 1924 for reform of the Luna Park:

The joy in intense movement (flywheels alongside sleds and swings); the pleasure in surprise and sensation; the daring of bold skill; the delight in watching action, form, and color.... Direct the large slideways above, through, and around the main restaurants (take advantage of differences in the levels of the existing buildings).... design of the directional possibilities of standstill and movement, of fast and slow, of sudden and gradual as well as of horizontal and vertical, of up and down, of forward and backward, of rotating and swinging.... Distinction should be made between machines that are compelled to carry out particular courses of movement and those that call for active participation in mastering one's balance....[32]

Lesák has observed that the mobile audience ramp in Kiesler's 1924 Railway Theater proposal resembles a roller coaster.[33] That same year the Danish avant-gardist Knud Lönberg-Holm, while teaching at the University of Michigan, Ann Arbor, took his students on roller-coaster rides "in order to experience modernity."[34] It is within this context of artists' fascination with fairground rides during the 1920 that Moholy-Nagy's proposed structure is to be understood, rather than, as has generally been the case, as a proposal for a "theater."

Immersion/Participation

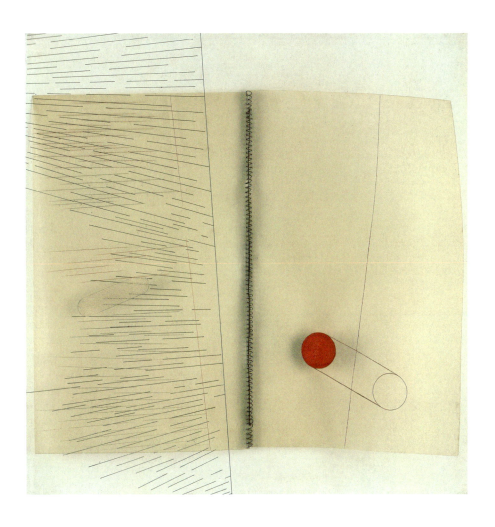

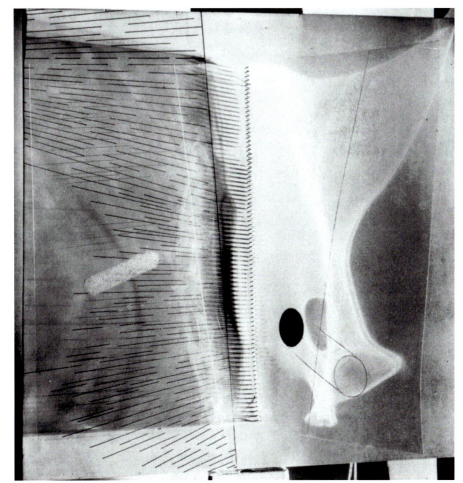

Film still from *Interview with Institute of Design students and display of student work, Chicago*, 1942. 16 mm film transferred to DVD, color, silent. On display is *Space Modulator*, 1942. Plexiglas and chrome-plated steel rods (lost).

Mobile, 1942. Wood and chrome-plated steel rods (lost?). Gelatin silver documentary prints.

Top: *Light Painting*, 1937. Pigment, acetate, wire, board, 50 × 51 cm. Bottom: Moholy-Nagy illustrating *Light Painting* and demonstrating how the acetate "pages" may assume different positions, producing various light effects, in: Moholy-Nagy, 1947b, p. 146.

How new were Moholy-Nagy's ideas about immersion and participation? In her work on Oskar Schlemmer, Nancy Troy has pointed out that "in 1910, the Italian Futurists had been the first explicitly to reject the conventions of beholding, which had previously been determined by the requirements of perspectival illusionism in painting. Instead of an immobile spectator standing opposite a painted image, they aimed to 'put the spectator in the center of the picture.' Three years later," Troy continues, "Marinetti extended this idea to the Futurist Variety Theater which, he wrote, 'is alone in seeking the audience's collaboration. It [that is, the audience] doesn't remain static like a stupid voyeur, but joins noisily in the action.'"[35] While Lissitzky (with his *Proun Room*), Kurt Schwitters (with his *Merzbau*), Schlemmer, and others proposed and made immersive walk-in works of art and complex spectacles as artworks,[36] none of them suggested creating an artwork that contained little or no aesthetic content other than the participatory actions of the participants/visitors. If one discounts the brawls that sometimes occurred after their early performances, the Futurists never did realize a fully participatory artwork. In this sense, and in keeping with the theoretical statements pronounced in the manifesto he wrote with Kemény, Moholy-Nagy's proposal was new, and it is the clearest predecessor to post–World War II participatory art environments. Furthermore, the notion of viewer participation recurred in Moholy-Nagy's oeuvre. Examples include his 1922 *Zwei Konstruktionsysteme Zusammengefügt* (Integration of Two Systems of Construction) in which art consumers were encouraged to rearrange two elements in relation to each other (pp. 136–37, 148–49, 175), and also encompass what Eduardo Kac dubbed the "kinaesthetically interactive" works of his London period, such as *Gyros*, which viewers were intended to spin, as well as *Light Painting*, where the viewer was invited to manipulate the two hinged celluloid, spiral-bound sheets attached to the work.[37]

A number of authors have pointed out that the Kinetic-Constructive System was conceived with Tatlin's model for the Monument to the Third International in mind, noting that this proposal involves a structure based on a tilted external spiral form with inner platforms, with an elevator at its core. In addition, it was meant to rotate, just like the inner spaces of Tatlin's tower. Both his second book *Von Material zu Architektur* (published in an English edition as *The New Vision*) and Moholy-Nagy's photographic oeuvre contain numerous examples of spiral structures, staircases, elevator shafts, and the like. However, whereas Tatlin's monument was conceived at a superhuman scale, Moholy-Nagy's Kinetic-Constructive System was proportioned in relation to the human body. Moholy-Nagy's structure involves three nested spiral ramps and a movable fireman's pole; it is a site of physical challenge and fun rather than of

Vladimir Tatlin, model for *Monument to the Third International*, 1919. In Kassák and Moholy-Nagy, 1922.

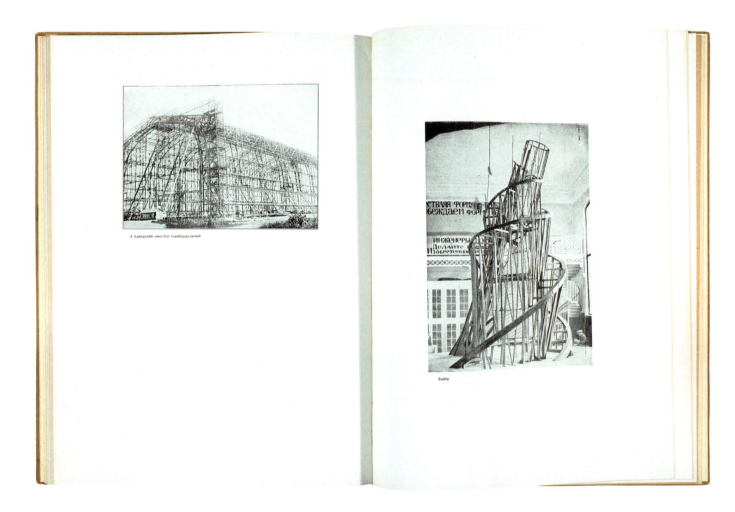

high-minded governance and propaganda, rendering it almost a parody, a carney version of Tatlin's deeply serious tower.

Bodily movement and immersion also appeared as themes in Moholy-Nagy's remarkable trilogy of metropolitan films from the early 1930s.[38] *Marseille, vieux port* (The Old Port of Marseille) includes brief sequences of a (probably Roma) woman dancing at a Marseilles café-restaurant, and of children playing. The latter motif recurs in *Berliner Stilleben* (Berlin Still Life) but with a more athletic touch, portraying children climbing on and spinning their bodies around carriage axles.

These themes are however most fully developed in *Grossstadt-Zigeuner* (Metropolitan Gypsies). In this film Moholy-Nagy thematizes the unguarded physicality of the Roma/Sinti people he focuses his camera on. Contrasting with the stiff, self-disciplined movements of Berlin's general populace, as depicted in the two Berlin films, the Roma use their bodies more freely. The children get into fights and play. The adults fight, too, but they also laugh, display affection, and use arcane, physical codes of hand-gestures while horse trading, with everything "crystallizing finally," as Sibyl Moholy-Nagy curiously phrased it, "into a dance."[39] Rather than documenting all this from outside the arena of movement, however, Moholy-Nagy immerses himself in it, steadying his handheld 1.5-kilo "Kinamo" camera on his shoulder, squatting and aiming it up, down and around.[40] Through him, the camera "dances" with the Roma men, women, and children. This kinaesthetically charged development of the medium, facilitated by handheld cameras, which had only recently become available, harkens back to Moholy-Nagy's and Kemény's calls for a new art of kinaesthetic bodily involvement. Though Charles Metain had demanded as early as 1926 in *G* magazine that "the camera … be set in motion! … Who will build us the film camera for handheld shots?"[41] the utilization of the camera during the dancing sequence in *Metropolitan Gypsies* was evidently inspired by the scenes of women's basketball and men's soccer in Dziga Vertov's brilliant 1929 film *Man with a Movie Camera*, in which Vertov situates the camera among the players. Like Vertov, Moholy-Nagy succeeds in interpolating the "camera eye" into the action, lending the sequence a dynamism that could not be attained even by the kind of complex montage invented by Sergei Eisenstein. *Metropolitan Gypsies* must surely be among the earliest documentaries ever made about the Roma in Germany. It is also arguably the first film in which the filmmaker positions himself both as an observer of the Roma (the man with the camera) and as a participant in their communal activity, "not by an outsider but by an equal participant" as Jeanpaul Goergen puts it.[42] Finally, it calls to mind Sibyl Moholy-Nagy's description of the Csárdás she danced with her husband-to-be. Moholy-Nagy did not merely view the physicality of the Roma as embodying his ideal of bodily movement; he also shared their propensity for bodily engagement.

The "Dynamic-Constructive Energy System" manifesto and the related proposal for a structure are evidence of Moholy-Nagy's attempt to transcend "art" (at least as "art" was traditionally understood) and to arrange instead for situations in which people could experience and develop both their physical and sensory capacities, honing their engagement with interoceptive senses such as kinesthesia and proprioception, for which there was not even a generally accepted terminology in common use at the time. The "system" he advocated was thus immersive, participatory, playful, and transformative, one within which "man, not the object, is the end in view" and within which "everyone is talented." Proposing an environment as a locus for experience, and avoiding the term *art*, Moholy-Nagy was creating a model for the Gesamtwerk, for the integration of art into life, and indeed a precedent for later immersive, participatory, and relational art.

Film stills from *Grossstadt-Zigeuner* (Metropolitan Gypsies), Germany 1932–33. 35 mm, black and white, silent, 12".

Immersion/Participation

Z VII, 1926. Oil on canvas, 95.3 × 76.2 cm.

Untitled, 1925. Photogram on developing paper, 23.9 × 17.9 cm.

Jaroslav Bouček, Installation photograph, *ausstellung l. moholy-nagy*, Mährischer Kunstverein, Brno, Czechoslovakia, June 1935. Gelatin silver print in a spiral-bound album (1934), 29.3 × 20.9 cm.

Projection Spaces

*I longed to have at my disposal a bare room containing twelve projectors,
the multi-coloured rays of which would enable me to animate its white emptiness.*[1]

László Moholy-Nagy's manifesto of media art, *Malerei, Photographie, Film* (*Painting, Photography, Film*) may be regarded as a manifesto of optophonetics.[2] As conceptualized with regard to its use in the fine arts (as the simultaneous deployment of sound and light), optophonetics is by its very nature projective–as is "film" itself. Furthermore, Moholy-Nagy's idea was that light is the immaterial material, so to speak, of all visual art, most obviously of photography and film, but also of painting, because light is of necessity, always projected, whether it is absorbed into or reflected off a surface (or both, depending on its wavelength and on the nature of the surface). Projected light is also the key factor in his "light modulators," which involve light rays passing through transparent surfaces onto opaque ground planes or onto the surfaces around the work, as in his Plexiglas sculptures[3] (pp. 95, 146–147). In an article published in *MA* in 1923, Raoul Hausmann wrote "we will make strides in optics right to the foundational phenomenon of light."[4] For his part, Moholy-Nagy announced in *Painting, Photography, Film* that "traditional painting has been rendered historical and is over with."[5] Moholy-Nagy was probably referring to nonabstract work when he used the term "traditional," and indeed he continued to paint for some time; however, when he returned from the Bauhaus to Berlin in 1928 to set up a freelance design practice, he seems to have stopped painting in order to focus on other media, not only advertising and stage design, but "painting" with light.

In 1930 one of his friends, art historian Franz Roh, captured the essence of this period when he wrote that "as the chief problem in 'painting' of the future Moholy bears in mind the forming of space by means of colored reflecting light." Citing the Light Prop that had just been completed, he continues: "in 1930 he exhibited in Paris an electric light appliance for change of color and motion technique."[6] As Moholy-Nagy himself put it, the Light Prop was essentially "ein Versuchsapparat zur Lichtmalerei," an experimental device for light painting, a project that he had formulated in his 1922–23 texts.[7] Projected, reflected, and refracted light was also a primary means of creation in his set designs of the previous couple of years, and the Light Prop's name was coined because it was to be displayed in a gallery featuring theatrical innovations. Roh was however probably not aware that later that very same summer, at La Sarraz in Switzerland, Moholy-Nagy returned to painting, and never abandoned it again. As he wrote late in his life, echoing his own words of 1922, "…abstract painting can be understood as an arrested, frozen phase of a kinetic light display leading back to the original emotional, sensuous

AEG Film Projector, in Moholy-Nagy and Kassák 1922.

Raoul Hausmann, *Jelzőállomás* (Messaging Station) (Transformers?), original media unknown. *MA* (Today) 7, nos. 4–5 (May 1, 1922).

AEG High-tension transmission towers, in Moholy-Nagy and Kassák 1922.

Konstruktion Z 1, ca. 1922–23. Oil and graphite on canvas, 75.5 × 96.5 cm.

meaning of color."[8] Evidently, Moholy-Nagy was interested both in the arrested moments of Lichtspiel as expressed on canvas and in kinetic "light plays" themselves, both live and recorded as film.

Projection or Lichtspiele, along with the creation of Lichtraum (light space) as Hans Richter phrased it,[9] were central themes in Moholy-Nagy's aesthetic. Think for example of photography (both exposure of the light-sensitive surface in the camera and printing by projecting light in an enlarger or to present the work as a slide), or film (again in terms of image-creation in the camera and subsequent projection for viewing) and, of course, the photogram (Moholy-Nagy's innovation of holding objects *above* the light-sensitive surface, as opposed to laying them *on* it and steering the light source to project, filter, or block light projection.)[10] It comes as no surprise that Moholy-Nagy conflates paintings and projection screens:

Here is to be found the interpretation of Malevich's last picture—the plain white surface. One cannot deny that this constituted the ideal screen for the light and shadow effects which … would fall upon it. The same thing is effected as by its big brother: the cinema screen. If the projection is fixed on a layer sensitive to light, a photograph or photogram results. It seems … that the picture painted by hand is surpassed by the purer 'pictorial' light projection. Ever since the invention of the motion picture, many painters have concerned themselves with this problem: projection, light, motion, interpenetration. Photography is doubtless a bridge to them.… In the continuation of this work we must … 'paint' colors with flowing, oscillating, prismatic light, instead of with pigments.[11]

In *telehor* he is even more direct: "Malevich['s last picture] … may serve as an example …: a white square on a square white canvas is clearly symbolic of the projection screen for slide and film presentations, symbolic of the transition from painting with pigment to light design. Unmediated and in motion, light can be projected onto this white surface."[12] In *The New Vision*, a photogram itself is likened to a projection screen.[13] Painting on the one hand, and the various forms of photography (including film and photograms), on the other, are manifestations of the same medium, he suggests, the medium of projected light. Moholy-Nagy was incorporating the two types of media (polemically set up as kinds of "opposite poles" at the time) to frame his thesis that they were essentially related and shared the same "material" basis, a particularly striking position at a time when photography was conventionally not held to be a fine art, or was considered wholly distinct from the traditional disciplines of painting, sculpture, and the graphic arts.

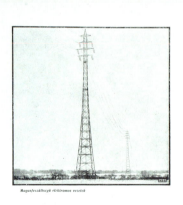

Projection Spaces

While light was key to Moholy-Nagy's conception of art, he did not limit himself to the visible range of the electromagnetic spectrum, nor even to that spectrum. He was inspired by Hausmann's article "PRÉzentizmus" (Presentism), which Moholy-Nagy sent to Kassák for publication in *MA*. In this article, Hausmann asked:

What is art? Nonsense, if it only provides us with aesthetic rules.... We're calling for an electric, scientific painting!!! Sound and light and electric waves distinguish themselves from each other only by their wavelength and oscillation; after Thomas Wilfred's successful experiments with freely floating color apparitions in America and the sound experiments of American and German radio stations, it would be a bagatelle to employ these waves, aided by the requisite transformers, into enormous color or musical aerial performances.... At night, huge, polychrome Light Dramas will be played out in our sky and during the day these transformers will be reset to sound, and will then sound the atmosphere!!! Electricity will allow us to transform all our haptic emanations into kinetic colors, into sounds, into a new form of music.[14]

Optophonetics and other intersensory translations aside, Moholy-Nagy engaged with a broad range of forms of transmitted energy: he noted the use of wireless telegraphy in producing images (via microwaves), proposed employing radio waves to transmit programs that would provide remote control lighting for his Light Prop for an Electric Stage (1930) and suggested that "light plays" be broadcast on television. On either side of the visible spectrum of light, he envisaged using ultraviolet and infrared light in art making, and toward the high-frequency end of James Maxwell's electro-magnetic spectrum, he both suggested and practiced utilization of X-ray energy.[15] Sound, when conveyed via radio waves or amplified electrically, also becomes a manifestation of electromagnetic energy, as are the electrons that create the image produced by an electron microscope: and all electromagnetic energy, whether considered as moving via waves or particles, is projected.[16] It is worth recalling here that Moholy-Nagy and Kassák's *Book of New Artists* began with images of a high-tension transmission tower and a movie projector.

Shortly after he arrived at the Bauhaus in late March 1923, Moholy-Nagy attended the Laternenfest (Lantern Festival) organized by the students, where he witnessed the projected light-and-shadow experiments of Kurt Schwerdtpfeger, Ludwig Hirschfeld-Mack, and Josef Hartwig. Hirschfeld-Mack's Farbenlichtspiele (colored light plays) included a musical dimension to the performance. Moholy-Nagy soon became aware of the tradition, dating back to the eighteenth century, of projected colored

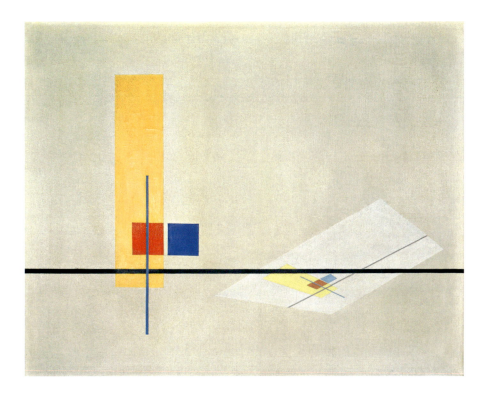

light, often in conjunction with music. Moholy-Nagy knew of Wilfred's silent Clavilux and of his Art Institute of Light, founded in New York in the 1930s. He will also have been acquainted with Czech artist Zdenek Pešánek's "kinetic light piano," and in *Painting, Photography, Film* he addressed related work by his compatriot Alexander László.[17] Some of his photograms and paintings resemble the photographs that capture glimpses of presentations by these artists. *A 19*, for example, depicts projected light on a flat surface and closely resembles both Hirschfeld-Mack's work and Moholy-Nagy's own more two-dimensional photograms of the time.

Space appears in a small group of paintings, including *Z VII* (p. 100) and *Construction A 19* (p. 107; not to be confused with *A 19*), which depict complex structures of color planes.[18] As Joyce Tsai puts it: "In paintings of the period, [Moholy-Nagy's] compositions provide the scaffolding for his exploration of effects of translucency, transparency, and luminosity. The colors, often within a restricted range, are all deployed to produce the illusion of an architectonic structure hovering in an infinite space or to render in paint the effect of overlapping shafts of light."[19] Analogies to these works can be found in some of the photograms, especially those made at Dessau during the mid-1920s, when he was producing these paintings. As Neusüss has informed us, these photograms were made in a darkroom using three-dimensional objects held at a distance from the light-sensitive paper, which gives them both their unmistakably hovering quality and their plasticity, creating a sense of Lichtraum (light space). These architectonic elements reappear in sketches for built spaces in Moholy-Nagy's sets, particularly those for Jacques Offenbach's 1881 opera *Les contes d'Hoffmann* (*The Tales of Hoffmann*) produced for the Staatsoper am Platz der Republik (Berlin) in 1929 (p. 107). The beautiful renderings were by the Hungarian architect István Sebök, who was working in Moholy-Nagy's studio at the time and was responsible for many of the drawings in Moholy-Nagy's oeuvre that required architectural or engineering expertise.

Lichträume, that is, spaces created by means of projected light, were not limited in Moholy-Nagy's imagination to projecting or constructing static edifices made up of flat color planes: "It is possible to enrich our spatial experience by projecting light on to a succession of semitransparent planes (nets, trellis-work etc.) [that is, scrims]. I did this in my scenic experiments for the *Kaufmann von Berlin* performed at Piscator's theater in 1929," wrote Moholy-Nagy (pp. 122, 123). The projections could also be aimed at "gaseous formations such as smoke or steam …"[20] or they could be cinematic in nature. In Charlotte Lusk's interpretation, Moholy-Nagy's photomontage *Die Lichter der Stadt* (The Lights of the City) figures just such a lustrous beam formed by radiating planes in different shades, emanating from a light projection apparatus, through which Charlie Chaplin's "Little Tramp" figure spies on two corpulent female figures in bathing suits, who look as if they were being carried aloft on these light streams (pp. 108, 109).[21]

In his writing about cinematic projection spaces, Moholy-Nagy was critical of thinking that did not fully take account of the medium's technical possibilities. He thought in radically new ways about both the configuration films could take, given the possibilities of projection, and about the ensuing narrative implications – though in general he opposed the notion of narrative. He speculated in *Painting, Photography, Film* on these new potential constellations:

One should construct a cinema, with a concave projection screen in place of today's flat, rectangular variety. This concave surface must have a very large radius, that is, it should be shallow, and should be positioned toward the audience at a 45-degree angle. Several films would be projected onto this projection surface (perhaps only two during the initial, experimental phase), and in fact not projected onto one spot, but rather tracking continually from left to right, right to left, down up, up down, and so on. Using this procedure one or more initially autonomous events meeting at predetermined points of intersection when it makes sense for them to do so, could take place.[22]

Though the idea may be traced back to the phantasmagoric multiprojection performances introduced in the late eighteenth century in France, nothing like this had, to the best of my knowledge, ever been thought of before within avant-garde art discourse, and even film historians have not remarked on the importance of Moholy-Nagy's suggestion.[23] As part of the project *Sensing the Future*, two of my colleagues at the University of Manitoba, Patrick Harrop and Lancelot Coar, have risen to the challenge and have developed a *Polycinema*. It responds to the multiple challenges thrown down by Moholy-Nagy, changing conventional projection surfaces and using projector-tracking, while incorporating kinetic light and shadow reflections into

fischgrät – S.S. Kettenläden AG für Herrenkleidung, advertising design for Schroeder-spezial gmbh, ca. 1930. Offset print, 24.8 × 34.9 cm.

Unknown photographer (Letteverein, Berlin), X-ray of a fish, 1924. 24 × 37 cm.

X-ray photograph of a pen, 1925. Collaboration between László Moholy-Nagy and Dr. Moses, in *Photographische Korrespondenz* no. 9 (1927), p. 260.

Projection Spaces

A 19, 1927. Oil on canvas, 80 × 95.5 cm.

Untitled, 1925. Contact prints (above: positive; below: negative) from vintage copy negative of a lost photogram, 18 × 24 cm each.

Ludwig Hirschfeld-Mack, photograph of one phase of *Farbensonatine II* (Rot). Photo: Atelier Eckner, Weimar, n.d. (ca. 1922–24), 18.4 × 13.3 cm.

the mix (pp. 165, 167). In the second edition of *Painting, Photography, Film*, Moholy-Nagy elaborated on this idea:

A cinema should be built equipped for various experimental purposes with respect to projectors and projection surfaces. One can, for example, imagine—with the use of a simple adaptor—the normal projection plane being divided into various planes and curved surfaces at angles to each other like a landscape of hills and valleys. It would be based on the simplest possible principle of division in order to be able to control the resulting projection distortions.[24]

At this point he reiterated the idea articulated in the first edition, which is quoted above. He formulated several more versions of this notion over the coming years. In a later text he phrases it thus:

It is also quite possible to replace a single flat screen by one (or more) concave or convex surfaces; spherical surfaces and fragments (perforated or not) that shift with respect to each other. (It would be possible, for example—as I had previously advocated for the silent cinema—to hold all the walls of the cinema under the crossfire of multiple film projections: "simultaneous cinema.")[25]

This striking notion was costly and technically difficult to realize, and Moholy-Nagy never attempted to do so. He did publish a schematic diagram for the triple-tracking film projection idea (Polycinema) in *Painting, Photography, Film* and illustrated the idea of multiple projections on concave surfaces in at least one artwork from this period, *Mord auf die Schienen (Liebe deine Nächsten)* (Murder on the Tracks. [Love Your Neighbor]). As Eleanor Hight observes, this resembles a spherical space within which there are multiple projections (p. 111).[26] The themes of "shooting" and violence recur in the imagery of this discourse, calling to mind Friedrich Kittler's observation that the invention of the movie camera drew on the mechanics of the machine gun.[27] Thinking back to the multiple sensory inputs experienced by the provincial figure caught in the "crossfire" of sights and sounds of Potsdamer Platz in Berlin, as cited in the introduction to this book, an analogy emerges here, with the cinematic space being "held" in the "crossfire" of multiple cinematic projections—a powerful metaphor for anyone who had experienced the horrors of trench warfare during World War I, as Moholy-Nagy had. In a similar vein, a sharpshooter is positioned within the multicinematic sphere of *Murder on the Tracks*.

Centered on the twofold sense of the term "shooting," and underscored by the inscription "kinoplakat" (film poster) written on the sheet in the artist's hand, this line of thinking might also suggest a reinterpretation of *Neue Einrichtungen in Museen: Jeder kann sich sein Bild schiessen* (New Museum Installations: Everyone Can Shoot His Own Picture, p. 110). If we mentally transpose the rifles in the latter image into projectors, and the photographs on the museum walls into films, the configuration of this "photoplastic" (as Moholy-Nagy called these works) invokes the idea of multiple projections. This is a plausible association in Moholy-Nagy's mind, given that some of the photos incorporated here, such as the lynx and the dancing girls, are borrowed from his 1925 film script "Dynamic of the Metropolis." Moholy-Nagy is, in a sense, acknowledging the violence inherent in his larger project: the sensory "violence" of modernity and the corresponding "violence" of his therapeutic intervention, with the audience subjected to an aesthetics of simultaneous multisensory inputs, a "crossfire" of cinematic projection. Shortly before her death, responding to the intensity of Op and Kinetic art, Sibyl Moholy-Nagy wrote that for Moholy-Nagy "perception had to feed the senses, not to brutalize them." She must have had in mind the subtlety of his late Plexiglas "light modulators" rather than the intensity of his proposals of the 1920s.[28]

Andreas Hapkemeyer points out that Hirschfeld-Mack's color-light play performances—though projected onto flat screens—induced an illusion of depth, of the third dimension.[29] This may have inspired Moholy-Nagy to think along similar lines.

The first concrete proposal clearly based on Moholy-Nagy's ideas of a multiscreen space was made by Walter Gropius for Erwin Piscator's new theater, a space intended to dissolve the barrier between audience and performer. To be sure, employing film projections within theatrical productions was not an entirely novel idea. Friedrich Kiesler included a film in the set for his production of Karel Čapek's *R.U.R. (Rossum's Universal Robots)* in 1923.[30] Furthermore, the notion of simultaneous projection began to take off soon after Moholy-Nagy published *Painting, Photography, Film* in 1925.

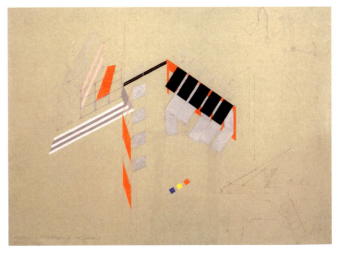

Construction A 19, 1927. Oil on canvas 75 × 95 cm. Reproduced in *telehor* 1, nos. 1–2 (1936), page 77.

Untitled, 1925. Photogram on developing paper, 20 × 15.5 cm.

Set design for Jacques Offenbach, *Les Contes d'Hoffmann*, Act 1, Staatsoper am Platz der Republik ("Kroll-Oper"), Berlin, 1928. Graphite, tempera, and ink on faded whiteprint mounted on card; paper: 41.7 × 59 cm.

Set design for Jacques Offenbach, *Les Contes d'Hoffmann*, Act 2 (Giulietta's palace in Venice), Staatsoper am Platz der Republik ("Kroll-Oper"), Berlin, 1928. Tempera and ink on faded whiteprint mounted on card; paper: 42 × 55.9 cm; card: 44.3 × 58.2 cm.

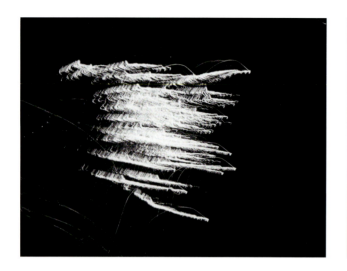 

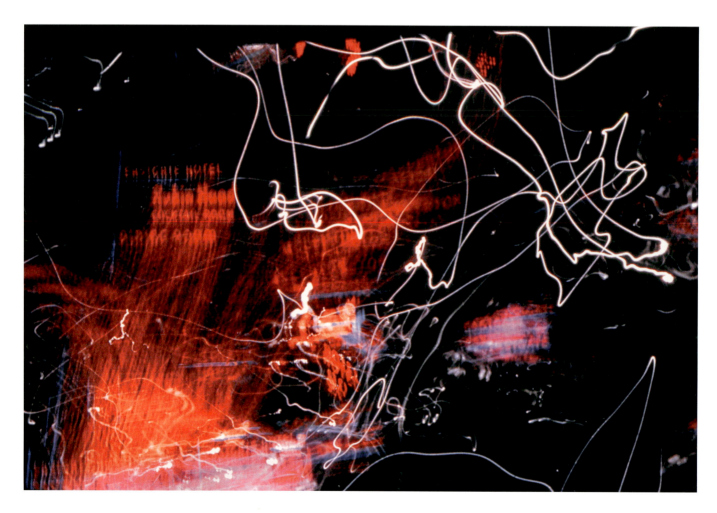

Eton Fireworks – Slow Motion, 1936. 15.7 × 20.7 cm.

Untitled (Fireworks, New York World's Fair), 1939. Kodachrome copy slide, 24 × 36 mm.

Untitled (Traffic, City Lights Eastgate Hotel, Chicago), 1937–46. Original Kodachrome glass slide in cardboard mount, 24 × 36 mm.

City Lights, dated 1926 [1927–28]. Photocollage using magazine clippings and tempera on card; paper: 61.5 × 49.5 cm.

Projection Spaces

Public, like waves in the sea.

Girls.
Legs.

AN ANGRY LYNX.

The wheels. They turn to the point when the vibration fades.

New Installations in Museums: Everyone Can Shoot His Own Picture, 1925. Gelatin silver copy print of a photomontage, 27.4 × 37 cm. Munich. Galerie Klihm, 1973.

Two details from "Dynamic of the Metropolis," in Moholy-Nagy, 1969, pp. 130 and 127.

Murder on the Tracks (Love Your Neighbor), 1925. Photomontage design for a film poster. Graphite, photographic reproductions cut from magazines, mounted on paper, 47 × 31 cm.

Schematic diagram for the "Simultaneous or Poly-cinema," in Moholy-Nagy 1926, pp. 40–41.

Um recht deutlich zu werden, teile ich eine schematische **Skizze** mit:

Von links nach rechts läuft der Film des Herrn **A**: Geburt, Lebenslauf. Von unten nach oben läuft der Film der Dame **B**: Geburt, Lebenslauf. Die Projektionsflächen der beiden Filme schneiden sich: Liebe, Ehe usw. Die beiden Filme können dann entweder sich kreuzend, in durchscheinenden Geschehnisfolgen oder parallel nebeneinander weiterlaufen; oder es kann ein neuer gemeinsamer Film der beiden Personen an die Stelle der beiden ersten treten. Als dritter bzw. vierter Film könnte der Film des Herrn **C** gleichzeitig mit den Vorgängen **A** und **B** von oben nach unten oder von rechts nach links oder auch in anderer Richtung laufen, bis er die anderen Filme sinngemäß schneiden bzw. decken kann, usw.

Ein solches **Schema** wird natürlich für ungegenständliche Lichtprojektionen in der Art der Fotogramme ebenso geeignet, wenn nicht geeigneter sein. Mit Ein-

schaltung farbiger Wirkungen können hier noch reichere Gestaltungsmöglichkeiten entstehen.

Die technische Lösung solcher Projektionen wie die des Autos oder der erwähnten Skizze ist sehr einfach und gar nicht kostspielig. **Es muß nur ein drehbares Prisma vor die Linse der Filmprojektionsapparate eingeschaltet werden.**

Die große Projektionsfläche ermöglicht auch eine simultane Wiederholung einer Bilderfolge, indem weitere Kopien des laufenden Filmstreifens durch nebeneinanderstehende Apparate, neu von vorn beginnend, auf die Fläche projiziert werden. Man kann so den Anfang einer Bewegung während ihres Weiterschreitens — stufenweise überholt — immer wieder zeigen und damit neue Wirkungen erzielen.

Die Verwirklichung derartiger Pläne stellt neue Anforderungen an die Leistungsfähigkeit unseres optischen Aufnahmeorgans, des Auges, und unseres Aufnahmezentrums, des Gehirns.

Durch die Riesenentwickelung der Technik und der Großstädte haben unsere Aufnahmeorgane ihre Fähigkeit einer simultanen akustischen und optischen Funktion erweitert. Schon im alltäglichen Leben gibt es Beispiele dafür: Berliner queren den Potsdamer Platz. Sie unterhalten sich, **sie hören gleichzeitig:**

die Hupen der Autos, das Klingeln der Straßenbahn, das Tuten der Omnibusse, das Hallo des Kutschers, das Sausen der Untergrundbahn, das Schreien des Zeitungsverkäufers, die Töne eines Lautsprechers usw.

und können diese verschiedenen akustischen Eindrücke auseinanderhalten. Dagegen wurde vor kurzem ein auf diesen Platz verschlagener Provinzmensch durch die Vielheit der Eindrücke so aus der Fassung gebracht, daß er vor einer fahrenden Straßenbahn wie angewurzelt stehen blieb. Einen Analogfall optischer Erlebnisse zu konstruieren liegt auf der Hand.

Ebenso analog, daß moderne Optik und Akustik, als Mittel künstlerischer Gestaltung verwendet, auch nur von einem für die Gegenwart offenen Menschen aufgenommen werden und ihn bereichern können.

Piscator, 1929; cover designed by László Moholy-Nagy. The cover and accompanying photograph show Traugott Müller's designs for the production of Erwin Piscator's play *Rasputin*, Piscatorbühne, Berlin, 1927. Müller employed three simultaneous film projections with live actors.

Illustration showing three films projected simultaneously in László Moholy-Nagy's production of Walter Mehring's play *Der Kaufmann von Berlin*, 1929. Film direction: László Moholy-Nagy; camera: Alex Strasser. In Strasser, "Film im Theater," *Filmtechnik*, 20 (September 1929), pp. 417–19.

Moholy-Nagy's friend Alexander László had collaborated with Oskar Fischinger in 1926, shortly before Fischinger presented *Raumlichtmusik* (later *Raumlichtkunst*), which was probably a three-screen projected work consisting of three to five abstract films, both black-and-white and tinted. It is certain that Alexander László attended at least one performance of *Raumlichtkunst*. This makes it possible that Moholy-Nagy at least knew of these performances.[31] Furthermore, Abel Gance's film *Napoleon*, widely distributed in 1927, famously ends with three films projected simultaneously, side-by-side, and Moholy-Nagy explicitly referenced this in the second, 1927 edition of *Painting, Photography, Film*. Moholy-Nagy's 1929 production of Walter Mehring's play *Der Kaufmann von Berlin* (The Merchant of Berlin) for Piscator's theater also included a tripartite projection. However, these examples entail projecting three adjacent films onto one single, flat surface. In Traugott Müller's globular set design for Piscator's play *Rasputin* (1927), the film projections were stacked, overlapping, and combined with live actors, but still stationary and on a single flat surface. Moholy-Nagy configured an enormous trapezoidal screen employed for both films and shadows as the backdrop to his 1929 production of *The Tales of Hoffmann*, but once again this is one large flat surface (p. 114). That same year Alex Strasser shot a film for Moholy-Nagy's production of *Der Kaufmann von Berlin*. This film, along with slides, was projected onto a series of scrims, from the front and behind, as well as to the sides of the stage, introducing a spatial dimension.[32] It was not until June 4, 1929, however, when he arranged a special screening of Dziga Vertov's *Man with a Movie Camera*, that Moholy-Nagy endeavored to move away from flat projection surfaces in actual practice; the film was projected onto the concave interior of the domed planetarium at the top of Hannover's Anzeiger-Hochhaus.[33]

Walter Gropius's theatrical scheme, referencing Moholy-Nagy's Polycinema idea, envisaged surrounding the combined space of the audience and stage with twelve giant projection screens. Just as Moholy-Nagy had adapted Gropius's term Gesamtwerk in 1924–25, Gropius adapted Moholy-Nagy's 1925 suggestion of a "Theater der Totalität," integrating it into this 1927 scheme for Piscator's dream of a Totaltheater.[34] Gropius writes that this "can set the entire auditorium—walls and ceiling—within the film.... [I]n place of the projection surfaces in use until now, a *projection space* emerges..." (italics added).[35] In Piscator's vision, furthermore, the screens could be animated either by simultaneous, coordinated film projections from outside the audience space, or by means of a central column within that space, fitted with a dozen projectors, echoing Moholy-Nagy's categorization of "light displays" as both interior and exterior.[36] In other words, the walls surrounding the theatrical space of the Totaltheater were to dissolve into screens; as these walls-cum-screens were inherently translucent, at night, when the direction of projection was reversed, the films would have been visible to the city through the theatre's glazed exterior, transforming its urban surroundings into an activated, cinematic space. Javier Núñez and Javier Navarro de Zuvillaga's digital animation of Gropius's proposal (p. 114) gives us a clear idea of quite how groundbreaking this project was.

Perhaps the most radical notion of all in Moholy-Nagy's Polycinema proposal was the idea that pivoting mirrors in front of the projector, or indeed pivoting the projector itself, would offer a means to make the projected image move about. Projector-tracking conjured up a whole host of scenarios in Moholy-Nagy's imagination, for example, with three films, all components of a single story, unfurling independently of one another on different parts of the cinema's interior, and conjoining at specific moments of contact between characters. The possibilities are dizzying, also affording enormous scope for nonnarrative tracking projection of abstract films. This is where the Polycinema, an idea Moholy-Nagy first proposed in 1925 and, as we have seen, elaborated repeatedly subsequently, intersects with the idea of "light painting" or "light formation," and the means to achieve this: the Light Prop for an Electric Stage.

Around 1929 the German government entrusted the Deutsche Werkbund with organizing Germany's contribution to the Salon des artistes décorateurs scheduled for the summer of 1930. This was an enormously important event, for it was the first exhibition of German decorative arts and design in Paris since World War I.[37] Gropius was invited to head the exhibition team. Moholy-Nagy was asked to design "Raum 2" (Gallery 2). His proposal for this lighting, photography, ballet, product design, and theater gallery featured Oscar Schlemmer's designs for the Bauhaus stage as well as Gropius's designs for the Totaltheater. The funding available for a prestigious undertaking such as this also presented Moholy-Nagy with an opportunity to finally realize his long-standing plans for a "light painting" machine. In his article on this project for the

Projection Spaces

German Werkbund's journal *Die Form*, Moholy-Nagy reports that it was financed by AEG (Allgemeine Elektrizitätsgesellschaft), with the firm's "theater department" taking charge of its production.[38]

Moholy-Nagy had been thinking since 1922 about how a light painting machine might look, long before István Sebök prepared the working drawings in 1930.[39] Right from the outset the notion of such a machine was closely connected with making abstract films: In 1925, referring to use of light play in this context, he writes:

The practical prerequisites for abstract film formation are excellent preparations and the most advanced equipment. More than anything else, its realization has been made difficult by abstract light plays being made using either laborious animation techniques or light-shadow plays that are difficult to record. An apparatus that could rotate mechanically or otherwise operate continuously would be necessary. The variety of light phenomena can also be intensified through the use of movable light sources.[40]

In order to create an abstract ("absolute") film, he sketches out an apparatus here that would produce effects rather different, on the one hand, from those in abstract animated films by Hans Richter, Viking Eggeling, or Walter Ruttmann, and that would, on the other hand, also be distinct from the "light-shadow plays" of Hirschfeld-Mack and Schwerdtpfeger. Abstract film animation is intrinsically two-dimensional: it involves painting sequences of images that are then shot in order to produce the illusion of movement. The "light-shadow plays" meanwhile involved two-dimensional templates that are moved up and down within a single planar dimension; the projection of light through these templates does however accord the resulting Farbenlichtspiel a certain three-dimensional effect.[41]

In contrast, Moholy-Nagy is implying that it would be preferable to work with a rotating, and therefore three-dimensional, apparatus around which the light sources could be moved in order to achieve entirely different effects. There is some evidence that Moholy-Nagy was thinking about the configuration of this rotating, three-dimensional apparatus as early as 1922. A lithograph from the *Kestnermappe* commissioned by Alexander Dorner, director of the Kestnergesellschaft in Hannover, and produced early in 1923, prefigures one of the three components that made up the final Light Prop apparatus; the same configuration is also repeated in two paintings dated to 1922–23. Moholy-Nagy would later describe this section of the device as consisting of "three panels moving in an endless sequence with a rocking motion (due to the slight difference in plan between the base track and top track)."[42] The three panels are most clearly visible in the lithograph, but the base track is visible in all three works of art. Gottfried Jäger and Karl Martin Holzhauser's stately animation of *K XVII* (pp. 116, 117) also demonstrates how the device would have moved, as well as revealing Moholy-Nagy's conception of his paintings as snapshots of a kinetic evolution of color and form.

Rather than as a freestanding, moving object, however, as he writes in his *Die Form* article, the Light Prop was to be contained within a 1.2-meter-square box with a circular opening on its front (p. 119). Within the box was to be an array of, as he put it in *Vision in Motion*, "140 lightbulbs connected with a drum contact. This was arranged so that within

Abb. 1—3. Diese drei Bilder wurden — in so verschieden abgedecktem Format — gleichzeitig projiziert.

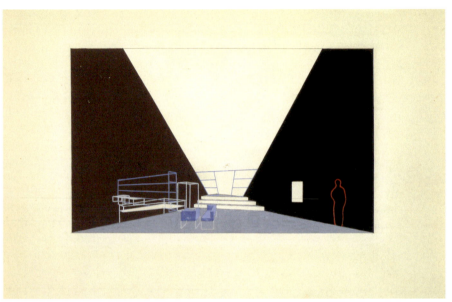

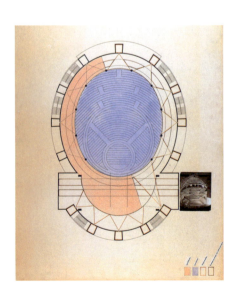

Set of Jacques Offenbach, *Les Contes d'Hoffmann*, Act 3 (In the house of Crespel), Staatsoper am Platz der Republik ("Kroll-Oper"), Berlin, 1929. Director: Ernst Legal. Photo: Lucia Moholy, gelatin silver print with collage, 21.2 × 38 cm.

Set for Jacques Offenbach, *Les Contes d'Hoffmann*, Act 3 (Antonia), Staatsoper am Platz der Republik ("Kroll-Oper"), Berlin, 1928. Tempera and ink on paper. Paper: 35.5 × 52.9 cm, image: 21.2 × 36 cm.

Walter Gropius, plan for a Totaltheater, 1927. Mixed media on paper, 100 × 80 cm. Designed for Erwin Piscator. Executed by István Sebök.

Digital animation of Walter Gropius, *Total-Theater, for the Piscatorbühne of Erwin Piscator*, 2006. Director: Javier Navarro de Zuvillaga; animation: Javier Núñez.

Projection Spaces

Realistische, filmplastische Elemente
aus dem Film „Mirakel" (Hoffmanns Erzählungen) von Moholy-Nagy (1929)

rade diese Fläche muß g e s p r e n g t werden, um hinter ihr die n e u e T i e f e, das raum-zeitliche Filmkontinuum zu entdecken. Dort und nirgends anders liegt die schöpferische Sphäre des gestaltenden Films! Der poly-dimensionale Raum, den die Bildhauer seit Michelangelos „Grablegung" vergeblich zu gestalten versucht haben, wird einmal mittels raffinierter Filmtechnik lebendig werden.

Die neuen Filmversuche der letzten zehn Jahre verdanken wir einerseits den Fortschritten des fotografischen Verfahrens, andererseits den Fortschritten der Malerei. Aus Foto und Bühne entwickelte sich der moderne illusionistische und Spielfilm, aus der neuen Malerei (Kubismus, Neo-Plastizismus, Futurismus) entwickelte sich eine abstrakte Filmornamentik. In beiden Fällen hat man n u r (und zwar innerhalb des Bildrahmens) die Projektions- oder Bildfläche geschüttelt und dadurch zwar neue Proportionen oder dynamisch-plastische und dynamisch-ornamentale Wirkungen erreicht, aber der Filmraum blieb unberührt. Wir wissen, daß sämtliche Filmversuche, sei es auch mehr intuitiv als bewußt auf der Tendenz beruhen: die W e l t a u s e i n e r n e u e n D i m e n s i o n z u b e t r a c h t e n. Räumliches Multiplizieren mittels Überschneidung, Repetieren des Gegenstandes mittels Durch-, Neben- und

247

"Photogramm und Grenzgebiete," *Die Form* 4, no. 10 (May 15, 1929), reproducing images from the short films included in László Moholy-Nagy's set design for Jacques Offenbach, *Les Contes d'Hoffmann*.

Detail of installation photograph, "Raum 2," "Section allemande," *Salon des artistes décorateurs*, Paris, 1930, showing model and plans for Walter Gropius, Totaltheater, 1927, designed for Erwin Piscator. Executed by István Sebök.

a two-minute turning period, various colored and colorless spotlights were switched on, creating a light display on the inside walls of a cube."⁴³ I have always been puzzled by this proposal, since viewers would not have been able to experience the light environment created if it were enclosed in a box. And in any case, given the opposition to the Guckkastenbühne (Proscenium Stage) that he expressed in his book *Die Bühne im Bauhaus* (The Bauhaus Stage), why would he propose one here?⁴⁴ Jan Sahli states that " … the [colored light reflections] would have been easily visible on the interior walls" of the housing.⁴⁵ I have seen this arrangement in action, and must disagree with Sahli's view. It is not easy to see these reflections—one must stoop and crane one's neck. In his insightful dissertation, Noam Elcott, in effect, states this problem when he writes that "the viewers might be interpreted as being encouraged to thrust their heads through the circular aperture and enter the light-space of the *Light Space Modulator*, to see not the apparatus, but its effects—shadows, superpositions, and light." Nonetheless, as Elcott is implying, this hardly makes sense, and would, in any event, have been dangerous (pp. 118, 124).

In his *Die Form* article Moholy-Nagy describes an alternative way of presenting the prop, which involved darkening the room and removing the back of the box, allowing the "light play" to be projected onto a screen specially set up for this purpose. Naomi Crellin has made a digital animation of just such a projection, assuming an eight-foot distance from box to wall (p. 125).

The *Die Form* article makes it clear, however, that the principal means of viewing the prop in operation was to be through the round opening on the "audience side" of the box. The photograph published in *Die Form* of the apparatus within the box in the workshop—with a man, presumably Otto Ball, underneath working on it—has misled us into believing that it was exhibited with an uncovered circular opening. I would contend that the device itself was *not* meant to be seen. Rather, *the opening was to be covered by a translucent layer onto which the shadows and light projections from the interior—produced by the prop—would be projected*. In other words, there is no reason to believe that a workshop photo (presumably the only one available to Moholy-Nagy at the time of the press deadline for his article in *Die Form*) would indicate the intended display mode for the prop.

As we have seen in the passage quoted above, Moholy-Nagy had always thought of the device in cinematic terms. Its reification as the *Light Space Modulator*, a "kinetic sculpture," after Moholy-Nagy's death, has blinded us to what Moholy-Nagy himself would have seen as obvious: the device was meant to make "light paintings." These would either have been "live" abstract films (when the device was displayed in its box), or abstract films made by recording the light patterns, that is, "light paintings" that were projected onto the round, translucent surface of the box's opening (or onto a wall outside the rear of the box, as Naomi Crellin has demonstrated).

I am not the first to note that Moholy-Nagy thought of the Light Prop in cinematic terms. Noam Elcott writes that "the *Light-Prop for an Electrical Stage* … is a film projector without film.…"⁴⁶ He argues for it as a device enacting the characteristics of what should be registered on film, but without film:

Light Prop for an Electric Stage, 1930. Collage on light print, ink, colored papers on card, 65.2 × 49.9 cm. Executed by István Sebök.

Sheet from *6. Kestnermappe – 6 Konstruktionen*, 1923. Album of lithographs, 61 × 45 cm (Hannover: Verlag Ludwig Ey), edition of 50. Printer: Rob. Leunis u. Chapman, G.m.B.H. Hannover.

Composition K XVII, 1923. Oil on canvas, 95 × 75 cm.

Opposite: Gottfried Jaeger and Karl Martin Holzhauser (with Andreas Dress and Ralph Flowerday), *Animato: Das Kunstwerk im Zeitalter seiner elektronisches Manipulierbarkeit. Paraphrasen über das Gemälde K XVII aus dem Jahre 1923 von László Moholy-Nagy*, 1995. Digital animated film.

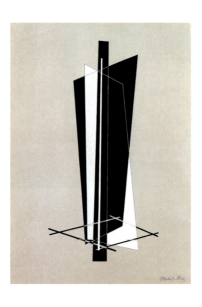

Projection Spaces

The overlapping layers, mechanical repetitions, bright reflections, and dark cast shadows of the Light-Prop anticipate the use of double exposure, serial repetition, high contrast, and negative footage in the film Lichtspiel: Schwarz, Weiss, Grau. *In other words, the Light-Prop makes over the pro-filmic—that which lies before the camera—according to the dicta of the filmic—the manipulations available only to the cinematic medium. Film becomes productive the moment it reproduces a reality created in its own image.*

If, as Elcott remarks, the Light Prop was meant at this time to be shown in the display box and not in the round (as it is illustrated in the 1938 edition of The New Vision, the caption to the photograph of the Light Prop he references), why would Moholy-Nagy not have planned for a "productive" presentation, projected from the interior onto a translucent layer covering the opening? Scrims and walls, in other words, *screens*, onto which the light is projected, also appear in the photogrammatic[47] stage lighting, complex as it is, that Moholy-Nagy designed for The Tales of Hoffmann (so beautifully photographed by Lucia Moholy). It is impossible to make a photogram without a projection surface, even if it is a photogram in "space-time" rather than "on the sensitive plate."[48] Unless steam or smoke or the like is used, the "Raum" in Lichtraum is defined by the solid reflecting or refracting surface. Without the screen (as van Doesburg found out when he built Café Aubette in Strasbourg), there is no Lichtraum.[49]

It is no coincidence that the only use that Moholy-Nagy made of the device (apart from a few photographs) after its initial display in Paris was in the production of a film. Around 1931–32, with his studio assistant György Kepes, Moholy-Nagy made one section of his planned five-part movie about the Light Prop, Lichtspiel Schwarz Weiss Grau (Lightplay Black White Grey), the only portion realized. It is telling that the apparatus is not to be seen in its entirety even once—we see only details, close-ups. The "light and shadow are the 'stars'" of the film, as Elcott remarks.[50] Instead of being depicted as an object, the Light Prop was used exclusively as a device to produce "light play" in the film, enhanced by the cinematic special effects Elcott lists above. All this served to obscure the device rather than to showcase it, or rather, it served to underline the fact that, in the film as in real life, the apparatus was a prop for making a film. Moholy-Nagy had dreamed of "film without film" in his 1925 proposal for a Mechanical Eccentric, where he described white canvas screens onto which live light plays were to be projected from behind (p. 120). He terms this shadow play "Flächenfilm" (planar film): a "film" brought about through the use of reflective projections.[51] He had in fact realized such projections on the translucent screens employed in his set designs of the late 1920s, particularly The Tales of Hoffmann and The Merchant of Berlin.

Despite this experience with the stage, naming his device a theatrical "Requisit" (prop) was driven primarily by his desire to have his Experimental Device for Light Painting built, rather than by any particular motivation to actually use it theatrically (which he never did). Let us examine how it was designated on the only occasion it was exhibited during Moholy-Nagy's lifetime. On display in Paris, it was identified in two ways: firstly, as a "poste d'illumination d'une scène electrique" (a text clearly visible in one of the photographs of the gallery, pp. 115, 120), and secondly, in this case on a wall text visible in another installation photo as a "modèle des accessoires d'éclairage d'une scène electrique."

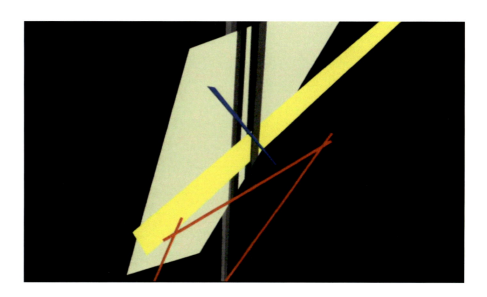

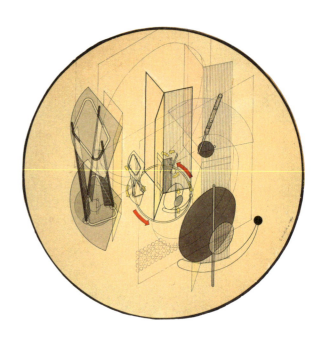
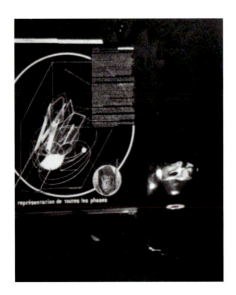
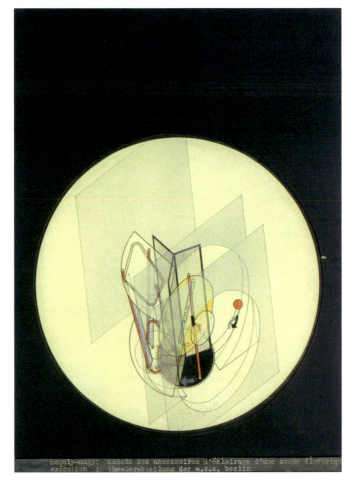

Design for the Light Prop for an Electric Stage, 1930. Collage on light print, ink, watercolor, colored papers on card, 60.4 × 59.5 cm. Executed by István Sebök.

Design for the mechanics of the Light Prop (exploded axonometric view of the Light Prop for an Electric Stage), 1930. Watercolor, ink, and graphite on cut-out circular paper, mounted on board, diameter: 52 cm; support: 71 × 71 cm. Executed by István Sebök.

Detail of installation photograph, "Raum 2," "Section allemande," showing poster and wall text for Light Prop for an Electric Stage. *Salon des artistes décorateurs*, Paris, 1930.

LICHTREQUISIT EINER ELEKTRISCHEN BÜHNE

MOHOLY-NAGY

Das regulierbare künstliche elektrische Licht erlaubt uns heute mühelos, reiche Lichteffekte zu schaffen. Mit elektrischer Kraft kann man vorberechnet verschiedene Bewegungen durchführen, die sich unveränderbar immer wiederholen lassen. Licht und Bewegung werden, gemäß der heutigen Beziehungen, wieder Elemente der Gestaltung. Die Springbrunnen der Barockzeit, die Wasserfontänen und Wasserkulissen der Barockfeste können durch Lichtfontänen und mechanische elektrische Bewegungsspiele schöpferisch erneuert werden. Diese Möglichkeiten werden in naher Zukunft wahrscheinlich als Reklame oder bei Volksfesten als Unterhaltung, im Theater als Erhöhung der Spannungsmomente verwendet. Es ist sogar vorauszusehen, daß diese und ähnliche Lichtspiele durch Radio übertragen werden. Teilweise als Fernsehprospekte, teilweise als reale Lichtspiele, indem die Empfänger selbst Beleuchtungsapparate besitzen, die von der Radiozentrale mit elektrisch regulierbaren Farbfiltern ferngelenkt werden. Es sind zum Beispiel auch Schablonenspiele vorstellbar. Ausgestanzte Kartons werden in die Apparate gesetzt, die — wie heute die Kunstbeilagen — den Radiozeitschriften beigegeben werden.

Bei den ersten Versuchen solcher Lichtspiele wird man sich auf sehr einfache Licht- und Bewegungsvorgänge beschränken müssen, da die meisten Menschen in der Aufnahme solcher Erscheinungen nicht vorbereitet, geschweige geübt sind. Einen solchen Anfangsschritt stellt das „Lichtrequisit einer elektrischen Bühne" dar, das die AEG für die Pariser Werkbundausstellung stiftete und das die Theaterabteilung der AEG ausführte.

Dieses Lichtrequisit ist ein Apparat zur Demonstration von Licht- und Bewegungserscheinungen. Das Modell besteht aus einem kubischen Kasten, 120 × 120 cm, mit einer kreisrunden Öffnung (Bühnenöffnung) auf der Vorderseite. Um die Öffnung herum, auf der Rückseite der Platte, sind eine Anzahl gelb-, grün-, blau-, rot-, weißfarbiger elektrischer Glühbirnen montiert (ca. 70 Illuminationsbirnen von je 15 Watt und 5 Stück Scheinwerferbirnen je 100 Watt). Innerhalb des Kastens, parallel zu der Vorderseite, befindet sich eine zweite Platte, ebenfalls mit einer kreisrunden Öffnung, worauf auch um die Öffnung herum die verschiedenfarbigen elektrischen Glühbirnen montiert sind. Einzelne Glühbirnen leuchten auf Grund eines vorbestimmten Planes an verschiedenen Stellen auf. Sie beleuchten einen kontinuierlich sich bewegenden Mechanismus, der teils aus durchscheinenden, teils aus durchsichtigen, teils aus durchbrochenen Materialien aufgebaut ist, um möglichst lineare Schattenbildungen auf der Hinterwand des geschlossenen Kastens zu erzielen. (Wenn die Vorführung in einem verdunkelten Raum vor sich geht, kann die Kastenrückwand entfernt und die Farben- und Schattenprojektion hinter dem Kasten auf einem beliebig großen Schirm vorgenommen werden.)

Der Träger des Mechanismus ist eine kreisrunde Platte, worauf ein dreiteiliger Rahmen aufgebaut ist. Die Trennwände bestehen aus durchsichtigem

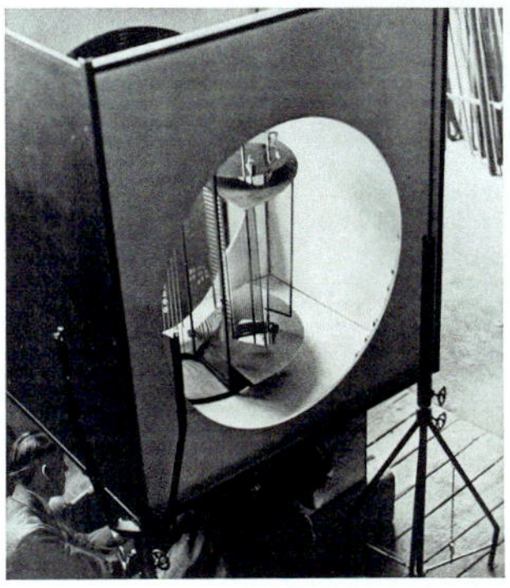

Lichtrequisit einer elektrischen Bühne 1922 / 30
Entwurf: Moholy-Nagy, Berlin. Durchkonstruiert von Dipl.-Ing. Stefan Sebök. Ausführung: A.E.G. Theaterabteilung. Ausgestellt auf der Pariser Ausstellung

Poste pour l'illumination d'une scène electrique 1922 / 30
Projet: Moholy-Nagy, Berlin. Plan et construction de M. Stephan Seboek, ing. dipl. Exécution: A.E.G. (section théatrale). Présenté à l'Exposition du « Deutscher Werkbund » à Paris

Lighting requisite for an electric stage, 1922 / 30
Designer: Moholy-Nagy, Berlin. Constructed by Stefan Sebök, dipl. ing. Carried out by A.E.G., theater department. Exhibited of the Exhibition of the German "Werkbund" in Paris

297

Zeichnerische Darstellung des Lichtrequisits
Dessin représentant le poste d'illumination
Graphic demonstration of the lighting requisite

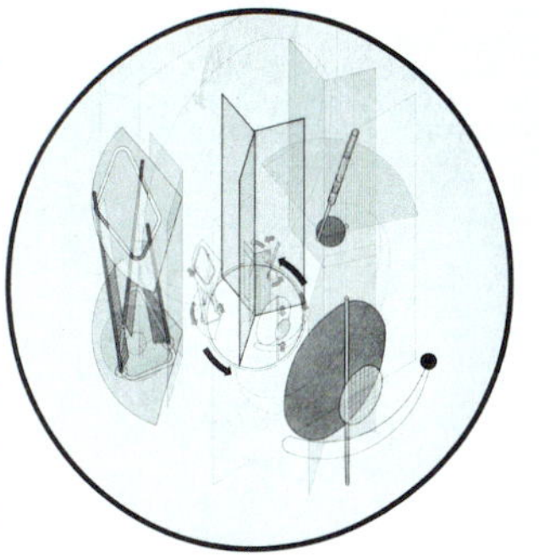

Zellon und aus einer Metallwand, die durch vertikale Stäbe gebildet ist. Jeder der drei Sektoren des Rahmens enthält ein Bewegungsspiel, das jeweilig in Tätigkeit tritt, wenn es auf der sich drehenden Grundscheibe vor der Bühnenöffnung erscheint.

Das Bewegungsspiel des ersten Sektors: drei Stäbe bewegen sich schaukelnd (da Deckengrundriß und Bodengrundriß etwas Verschiedenes sind) auf einer endlosen Bahn. Auf den drei Stäben sind verschiedene Materialien, durchscheinender Siebstoff, parallele Horizontalstäbe und Maschendraht montiert.

Das Bewegungsspiel des zweiten Sektors: in drei hintereinanderliegenden Ebenen befindet sich eine große Aluminiumscheibe unbeweglich; davor eine kleinere vernickelte und polierte Messingscheibe, durchlöchert, die sich auf- und abbewegt; währenddessen — zwischen den beiden — eine kleine Kugel auf einer Achterbahn geschleudert wird.

Das Bewegungsspiel des dritten Sektors: ein Glasstab, worauf eine Glasspirale aufgewickelt ist. Diese beschreibt eine der großen Scheibe entgegengesetzte Kegelbewegung. Die Spitze des Kegels berührt den Boden, der aus einer schräggestellten sektorförmigen Glasscheibe besteht. Diese schwebt über einer spiegelnden kreisrunden Platte.

Das Lichtrequisit könnte zu zahlreichen optischen Feststellungen ausgewertet werden, und es scheint mir richtig, diese Versuche planmäßig weiterzuführen als Weg zur Licht- und Bewegungsgestaltung.

EXTRAIT DE TRADUCTION:

INSTALLATION LUMINEUSE D'UNE SCÈNE ÉLECTRIQUE

L'installation lumineuse en question est un appareil devant servir à la démonstration de phénomènes lumineux et de mouvements. Le modèle consiste en une caisse cubique de 120×120 cm, munie à l'avant, d'une ouverture en forme de cercle (ouverture donnant sur la scène). Autour de l'ouverture, sur le côté-arrière de la plaque, est montée toute une série de lampes à incandescence électriques jaunes, vertes, bleues, rouges, blanches (environ 70 ampoules d'illumination de 15 watt chacune et cinq ampoules de projection, de 100 watt chacune). A l'intérieur de la caisse, parallèlement au côté-avant, se trouve une seconde plaque également munie d'une ouverture en forme de cercle, sur laquelle sont montées — également autour de l'ouverture — des ampoules électriques à incandescence de différentes couleurs. Certaines ampoules, en vertu d'un plan déterminé, s'allument à différents endroits. Elles éclairent un mécanisme à mouvement continu, construit partie en matériaux translucides, partie en matériaux transparents, partie en matériaux à jour, afin de pouvoir obtenir des jeux d'ombre aussi linéaires que possible sur la paroi-arrière de la caisse fermée. (Lorsque l'opération s'exécute dans un local rendu obscur, la paroi-arrière de la caisse peut être enlevée et la projection des couleurs et des ombres peut être faite, derrière la caisse, sur un écran d'une grandeur quelconque.)

Le support du mécanisme est une plaque circulaire sur laquelle est établi un cadre tripartite. Les parois de séparation consistent en une matière transparente, appelée « cellon », et en une cloison de métal formée de tiges verticales. Chacun des trois secteurs du cadre contient un jeu de mouvements qui entre en activité chaque fois que, sur le disque de base tournant sur lui-même, il passe devant l'ouverture donnant sur la scène.

Le jeu de mouvements du premier secteur s'opère de la façon suivante: trois tiges exécutent un mouvement de balancement sur une voie sans fin étant donné que la surface du disque supérieur diffère de la surface du disque de base. Sur les trois tiges sont montés différents matériaux: tissus à tamis transparents, tiges horizontales parallèles et treillis de fils de fer.

Le jeu de mouvements du deuxième secteur s'opère comme suit: sur trois plans placés l'un derrière l'autre se trouve un grand disque d'aluminium, immobile; par devant, est disposé un plus petit disque de laiton nickelé et poli, ajouré, qui monte et descend; et pendant ce temps là on fait courir une petite boule sur une bande en forme de huit passant entre les deux disques.

Le jeu de mouvements du troisième secteur s'opère de la façon suivante: Sur une tige de verre s'enroule une spirale en verre. Celle-ci décrit un mouvement parabolique, en sens inverse à celui du grand disque. L'extrémité du cône touche le fond qui consiste en une plaque de verre en forme de secteur et placée en biais. Celle-ci est suspendue au dessus d'une plaque miroitante en forme de cercle.

298

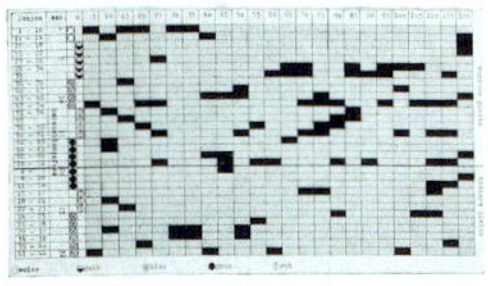

Beleuchtungsplan für eine Umdrehung der Schalttrommel des Lichtrequisits. Dauer zwei Minuten in 31 Beleuchtungsphasen
Plan d'éclairage pour un tour de rotation, des tambours de lancement du poste d'illumination. Durée: 2 minutes pour 31 phases différentes d'illumination
Plan of illumination for one rotation of the switchboard of the lighting requisite. Duration two minutes, 31 phases of illumination

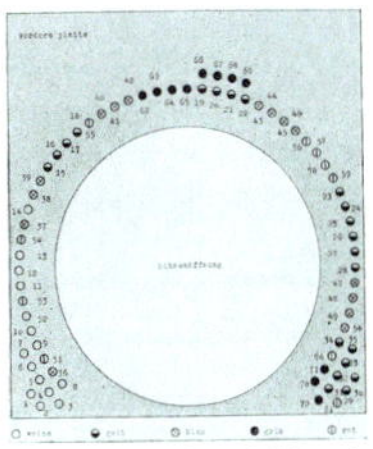

Lage der Glühbirnen, Rückansicht der vorderen Platte
Position des ampoules à incandescence, revers de la plaque de devant
Position of the electric bulbs, rear view of the front plate

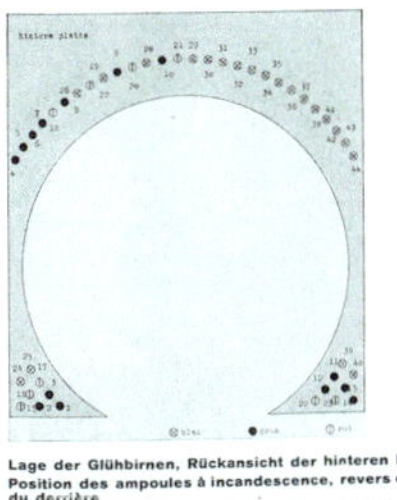

Lage der Glühbirnen, Rückansicht der hinteren Platte
Position des ampoules à incandescence, revers de la plaque du derrière
Position of the electric bulbs, rear view of the back plate

ABRIDGED TRANSLATION:

LIGHTING REQUISITE FOR AN ELECTRIC STAGE

The Lighting Requisite is an apparatus for the demonstration of special lighting and motion effects. The model consists of a box in cubic form, dimensions 120×120 centimetres, with a circular opening, representing the opening towards the stage, in front. Surrounding this opening on the back of the sheet a number of electric bulbs are mounted, yellow, green, blue, red and white. (About 70 illumination bulbs, each 15 watt power and 5 searchlight bulbs, each 100 watt.) In the interior of the box, parallel to the front side, there is a second sheet, also provided with a circular opening, which is also provided with electric bulbs of various colors ranged round the opening. Solitary bulbs flash up in various places according to a pre-arranged plan. They illuminate a mechanical device which is in constant movement and which is built up, partly of transparent material, partly of material pervious to light, and partly of perforated material, in order to attain the projection of shadow-forms as linear as possible, on the rear wall of the closed box. (If the projection take place in a darkened room, the rear wall of the box may be removed and the colors and shadows thrown behind the box upon a sheet of any size.)

The mechanism is built up on a circular plate upon which a frame in three sections has been secured. The dividing walls consist of transparent zellon and one wall of metal, built up of vertical staves. Each of the three sectors into which the frame is divided, contains a moving picture, which comes into action when this section of the revolving plate is facing the opening to the stage.

The moving picture in the first sector: Three staves move in swinging curves (since the outline of the ceiling differs from the outline of the floor) along an endless track. Various materials, such as transparent gauze, parallel horizontal staves and wire netting are mounted on the three staves.

The moving picture in the second sector: A large, immoveable plate of aluminium lies in each of three planes lying behind one another; before this is a smaller, perforated nickel-plated brass plate which moves up and down; meanwhile, between the two, a small bullet is cast on a slanting track.

The moving picture in the third sector: A glass staff, wound about with a glass spiral. This describes a conical movement in a contrary direction to the large sheet. The point of the cone touches the floor, which consists of a slanting, bisected glass plate. This plate is suspended above another circular plate which reflects the movements above.

Translated by E. T. Scheffauer

299

"Modèle d'accessoires d'éclairage d'une scène électrique", 1930. Collage, ink, watercolor, injection molding on paper, 40 × 30 cm. Executed by István Sebök.

"Lichtrequisit einer elektrischen Bühne," *Die Form* 5, nos. 11–12 (1930), p. 297 (top) and pp. 298–99 (bottom).

L. MOHOLY-NAGY:
MECHANISCHE EXZENTRIK
Eine Synthese von Form, Bewegung, Ton, Licht (Farbe)

Das bisherige Theater ist Mitteilung von | Geschehnissen | Bericht oder
Lehren | Propaganda.

FORM BEWEGUNG TON LICHT (Farbe) waren vollkommen dieser Mitteilung oder Propaganda untergeordnet.
Das Erzählungsdrama der Frühzeit wuchs rasch zum Aktionsdrama und so begannen die Elemente der Bewegungsdrama-Gestaltung sich zu klären. D. h. der ursprüngliche Zweck des Dramas: Bericht, Propaganda wurde langsam ausgeschaltet und die Mittel dieser Mitteilung versuchte man primär zu gestalten.
Bei August Stramm entwickelte sich das Drama z. B. zu Explosionen, wo nicht mehr Mitteilung, nicht mehr Propaganda, nicht Charaktere gestaltet werden sollten, sondern schon Gestaltungsversuche an BEWEGUNG UND TON (Sprache), allerdings noch durch die Stoßkraft menschlicher Energiequellen (Leidenschaft).
Das Theater gab bei Stramm keine richtig erzählbare Geschichte, sondern ETWAS ANDERES: Aktion und Tempo, welche ohne Vorbereitung aus dem Impuls des Bewegungswunsches fast AUTOMATISCH und in quellender Folge hervorbrachen, obwohl noch mit literarischer Belastung.
Das dadaistische und futuristische Theater der Überraschungen ist noch weiter gegangen, indem es versucht hat, das Literarische ganz zu streichen. Aber in diesen Stücken spielen noch die menschlichen Leistungen — ebenso in der Aktion, wie in der Rezeption — die Hauptrolle.
Demgegenüber soll das heutige Theater mit der unauflösbaren Einheit der dynamisch-kontrastierenden Phänomenrelationen von Form Bewegung Ton und Licht gestaltet werden.
Die Konsequenz ist, daß es mit dem Theaterschriftsteller und mit seiner Literatur zu Ende sein muß.
Form-, Bewegungs-, Ton- und Lichtgestaltung einer dynamischen Aktionskonzentration wird die MECHANISCHE EXZENTRIK sein.
Demgegenüber ist die heutige Exzentrik nur eine auf den menschlichen Mechanismus bezogene Bewegungsorganisation. Ihre Wirkung besteht im Wesentlichen darin, daß der Zuschauer erstaunt oder erschrocken ist über die ihm vorgeführten Möglichkeiten seines eigenen Organismus (Material = Mensch), also vollkommen subjektive Wirkung. Dem objektiven Gestaltungswillen gegenüber ist dieses Material aber unerhört begrenzt und da es in dieser Begrenzung zudem noch mit secundären (literarischen) Elementen vermischt ist, bietet es ihm verhältnismäßig nur ganz minimale Möglichkeiten. Allerdings ist unsere Zeit als Übergangsperiode ziemlich günstig für diese Art menschlicher Überraschungen, und zwar auf einem spannenden Niveau, das erreicht wird durch selten gebrauchte, überkultivierte Form (amerikanische Clownerie, Chaplin, Fratellini etc.).
Die richtige heutige Forderung ist: eine wirkliche Form- und Bewegungsorganisation, welche gleichwertig den heute erzeugbaren akustischen und optischen (elektrischen) Phänomenen beigeordnet ist und die Bewegung nicht als Träger literarischer und gefühlsmäßiger Ereignisse mißbraucht.

Nebenstehend eine PARTITUR-SKIZZE zu einer mechanischen Exzentrik, wie ich sie schon heute für verwirklichbar halte. Das Manuskript stellt den Bühnenraum und die darin sich abspielenden Vorgänge dar. Die Bühne ist in drei Teile gegliedert. Der untere Teil für größere Formen und Bewegungen: I. BÜHNE. Die II. BÜHNE (oben) mit aufklappbarer Glasplatte für kleinere Formen und Bewegungen. (Die Glasplatte ist zugleich präparierte PROJEKTIONSWAND für von der Rückseite der Bühne kommende Filmvorführungen.) Auf der III. (Zwischen-) BÜHNE mechanische Musikapparate; meist ohne Resonanzkasten, nur mit Schalltrichter (Schlag-Geräusch- und Blas-Instrumente). Die Wände der Bühne sind mit weißer Leinwand bespannt, welche farbige Lichter aus Scheinwerfern und Lichtbäumen durchlassen und zerstreuen ● Die 1. und 2. Kolonne der Partitur bedeuten in senkrecht abwärtsgehender Kontinuität Form- und Bewegungsvorgänge ● Die 3. Kolonne zeigt einander folgende Lichtwirkungen. Die Breite der Streifen bedeutet die Dauer. Schwarz = Finsternis. Die in den breiten Streifen vorhandenen schmalen vertikalen Streifen sind gleichzeitige Teilbeleuchtungen der Bühne. Die 4. Kolonne ist für Musik vorgesehen; hier nur in den Absichten angedeutet. Die farbigen Vertikalstreifen bedeuten verschiedenartig heulende Sirenentöne, die den größten Teil der Vorgänge begleiten ● Die Gleichzeitigkeit ist in der Partitur aus der Horizontale zu lesen.

FOLGE:
1. KOLONNE
PFEILE STÜRZEN
LAMELLEN ÖFFNEN SICH
KREISE ROTIEREN
ELEKTRO-APPARATE
BLITZ DONNER
GITTERSYSTEME VON FARBEN
SCHIESSEN AUF - AB
HIN - HER
PHOSPHORESZENZ
RIESEN - APPARATE
SCHWINGEN
BLITZEN
GITTER WEITER
RÄDER
EXPLOSIONEN
GERÜCHE
CLOWNERIE
MENSCHMECHANIK

2. KOLONNE
PFEILE STÜRZEN
LAMELLEN ÖFFNEN SICH
KREISE ROTIEREN

KINO AUF TAGESWAND
RÜCKWÄRTS GEDREHT
AKTION
TEMPO
WILD

3. UND 4. KOLONNE
SIND OHNE
SCHLAG-
WORTE
DEUTLICH

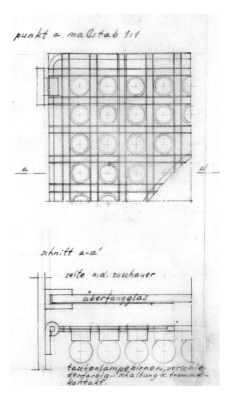

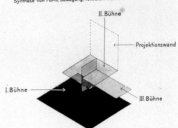

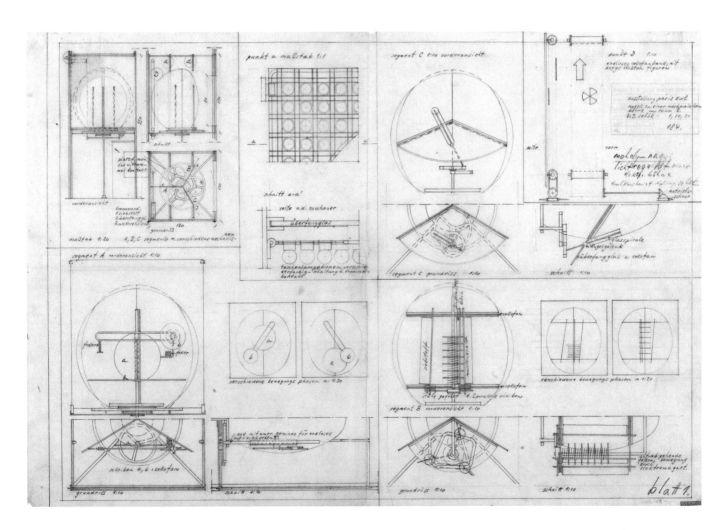

Werkbundausstellung Paris, 1930, Saal Theaterabteilung, 17.2 × 23 cm.

Left, opposite: Information sheet for the Mechanical Eccentric, printed paper. Opposite, lower right: Detail of "Partiturskizze zu einer mechanischen Exzentrik" (1924–25) bound into Moholy-Nagy, Molnár, and Schlemmer 1925, p. 44.

Werkbundausstellung Paris, 1930, Saal Theaterabteilung, 17 × 22.7 cm.

Working drawings for Light Prop for an Electric Stage, 1930. Graphite and stamping ink on tracing paper, 41.8 × 61 cm. Technical visualization by István Sebök. Detail, opposite, center-right.

A third translation, used in the French text in the *Die Form* article, is "installation lumineuse d'une scène electrique." While the terms "installation" and "accessoires" suggest stage props, "poste d'illumination" carries the technical connotation of a "lighting box" or "lighting station," invoking apparatus such as telephones, signal boxes, public fire reporting stations, and radio sets. In any case, none of this nomenclature suggested visible moving mechanical parts, or even an art object. All three French designations, as well as the German ones, connoted lighting devices. It is not surprising then, that not a single reviewer actually describes the apparatus or even reports seeing it.[52] Sigfried Giedion mentions it in passing and parenthetically: "(Moholy-Nagy showed a kinetic light prop for an electrical stage)."[53] In his review for *Neue Pariser Zeitung* (May 24, 1930) Hans Heilmaier wrote: "Highly instructive are the models [sic] of a lighting station for an electric stage by Moholy-Nagy...." Quoting from the wall text mentioned above, he continues: "the presentation of all the phases of movement offers a clear idea of the possibilities of stage lighting of the future."[54] These two quotations from texts provided to the visitor are as close to a description as it gets in the reviews! So was the Light Prop even there?

As Klaus Weber has pointed out, the Light Prop was definitely in the Trolit box in which it was supposed to be housed:[55] the crankshaft is clearly visible under the box in the side view, as is the cord plugged into a wall outlet, and indeed its label, in white on the black Trolit, is visible through the clear display case containing Gropius's Totaltheater model (p. 115). Looking through that glass case, though, no opening, round or otherwise, is visible on the glossy, dark surface of the housing. Moving on to examine the side-view photograph, there is no reflection of a round opening off the glass surface of the Totaltheater display case across from it (p. 120).

If Trolit, like Bakelite, is opaque, what was it that was covering the opening on the box? Why can we not see it? Careful examination of the working drawings for the Light Prop (p. 120) reveals that "überfangglas," ("flashed" glass) is specified on a plan detail of a corner of the display box on the side marked "seite n.d. zuschaer" (side toward the viewer). The round opening on the box was to be covered by glass with flashing—a layer of glass or film in a contrasting color applied to it. Flashing would have rendered the base glass darkly translucent, making it blend in with the dark, evenly colored Trolit. The light effects produced within the box, behind the dark flashed glass, would only have been visible when the lighting array on the interior of the box was switched on. The "poste d'illumination" would have appeared when the device and its lighting was engaged, a circular swirl of colored light, reflection and shadow playing though the semiopaque material, anticipating Frank Malina's Lumidyne System for "kinetic painting" by a couple of decades, as well as Otto Piene's Moholy-Nagy-inspired work of the 1960s.[56] This is the "installation lumineuse" seen by visitors to the Paris show: an abstract "film," a "Flächenfilm" constituted in real time while the visitor was watching.

Such a "planar film" presentation projected from behind onto a translucent surface would have realized, furthermore, Moholy-Nagy's dream of a "photogram film."[57] Rather than fixing the light display, as photograms did, the flashed glass arrangement, like the Lichtspiel film it so resembles, enables the spectacle to "unfold like a photogram set in motion."[58] This is why Moholy-Nagy referred to it as "ein Versuchsapparat für Lichtmalerei," an experimental device for light painting.

Set for Jacques Offenbach, *The Tales of Hoffmann*, Prelude and epilogue, Staatsoper am Platz der Republik ("Kroll-Oper"), Berlin, 1929. Director: Ernst Legal. Set design by László Moholy-Nagy. Photo: Lucia Moholy, later authorized print, 14.5 × 23.3 cm.

Set for Jacques Offenbach, *Les Contes d'Hoffmann*, Prelude and epilogue, Staatsoper am Platz der Republik ("Kroll-Oper"), Berlin, 1929. Director: Ernst Legal. Photo: Lucia Moholy, possibly a later, authorized print, 14.5 × 23.3 cm.

Projection Spaces

This solution to the problem of the presentation of the Light Prop was, in effect, suggested by Kai-Uwe Hemken and Jakob Gebert—even if only in passing—in their article on their realization of the Raum der Gegenwart (Room of the Present), the gallery that Alexander Dorner commissioned Moholy-Nagy in 1930 to design for the museum Dorner directed in Hannover.[59] Hemken and Gebert note that in Paris the Light Prop seemed to have been hidden behind a "translucent but opaque" dividing wall within the box. This is not the way the Light Prop was shown in their realization, however. Hemken and Gebert contrast the Paris presentation with their interpretation of its planned installation in Hannover, claiming that the round opening in the presentation box would have been uncovered. I disagree with this conclusion for a number of reasons.

The Raum der Gegenwart was to present films by Richter, Eggeling, and Ruttmann, as well as examples of Russian cinema, across from the box in which the Light Prop was to be housed. Rather than the usual rectangular format, they were to be rear-projected onto screens with round frames of the same diameter as the opening in the prop's Trolit housing. Why would Moholy-Nagy have proposed this if he did not intend to use the Light Prop as a device for making a "Flächenfilm", a "live" abstract film? Why the analogical mode of presentation if no analogy was actually to be drawn? A close look at the axonometric drawing of the Raum der Gegenwart, furthermore, reveals that no opening is sketched on the side of the presentation box facing the film presentations (pp. 124–25). A caption on the plan, however, states "öffnung hier," with an arrow pointing toward where the opening should be on the box. An opening that was invisible unless the Light Prop and its lighting array were switched on would solve this seeming contradiction in the plans.[60]

Finally, Moholy-Nagy's own depiction of the Light Prop in *Lightplay Black White Grey* shows the device as I am proposing it was shown in Paris and to be shown in Hannover: behind a translucent screen. When one reviews the film with my thesis in mind, one notes that in addition to "straight" shots of the device (the device, even if "doubled," clearly visible in its details), there are sequences of the Prop projecting its lights and shadows onto a translucent screen, a "Flächenfilm", a shadow-play film, in other words. In order to realize his dream of a photogrammatic film, Moholy-Nagy reverses the tonality of these shadow sequences. This is as close to a "photogram film" as he was able to get. It is important to emphasize that the reversed tonality sequences are not based on the "straight" shots of the prop. Rather, it is the tonality of the shadow sequences that is inverted. The divide between "straight" and "shadow" sequences is plainly visible, and he ends the film with a second shadow sequence (p. 127).[61]

As mentioned, Moholy-Nagy did think of an alternative way of presenting the Versuchs-apparat by removing the back of the housing to allow the prop to project onto an external surface. He also suggested that lighting programs for multiple Light Props be broadcast over the radio, opening up the possibility of remotely controlled and lit devices. This idea is explored by Ken Gregory in his work for *Sensing the Future, Prototype Electric Light Machine for a Modern Room* (p. 171).[62] Moholy-Nagy elaborated on this concept in *telehor*: "In all probability a special place will be reserved in the dwellings of the future for the reception of light frescoes, just as it is today for the radio."[63] By bringing the device "out of the box," it would have become something that could

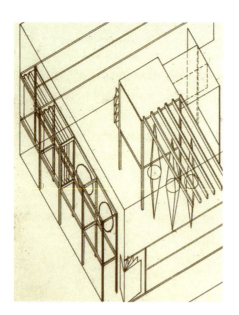

Raum der Gegenwart (Room of the Present), 1930. Isometric drawing, executed by István Sebök (detail).

View through opening of presentation box for Light Prop for an Electric Stage. Facsimile: Woodie Flowers, 1970 (edition of two) (Van Abbemuseum, Eindhoven), as presented in Jakob Gebert and Kai-Uwe Hemken's realization of Moholy-Nagy's design for the Raum der Gegenwart (Room of the Present), Kunsthalle Erfurt, 2009.

Naomi Clare Crellin, *(Re)Animating the Light Prop: A Digital Investigation of Moholy-Nagy's Light Space Modulator* (view through opening of presentation box), 2009. Digital file.

Projection Spaces

Naomi Clare Crellin, *(Re)Animating the Light Prop: A Digital Investigation of Moholy-Nagy's Light Space Modulator* (projection through anterior of presentation box), 2009, digital file.

Facsimile of Light Prop for an Electric Stage. Aluminum, chromed steel, Plexiglas, wood and electric motor, H: 91 cm. Facsimile by Woodie Flowers, based on the original in the Busch-Reisinger Museum, Cambridge, MA, 1970, edition of two. Photographed on display at the Bauhaus-Archiv, Berlin, Fall 1999, 35 mm slide.

View of projection of Sergei Eisenstein, *Battleship Potemkin*, 1915, as presented in Jakob Gebert and Kai-Uwe Hemken's realization of Moholy-Nagy's design for the Raum der Gegenwart (Room of the Present), Kunsthalle Erfurt, 2009.

transform a room utterly, when activated in the dark with lights directed at it, turning the space itself into a Lichtraum, a work of art, of "light art." These remain rather vague suggestions, of secondary importance to Moholy-Nagy, however, and the principal manner in which he intended to display the prop was within the box.

The designation of the Light Prop was tenuous and multifarious, ensnared as it was in the trap of its financing while at the same time left to float free on the waves of its fluid status as a mechanical device rather than a work of art worthy of a stable title. The many designations were never resolved into a title during Moholy-Nagy's lifetime. After his death in 1946, however, there was an increasing tendency to regard the device as a "kinetic sculpture," that is, as a work of art, a tendency that began in 1932, when a photograph of the prop itself appeared, perhaps for the first time in print, on the cover of two Czechoslovakian-Hungarian publications.[64]

In her posthumous biography Sybil Moholy-Nagy emphasized that "the Light Machine was not a piece of sculpture and was never exhibited in Moholy's lifetime as a work of art."[65] Her book still reflects the instability of its designation; she referred to it variously as "Light Machine," "Lichtrequisit," "light-display machine," and as "a construction–half sculpture and half machine." In the illustration caption, however, she dubbed it "Light Space Modulator." This designation, which emphasized its potential for being shown as an object in the round, a device for projecting shadows and light onto surfaces around it, is the one that stuck.[66] The device is to this day known mainly as the *Light Space Modulator*. While this is an excellent title for the way it has been shown since the 1960s, that is, as a kinetic sculpture, this framing of the machine served to obscure its original purpose as a device for projecting colored lights and shadows onto a translucent screen. The *Light Space Modulator* is a kinetic sculpture. The Light Prop was an "experimental device for light painting," a cinematic prop. We can choose how we wish to see it, but this should not blind us to the way in which Moholy-Nagy originally planned for it to be seen.

Projection and "projection spaces," as Gropius phrased it, are terms that relate to much of the art that Moholy-Nagy produced or foresaw during his career from about 1922 on. Like Gesamtwerk, immersion/participation, light, transparency, movement, the notion of art as a form of information, production/reproduction, and sensory education, it is a cornerstone of his aesthetic-pedagogical project. The Light Prop for an Electric Stage, his experimental device for light painting, the means of realizing a photogrammatic film, was perhaps the most completely realized of his works that sought to combine different media, concepts, and aesthetic effects into a single device.

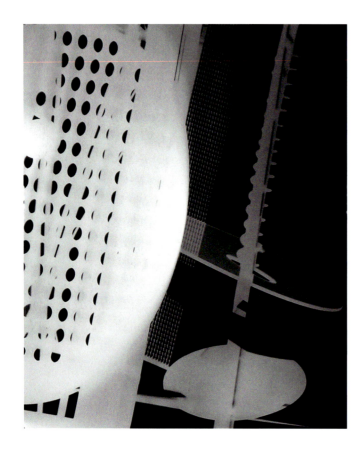

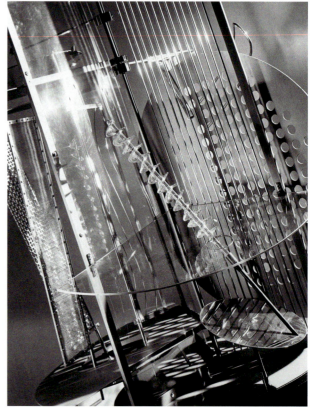

Projection Spaces

Kálmán Brogyányi, *A fény művészete* (The Art of Light) (Bratislava/Pozsony, 1932).

Forum no. 3, 1932 (Bratislava/Pozsony). Edited by Kálmán Brogyányi.

Floris Neusüss and Renate Heyne, Untitled (with the Light Prop of László Moholy-Nagy in the Bauhaus Archiv), 2005. Photogram, 50 × 50 cm.

"Light Prop for an Electric Stage", 1930. 30.2 × 23.4 cm; image: 27.2 × 20.8 cm.

Film stills from *Lightplay Black White Grey*, Germany, 1932. 35 mm, black and white, silent, ca. 5'30". Top: left: Shadow sequence; right: shadow sequence, tonally reversed, with double exposure. Middle: left: First shadow sequence, tonally reversed, double exposure; right: First straight sequence, double exposure; Bottom: left: End of second shadow sequence; right: Straight sequence, close-up of Light Prop.

Architektur I, n.d. [1922]. Oil, metallic oil pigment, and graphite on fine linen fabric, 65.2 × 55.4 cm.

MA (Today) 7, nos. 5–6 (May 1, 1922), with László Moholy-Nagy, *Üvegarchitektura* (Glass Architecture) on the cover.

Glasarchitektur III, 1921–22. Oil on cardboard, 84 × 61 cm.

Jaroslav Bouček, Installation photographs for *ausstellung l. moholy-nagy* (Exhibition 1. Moholy-Nagy), Mährischer Kunstverein, Brno, Czechoslovakia, June 1935. Gelatin silver prints in spiral-bound album, 1934, 29.3 × 20.9 cm.

128

Transparency/Reflection/Motion

The passion for transparency is one of the most spectacular features of our time. We might say, with pardonable enthusiasm, that structure becomes transparency and transparency manifests structure.[1]

I planned three-dimensional assemblages, constructions, executed in glass and metal. Flooded with light, I thought they would bring to the fore the most powerful color harmonies. In trying to sketch this type of 'glass architecture,' I hit upon the idea of transparency. This problem has occupied me for a long time.[2]

[In these paintings] form elements seem to float through an undefined space, as if weightlessly suspended and of such transparent substance as to allow freely balanced intersections to penetrate superimposed planes. [The paintings were] reflective in a way of the wondrous achievement of modern technology and science to have freed man from both the law of gravity and the pedestrian view of individual perspective.[3]

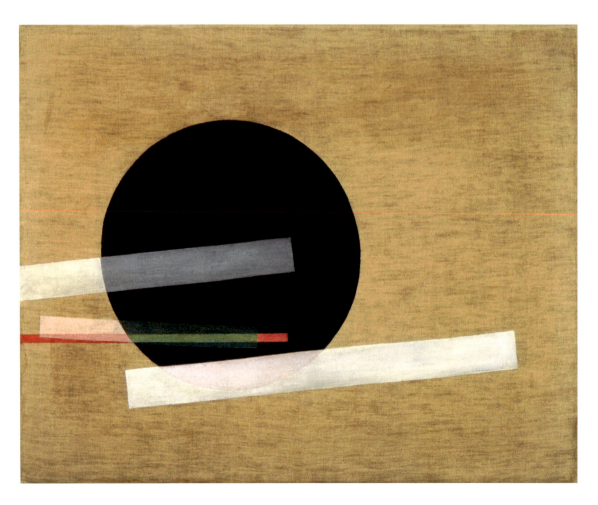

Variation on *Komposition A II*. Offset color print, in *Offset Buch & Werbekunst*, 1925, p. 347.

Komposition A 17, 1927. Tempera on canvas, 96.5 × 117 cm.

Komposition A II, 1924. Oil on canvas, 115.8 × 136.5 cm.

Komposition (variant on *Komposition A II*, 1924) Linocut or woodcut on paper; paper: 22.8 × 29.3 cm; image: 14.9 × 19.8 cm. Dedication: "für Heinrich Jacoby."

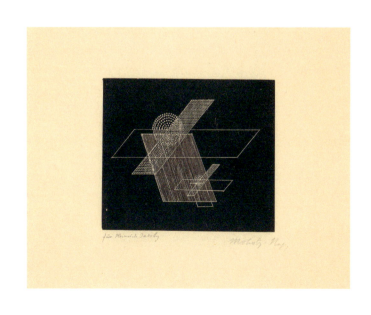

I became interested in painting-with-light, not on the surface of the canvas, but directly in space. Painting transparencies was the start. I painted as if colored light was projected on a screen, and other colored lights superimposed over it. I thought this effect could be enhanced by placing translucent screens of different shapes, one behind the other, and projecting the colored lights over each unit.[4]

At first sight ... one would see collages of transparent colored strips reproduced in oil or watercolor, first flat, later in more complex spatial combinations. However these "glass architectures" as he called them defy not only the laws of color composition, but also the graphical space representation techniques (perspective, axonometry, isometry). If one actually superimposed transparent colored planes made of glass or acetate, a darkening of color with the increasing number of layers would result. This is not the case in Moholy-Nagy's canvases where the effect is reversed, as if with colored light beams; the colors actually become clearer with the increasing number of layers, thus creating a depth of field and a characteristic spatial effect. But even then, the mixing of colors does not quite follow the rules of additive combination, no more than the composition and the relative position of elements follow those of linear perspective. The result depends only on an exquisitely subtle intuition and a deep sense of equilibrium.[5]

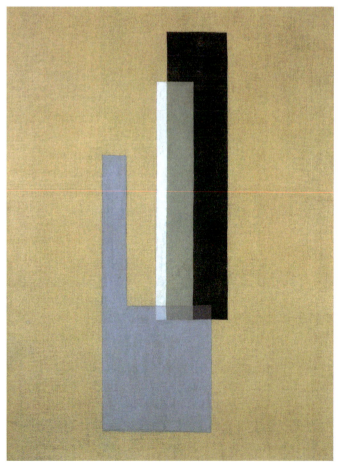

Untitled, ca. 1923. Tempera and blue paper on mahogany, 35 × 26 cm.

Komposition, n.d. [ca. 1923]. Oil on burlap, 66 × 50 cm.

From *Meistermappe des Staatlichen Bauhauses* 1923. Colored lithograph on paper. Paper: 39 × 28.8 cm, image: 36 × 25.5 cm.

Abstufungen (variation on *Konstruktion C VIII*), 1923. Lithograph on paper, 60.2 × 44 cm.

Em 3, 1923. Porcelain enamel on steel, 77.4 × 60.2 cm. Signed, dated and titled on verso. Present location unknown. Source: *The 1920s in Eastern Europe*, Cologne: Galerie Gmyrzynska, 1975, p. 158.

Untitled, n. d. (ca. 1925–28?). 22.5 × 17 cm.

Untitled, n. d. (ca. 1925–28?). Gelatin silver reverse print, 21.8 × 16.9 cm.

the new bauhaus: American School of Design. Prospectus, edited, designed, and photographed by László Moholy-Nagy, Chicago. The New Bauhaus, 1937.

Four sheets (nos. 3, 4, 6, 7) from *6. Kestnermappe – 6 Konstruktionen*, album of lithographs. Hannover: Verlag Ludwig Ey, 1923, 3. Edition of 50. 53 × 44 cm; 42 × 22.3 cm; 60 × 44 cm; 45 × 34 cm.

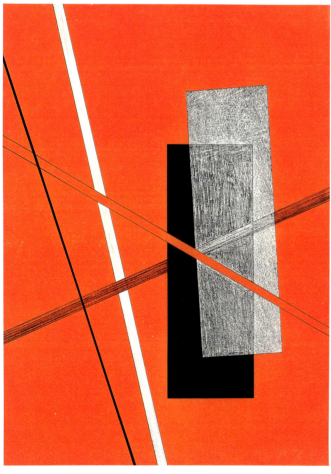

Moholy-Nagy wields his artistic means with ascetic transparency, leaving them to completely persist in their materiality. In his reliefs of wood, glass, metal, porcelain, fabric and paper, he combines found objects or formed materials into a construction.... Moholy-Nagy's Materialartistik [material artistry] shows itself above all in his sculptures; thus, in his Nickel Sculpture with Spring, the gleaming shine and mirroring of which refracts and variegates.[6]

Integration of two systems of construction (assembled from different metals: steel, copper, nickel, aluminum, zinc, and plate glass). An attempt to unite two independent and self-sufficient plastic compositions. The multiple reflection by mirrors creates the illusion of swaying. This experiment at the same time demonstrates the whole borderland lying between architecture and sculpture. If the experiment is carried further, bringing more and more new single pieces into relation with the two already present, spatial composition results.[7]

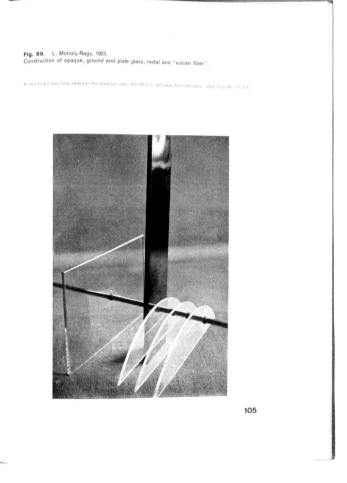

"Integration of two systems of construction (assembled from different metals: steel, copper, nickel, aluminum, zinc and plate glass)" and "Construction of Opaque, Ground and Plate Glass, metal, and Vulcan fiber" (both lost), in Moholy-Nagy 1932, pp. 104–5.

Staatliche Bildstelle, Berlin, *Bauhaus Exhibition, 1923: Gallery with Paintings and Sculptures by Moholy-Nagy*. Gelatin silver prints made in 2000 from original negative, 18 × 24 cm each.

Sculpture in Metal, ca. 1923. Dimensions and present whereabouts unknown. Reproduced in *Staatliches Bauhaus in Weimar 1919–1923* (Weimar, 1923).

Transparency/Reflection/Motion

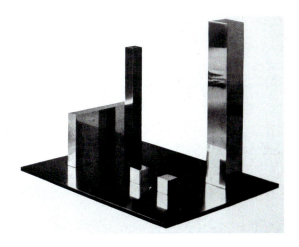

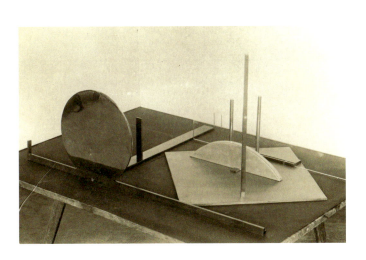

Vintage documentary photography of *Metal Sculpture*, 1922–23, also known as "Integration of two systems of construction (assembled from different metals: steel, copper, nickel, aluminum, zinc and plate glass),"
11 × 6.4 cm.

Nickel Construction with Spiral, 1921. Nickel-plated iron, welded, 35.9 × 17.5 × 23.8 cm.

I've been painting a few very nice paintings on highly polished sheets of silverit, an interesting effect: the colored planes float in an abstract space that is constituted only through reflections and mirroring.[8]

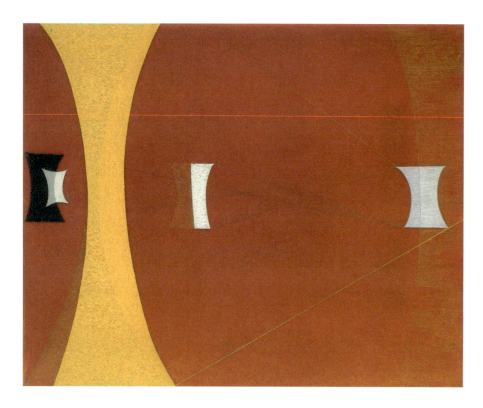

Sil 2, 1933. Oil and incisions into Silverit, 50.1 × 60.1 cm.

Rho + Ga CI I I, 1930. Oil pigment on Rhodoid and Galalith, 41.9 × 52.8 cm.

Sil I, 1933. Oil and incisions into Silverit, 50 × 20 cm.

Tp 1, 1930/42. Oil and incisions into plastic, 156 × 62.5 cm.

Transparency/Reflection/Motion

I began to paint on aluminum, highly polished nonferrous alloys, and on thermosetting and thermoplastics. If I had not been afraid that these latter materials were not permanent, I would never have painted on canvas again. In working with these materials—uniformly colored, opaque or transparent plastics—I made discoveries which were instrumental in changing my painting technique. This had inevitable repercussions on my thinking concerning light problems.... By producing real radiant light effects through transparent dyes on plastic and through other means, one has no need for translating light into color by painting and pigment.[9]

Cop 1, 1936. Oil on copper, 50.2 × 56 cm.

Konstruktion AL 6, 1933–34. Oil on aluminum, 60 × 50.2 cm (with detail).

Moholy-Nagy unifies engineer-like precision and the bounded surface-design of the image with a merry attitude towards life, which allows luminous signals to hover directly over boundless spatial expanses in his compositions. These delicate yet energetically taut color harmonies unleash – nearly without material constraint – the light held within them. Already the smooth and airy oil paintings achieve a transparent dissolution of substance such that, in the superpositions, forms appear to interpenetrate and pure colors are reciprocally broken. In order to create more intensive and purer light effects, Moholy-Nagy seizes enamel-galalite- and aluminum-surfaces and, ultimately, the direct manipulation of light itself.[10]

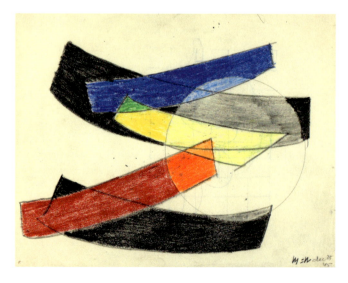

Dufay Color photograph, 1935. In Moholy-Nagy 1947b, pp. 170–71.

Untitled, 1945. Graphite and colored chalks on paper, 21.5 × 28 cm.

CH for Y Space Modulator, 1945. Oil on yellow Formica, 154 × 60.5 cm.

Transparency/Reflection/Motion

In my pictures I have tried to follow [a] line of space-time articulation by painting on waterclear, transparent plastics, introducing direct light effects, mobile reflections, and shadows, indicating a trend away from the static pigmentation of surfaces toward a kinetic "light painting." The problem is only how to control these colored "light paintings" with the same precision as the painter of yesterday controlled the effects of his pigments.[11]

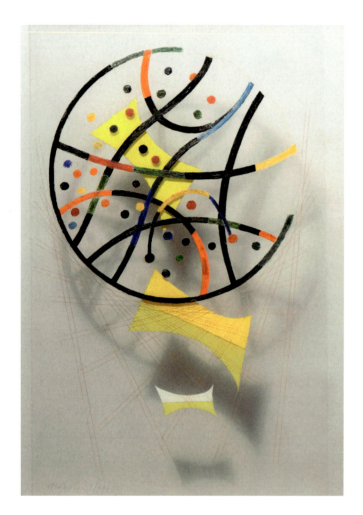

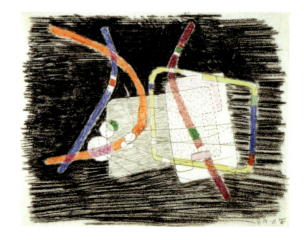

Untitled (Space Modulator), 1946. Oil on Plexiglas affixed to wood, 37 × 21.5 cm.

Untitled (study for a space modulator), 1946. Graphite and pencil crayons on paper, 28 × 21.5 cm.

Untitled (study for a space modulator), 1945. Graphite and colored chalks on paper, 21.5 × 28 cm.

Prehistoric Construction, 1941. Pigment and incisions on Plexiglas, mounted on wood, 25.5 × 62 cm. Reproduced by permission, from the Collection of the Queensland Art Gallery, Brisbane.

Untitled (sketch for Prehistoric Construction), 1941. Conté crayon on paper, 21.5 × 27.7 cm.

B-10 Space Modulator, 1942. Oil on incised and molded Plexiglas, mounted with chromium clips on painted plywood; Plexiglas: 45.1 × 30.5 cm.

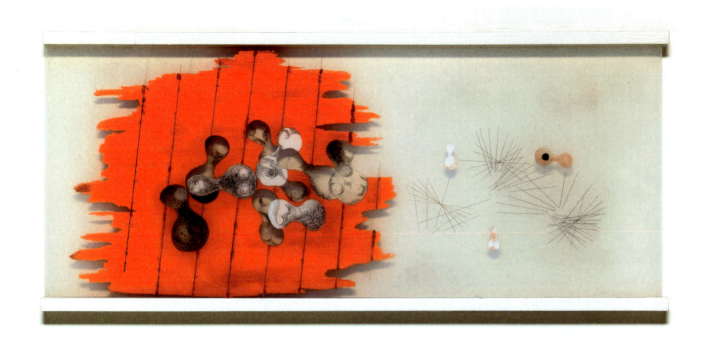

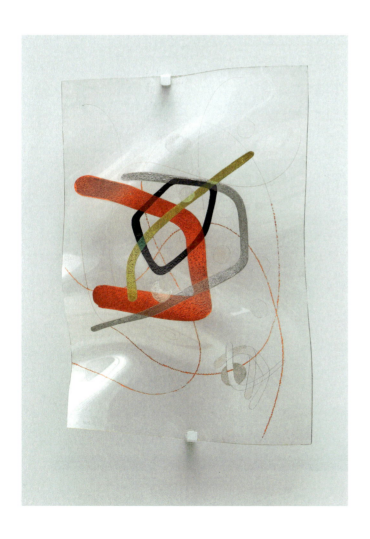

145

The new plastics allow a new type of visual experience to develop. Glass-like sheets, pliable, can be curved convex and concave. They can be perforated so that light and pigment will be fused into a new unity. Artificial light sources (spot lights, needle lamps) can continuously change the composition. This kind of picture is most probably the passage between easel painting and light display, a new branch of moving pictures.[12]

Space Modulator, 1940. Rhodoid and Plexiglas, dimensions and present location unknown. Illustrated in Moholy-Nagy 1947b, p. 235, figure 320.

The Spirals (1945/46), 1977 replica. Plexiglas, 49 × 37.5 × 40 cm.

Leda and the Swan, 1946. Plexiglas, 55.9 × 41.3 × 40 cm.

Twisted Planes, 1946. Acrylic and steel, 40.64 × 87.31 cm. Acquisition number 1949.2. Addison Gallery of American Art, Phillips Academy, Andover, MA. Museum purchase, 1949.12. Photo: Addison Gallery
© VG Bild-Kunst, Bonn

Transparency/Reflection/Motion

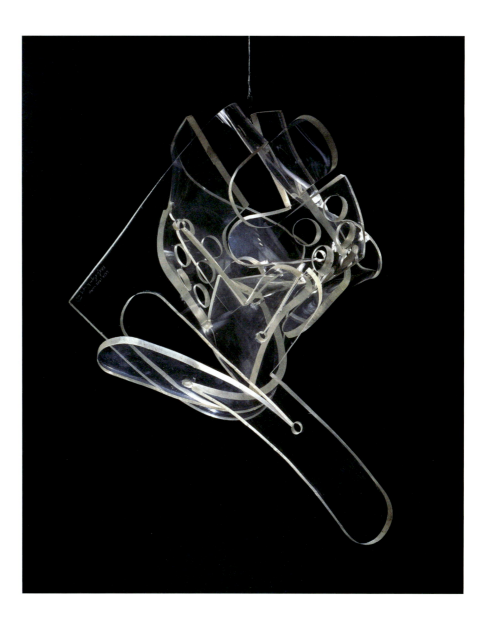

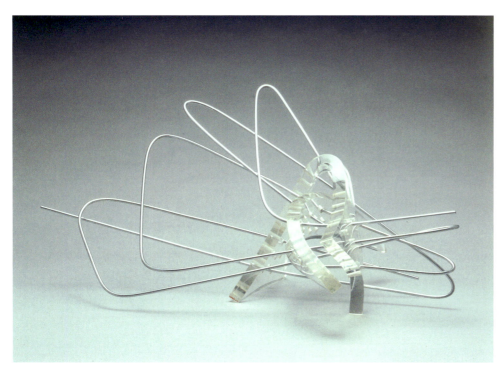

In mobiles, material is utilized not in its mass but as a carrier of movement. To the three dimensions of volume, the fourth, the time element, movement, is added. Depending upon the speed of motion, the originally heavy block of material—the solid volume—transforms itself into a kind of ethereal extension. The "mobile" is a weightless poising of volume relationships and interpenetrations.[13]

The [Light Prop] was designed mainly to see transparencies in action, but I was surprised to discover that shadows thrown on transparent and perforated screens produced new visual effects, a kind of interpenetration in fluid change. Also unexpected were the mirrorings of the moving plastic shapes on the highly polished nickel and chromium-plated surfaces. These surfaces, although opaque in reality, looked like transparent sheets when moving.[14]

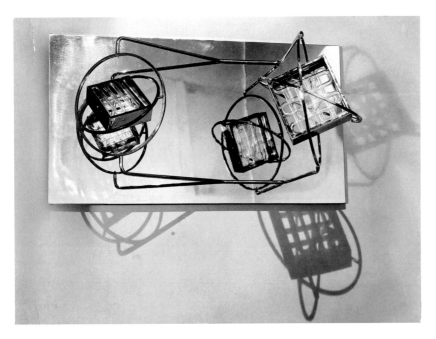

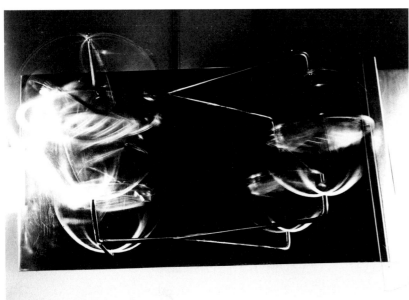

Two overhead views of *Gyros*, 1936. Stainless steel, glass tubes, liquid mercury. Top: Stationary, n. d. 16.4 × 22.5 cm; Bottom: in motion, n.d. 16.1 × 23.3 cm.

Space Modulator, 1943. Plexiglas and chrome-plated steel rods, 83 × 59 cm, gelatin silver documentary photograph.

Film still from *Lightplay Black White Grey*, Germany, 1932. 35 mm, black and white, silent, ca. 5'30".

Two illustrations of *Space Modulator* (1943), Plexiglas and chrome-plated steel rods, illustrated in Moholy-Nagy 1047b, pp. 242–43.

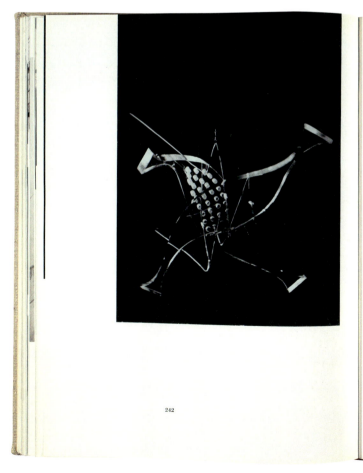

Figs. 329-330. ○ L. Moholy-Nagy, 1940
Space modulator with perforations and its virtual volume

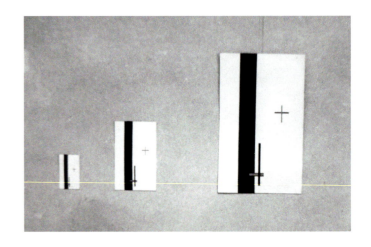

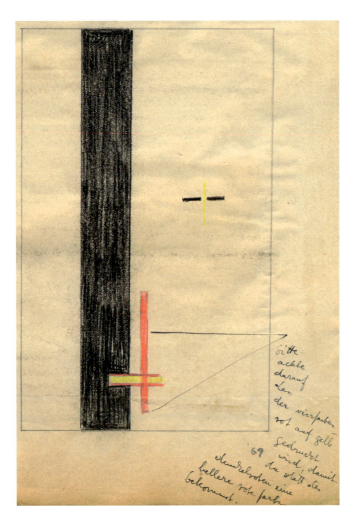

koliv kameře. dává nám naději na svéprávné, dosud naprosto neznámé optické formace. je nejvíce produševnělou zbraní v boji za nové vidění.

co jest to optická kvalita?

vývojem černo-bílé fotografie byly teprve správně objeveny světla a stíny a po teoretických poznatcích správně použity. (impresionismus byl v malířství k tomu souběžnou akcí barevnou.)

vývojem vysoce hodnotných umělých, zejména elektrických světelných zdrojů, jejich říditelnosti dospělo se k vystupňovanému použití plynulého světla a bohatě odstupňovaných stínů a tím k oživení plochy, optickému zjemnění. toto velké odstupňování hodnot je podstatným prostředkem optické tvůrčí práce. i tehdy, učíme-li se uvažovati a pracovati nejen v hodnotách černo-bílo-šedých, ale i v hodnotách barevných.

čistá barva položená vedle čisté barvy, tón vedle tónu, vyvolává totiž zpravidla dekorativní, tvrdý a plakátový dojem. tytéž barvy ve spojení se svými mezitóny uvolňují naproti tomu plakátové složení a vytvoří jemnější skladbu barevných účinů; černo-bílo-šedým podáním všech barevných zjevů přivedla nás fotografie — jak v šedé, tak v barevné škále — k poznávání nejjemnějších valérových rozdílů. to je nová kvalita optického výrazu, převyšující dosavadní standard.

to je ovšem pouze jeden bod z mnoha jiných. je to bod, při němž můžeme počítati spíše s vnitřní schopností dopracovati se optických účinů, spíše s funkcí stránky výrazové, umělecké než se zobrazovací funkcí tvorby. prozatím aspoň.

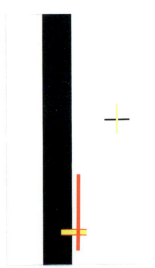

Art as Information / Information as Art

One of Moholy-Nagy's most provocative notions was that art was first and foremost a form of information. This idea tied in to his belief that the idea was primary in a work of art, whereas its execution was secondary, meaning there was no good reason not to subcontract the step of making an artwork:

People believe that they should demand hand execution as an inseparable part of the genesis of a work of art. In fact, in comparison with the inventive mental process of the genesis of the work, the question of its execution is important only insofar as it must be mastered to the limits. The manner, however—whether personal or by assignment of labour, whether manual or mechanical—is irrelevant.[1]

Removing the artist from actual production of the artwork was even more controversial a notion then than it is now. It may well have grown out of Moholy-Nagy's thinking on the relationship between painting and photography. He viewed it as problematic that painting—for example, Neue Sachlichkeit—continued to function as a mimetic or documentary medium, feeling it should instead defer to photography, which he considered to be innately suited to representation. Ever since its inception, an oft-repeated critique of photography on the part of established artists was that, being "machine-made," it lacked the artistry and craftsmanship that painting required. It was precisely such criticism that had induced the Pictorialist movement in photography to emphasize the craft of the medium. Moholy-Nagy responded to this accusation by turning the tables on traditional views on art. He insisted that craftsmanship intrinsically had very little to do with art, for the idea was paramount. His analysis of the proposed distinction between painting and photography took the wind out of the sails of critics of this new medium:

The representation of either the object or the human being has been perfected to such a degree in photography that the interpretation through manual means—painting—seems indeed primitive. The battle between brush and camera becomes ridiculous if one realizes ... that all representation is interpretation—that the choice of object, segment, light, shadow, even the choice of soft or hard photographic paper—are highly creative "artistic" decisions.[2]

The potential artistry in photography, Moholy-Nagy was suggesting, did not lie in attempts to make it emulate painting or the graphic arts, but in making decisions related to the medium, its intrinsic nature and to the tool it deployed, the camera. While this stance is not entirely unexpected for someone who, not having attended art school, lacked certain practical artistic skills, it also reflected the zeitgeist, including Marcel Duchamp's readymades, of course, and indeed the widespread belief in the early 1920s, particularly among the Russian Constructivists, that artists were akin to technicians: technicians did not fetishize manual dexterity, so why should artists?[3] As he wrote, referring to his Enamel series: "In this age of industrial production and technical precision we also strive to execute works of fine art with complete precision."[4]

Taking as the point of departure a conviction that the concept (rather than its execution) formed the core of an artwork, it was no great leap to assert that art was a form of knowledge, which, just like any other kind of knowledge, could be translated into information and transmitted, via an agreed code, to anyone willing and able to manufacture it. Against the backdrop of the invention of telegraphy in the early nineteenth century, and the development of binary codes (such as Morse), capable of transmitting any text using short and long bursts of electricity, all information could indeed be codified. Telegraphy had been superseded by analogue modes of communication, such as the telephone and the record player, but the core concept remained: information could be transmitted using other technological means, and there was no reason why art should be excluded from such operations.

Moholy-Nagy also pondered changes in information storage:

... there is a certain observable perspective in the development of our means of communication and the entire news service, leading to a substantial reduction in the

Installation photograph of László Moholy-Nagy's exhibition, Galerie Der Sturm, February 1924, with a detail (top) showing *Konstruktionen in Emaille 1, 1a* and *1b* (*EM* series), 1923. Porcelain enamel on steel, 24 × 15 cm, 47.5 × 30.1 cm, 94 × 60 cm.

Left: Sketch of the illustration of the *EM* series design (ca. 1922–23) for *telehor,* 1, nos. 1–2 (1936), with color instructions, 1935. Graphite and pencil crayon on paper. Right: Page as it appeared in *telehor,* p. 69.

role of typographical communication in the form of books, ... etc. The diffusion of film, the record player, and radio has led to a turning point. It is not utopian to say that film and record collections will often replace today's libraries. The improvement of phonographic techniques and the amplification tube as well as the development of a mechanical language phonetically best suited to such instruments, will probably result in future authors publishing their works in a phonetic-mechanical rather than an optical-typographical manner (for example, records, perforated tapes for the amplification tube, radio), or possibly by optophonetic means (sound film).[5]

Lazar el Lissitzky summed it up in a nutshell: "The new book demands the new writer. Inkstand and goose-quill are dead. The printed sheet transcends space and time. The printed sheet, the infinity of the book, must be transcended. THE ELECTRO-LIBRARY."[6]

Information and its various transmission media fascinated Moholy-Nagy. It was included as one topic he wished to tackle in the "synthetic" journal he proposed in 1922. In *Painting, Photography, Film* Moholy-Nagy mentioned what he dubbed a "drahtlose projizierte film zeitung," that is, a wirelessly transmitted film journal, and images of this featured later in the book. This procedure had been invented by a German, Arthur Korn, who demonstrated long-distance transmission of an image by means of radio waves as early as 1906. In 1913 Korn presented the telegraphic transmission of a film, going on to transmit a photograph across the Atlantic by wireless in 1923.[7]

The roots of this interest run deep in Moholy-Nagy's psyche. While he was still at high school, he won a copy of Charles Gilbert's *Modern Electricity* (in the Hungarian edition) as an academic prize, a book that discussed the various electrical means of information transmission in detail.[8] Many of Moholy-Nagy's early drawings of the Galician front during World War I depict telecommunications devices, such as the radiophone, in use. His poetry and short stories took communications technologies as one motif, often imbuing them with an erotic charge.[9]

Budapest had a tradition of innovative communication technologies. In 1876 Hungarian inventor Tivadar Puskás, while trying to develop a telegraph exchange, heard of Alexander Graham Bell's work on the telephone and traveled to New Jersey to work with him. Puskás went on to invent telephone exchange technology, installing the

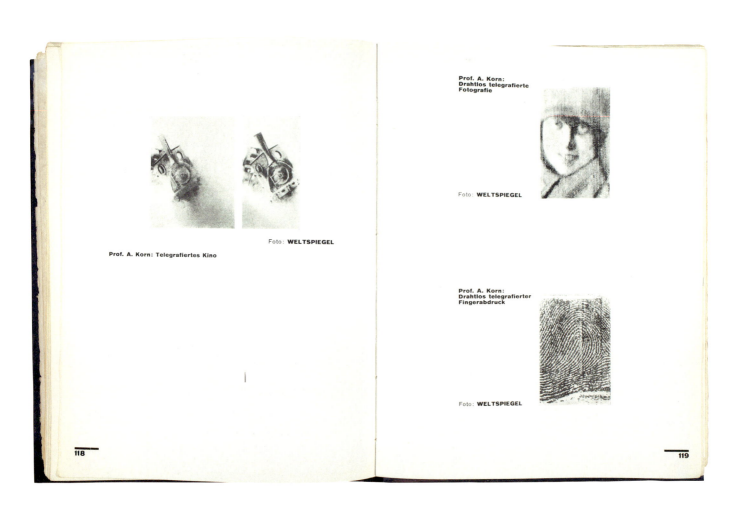

Art as Information / Information as Art

Reporters working on the *Telefonhírmondó* (telephone newspaper), Budapest. Thomas S. Denison, *World's Work* (April 1901), 640–43.

Mihály Dénes demonstrating the Telehor, Berlin, March 8, 1929.

Wirelessly transmitted still and moving images developed by Arthur Korn, in Moholy-Nagy, 1925, pp. 118–19.

"Some usable typographical signs" (at three scales), in *Gutenberg Festschrift* (Mainz: Gutenberg Gesellschaft, 1925), p. 315.

first European exchange in Paris in 1878. By 1881 his brother had opened the first exchange in the Austro-Hungarian Empire, in Budapest. In 1892 Puskás developed the first public broadcasting system, which was called the *Telefonhírmondó* (Telephone Herald), also in Budapest. Service began in 1893 and continued into the 1930s. During the early twentieth century it played an important role in Budapest's active journalistic scene, and pioneered broadcasts of news, weather, and live music performances.

In July 1919, during the Soviet Republic, Mihály Dénes from the Budapest Telephone Factory (Budapesti Telefongyár) demonstrated his mechanical television transmission technology, the telehor. In 1923 Dénes published *Das Elektrische Fernsehen und das Telehor* (The Electric Television and the Telehor) in Berlin, describing his invention, and in 1925 he moved to the German capital, where he secured a position with the AEG, the company that later sponsored production of Moholy-Nagy's Light Prop. Moholy-Nagy referred to the telehor in *Painting, Photography, Film* (p. 23) and his young Moravian friend František Kalivoda adopted it for the title of the journal devoted to Moholy-Nagy's work, a publication I shall address in more detail in the next chapter. Just as Moholy-Nagy's lifelong utopian and leftist ideas were shaped by the Budapest Galileo Circle, the Activists and his experiences with the Hungarian Soviet Republic in Budapest, his lifelong fascination with communications technology was forged primarily by his experiences in Budapest, the city of his youth.

Around 1923 Moholy-Nagy discovered the writings of Raoul Heinrich Francé, and these texts became crucial to him in integrating his enthusiasm for technology into a broader biocentric conception of the world.[10] Moholy-Nagy soon enacted a demonstration of this enthusiasm for technology in his art practice. Five of his best-known works, the *Konstruktionen in Emaille* (Constructions in Enamel) (the EM series), were made shortly after he and Lucia Moholy moved to Weimar.[11]

Sibyl Moholy-Nagy reports that Moholy-Nagy worked his way from Vienna to Berlin as a "letterer and sign painter" in 1920,[12] which suggests he would have been aware of the techniques for producing the most popular sign type of the day, using weather-resistant porcelain on metal—familiar to North Americans through the old Coca-Cola signs. Moholy-Nagy ordered the porcelain-enamel-on-metal works in the EM series from an enamel sign manufacturer, Stark & Riese, based in Tannroda, a village just south of Weimar. He first elaborated on this production methodology in 1923, just after the signs were made: "This [mechanical] means of producing pictures is only possible for works that are conceived with a view to being achieved by means of precise and impersonal technology. One can have works of this type made in a factory at any time using Ostwald's color charts and graph paper. In fact, one could order them by telephone."[13] Later in life he recalled how the process had worked:

In 1922 I ordered by telephone from a sign factory five paintings in porcelain enamel. I had the factory's color chart before me and I sketched my paintings on graph paper. At the other end of the telephone the factory supervisor had the same kind of paper, divided into squares. He took down the dictated shapes in the correct position. (It was like playing chess by correspondence.) One of the pictures was delivered in three different sizes, so that I could study the subtle differences in the color relations caused by the enlargement and reduction.[14]

The other two works in this series may have both had different designs, but as the fifth work of this series has not yet come to light, this cannot be determined with absolute certainty. The idea of reproducing an image at various scales was also apparent in the illustration accompanying an article on typography published by Moholy-Nagy in *Gutenberg Festschrift* in 1925.

Besides obviating the need for the artist's direct manual intervention, this production method suggested the pieces could be mass-produced. Berlin-based Hungarian critic Ernő Kállai acknowledged this possibility, comparing the Enamel series to a relatively new form of information storage, the gramophone record: "A sign of future strength and liveliness is the entirely pathos-free nature of this group of serially produced, standardized pictorial achievements that anyone can take home, keep, or exchange, just like they would a gramophone record."[15]

These works shifted the ground under the foundation of art in a further respect, too. Eberhard Roters realized this as early as 1965, writing that, given the way the *EM* pictures were made, "… the artist becomes a theoretician of communication.

Moholy-Nagy's thoughts anticipated many ideas which were only collected after World War II into a new scientific discipline, that of cybernetics."[16]

Though he could not have anticipated the digital per se, Moholy-Nagy was immersed in thinking that paved the way for such advances. Lev Manovich has famously proposed that " … avant-garde aesthetic strategies [of the 1920s] became embedded in the commands and interface metaphors of computer software. In short, the avant-garde became materialized in a computer."[17] Klemens Gruber and his team have conducted a systematic investigation of Soviet filmmaker Dziga Vertov as a forerunner of the digital.[18] However, both Manovich and Gruber focus on the Soviet avant-garde. Although Moholy-Nagy also worked with the techniques Manovich references (collage, montage, etc.), his aesthetic engagement with technology and his notion of art as information extended beyond these methods. As Eduardo Kac has pointed out, discussing Moholy-Nagy's Telephone Pictures, Moholy-Nagy's ideas, as expressed through this EM series, anticipated the emergence of digital thinking in the fine arts in a number of ways: breaking down the design into units of information ("pixelation"), transmitting this information electrically (via telephone), subcontracting production of the artwork, ordering the work in an open series of multiple sizes, thereby negating the notion of the "original" and of a fixed scale, and "pointing toward the new artforms that emerge in the age of mechanical reproduction." "Unlike Monet's sequential paintings, writes Kac, "the three similar telephone pictures are not a series. They are copies without an original" for which "scale … becomes relative and secondary … in the virtual space of the screen."[19] In engaging in these operations, Moholy-Nagy recognized art not as something transcendent and auratic, but as a form of information – sensory data; data for the senses.

Through his engaged focus on disseminating his thinking in publications, Moholy-Nagy also suggested that the equation worked both ways. Lavishing attention on his texts, he honed them over time as he would an artwork. The three articles chosen as the core content for *telehor*, for example, essentially recapitulated an argument he first published in a Leipzig exhibition catalogue and in the Czech journal *Pásmo* late in 1924 or early in 1925.[20] Emphasizing that optical art was concerned with light as its raw material, and highlighting the arc of optical possibilities (ranging from painting through photography to film) that the contemporary artist should draw on, along with any technical means at their disposal, he underscored points that in turn formed the basic line of argument in his first book *Painting, Photography, Film*. The constant reworking of his ideas in written form was typical of Moholy-Nagy's modus operandi.[21] It could even be argued that, after his initial burst of writing activity in 1922–24, he spent the rest of his career refining the ideas first put forward during the early 1920s. The specifics and technological references may have changed over time, but the core messages remained constant. Just like his first book, his second, *Von Material zu Architektur* (From Material to Architecture, 1929), also appeared in several subsequent revised editions, in English as *The New Vision* (1932, 1938, 1947). While developing some new ideas, his posthumous volume *Vision in Motion* also recapitulated what he had written previously (1947).

In addition to honing his thoughts, Moholy-Nagy put much effort into ensuring that his publications were designed and printed to the highest standards. In this respect he learned a great deal from working with Lajos Kassák, a pioneer of the new typography and book design, who first set the standards Moholy-Nagy would subsequently follow. Later collaborators involved in Moholy-Nagy's publications, from Herbert Bayer to Jan Tschichold and György Kepes, would just keep on raising the bar. Wrapping his broad-based notion of integrating art and life, the Gesamtwerk, in beautifully designed objects, Moholy-Nagy effectively aestheticized his publication series, drawing them into the realm of the Gesamtkunstwerk. While his conception of the Enamel pictures suggested the notion of "art as information," his publication projects of the 1920s landed foursquare in the realm of "information as art."

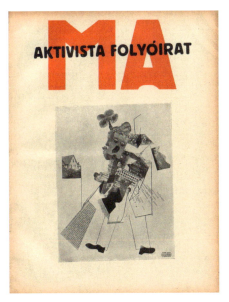
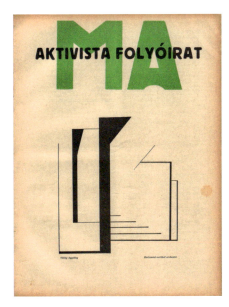

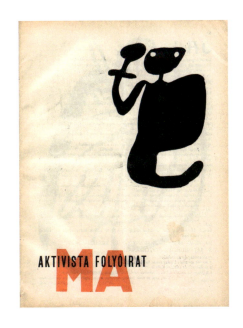
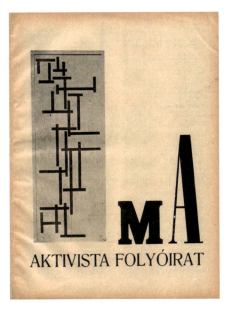

MA (Today) vols. 7 and 8, (1921–22). Editor and designer: Lajos Kassák. Berlin correspondent: László Moholy-Nagy. Cover art, vol. 7: no. 6 (April 25), Alexander Archipenko; no. 7 (June 1), George Grosz; no. 8 (August 1), Viking Eggeling; no. 9 (September 1), László Moholy-Nagy. Cover art, vol. 8: no. 1 (November 15), Lajos Kassák; no. 3 (February 1), Ivan Puni; no. 4 (March 15), Hans Arp; no. 7 (July 1), Theo van Doesburg; no. 8 (August 30), El Lissitzky.

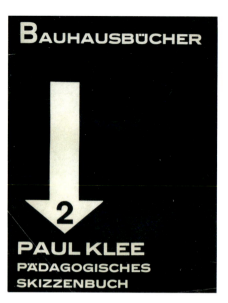

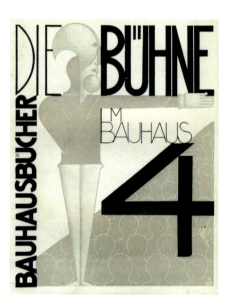
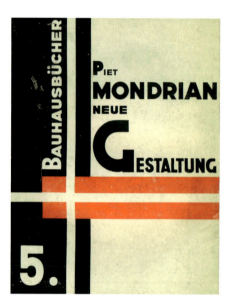
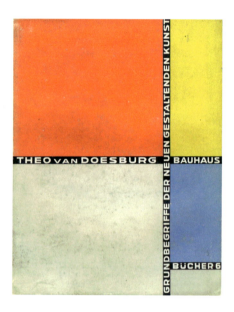

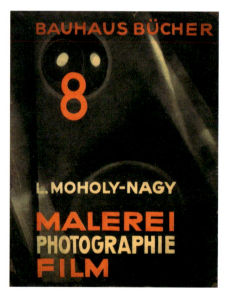
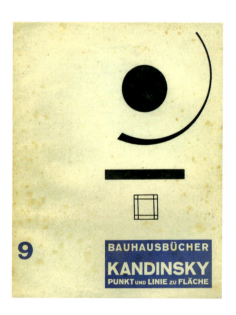

Bauhausbücher, vols. 1–14 (Munich: Albert Langen Verlag, 1925–29). Edited by László Moholy-Nagy and Walter Gropius, designed by László Moholy-Nagy (except: vol. 1, by Farkas Molnár; vol. 2, by Oskar Schlemmer; vol. 6, by Theo van Doesburg; vol. 9, by Herbert Bayer).

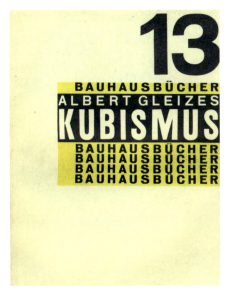

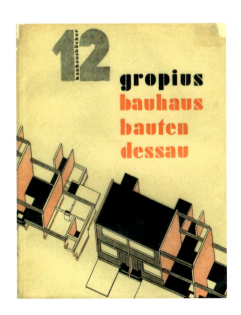

bauhaus nos. 1–3, Dessau, 1926–27. Edited by László Moholy-Nagy and Walter Gropius, designed by László Moholy-Nagy.

Front of the unique documentary album of photographs of the installation for *ausstellung l. moholy-nagy*, Mährischer Kunstverein, Brno, Czechoslovakia, June 1935. Spiral steel binding, celluloid protective cover, 29.3 × 20.9 cm. Edited and designed by František Kalivoda.

telehor 1, nos. 1–2 (1936). Designed by František Kalivoda. On the cover: *Z VII*, 1926. Oil on canvas.

telehor 1936 and the Crisis of Media Art

dear kalivoda: you are surprised that i am again arranging a growing number of exhibitions… it is true that for a number of years i ceased to exhibit, or even to paint. i felt that it was senseless to employ means that i could only regard as out of date and insufficient for the new requirements of art at a time when new technical media were still waiting to be explored.

That is how Moholy-Nagy begins his first text in *telehor*, a journal launched in 1936, in Brno/Brünn, Czechoslovakia, by the young Moravian architect and film enthusiast František Kalivoda.[1] Reading it today, one cannot help but think that the words do not appear to reflect the political and artistic reality of mid-1930s Europe, a time of a significant lurch to the right in politics, a seemingly inexorable slide toward authoritarianism, fascism, and totalitarianism. This passage seems, in a sense, to be outside time. It is apparently oblivious to the political realities of the day, but at the same time, it is a prescient, pioneering statement of the tensions between traditional and "new" media in art, tensions that would come to characterize artistic debates of the second half of the century.

The journal's title *telehor*, the Czech term of the era for what would become known as "television" (adopted from the terminology of Hungarian physicist and television pioneer Dénes Mihály), already points toward the future. Opting to use this terminology here signaled the journal's forward-looking focus on the question of media in art. This first (and, as it turned out, only) issue of *telehor* was devoted exclusively to the work of Moholy-Nagy, principally a strategic selection of his texts, which the journal published in four languages: the original German, plus translations into Czech, French, and English. Important as the texts were, the reproductions (nine in color) of some fifty examples of his works were also crucial; these included multiple frames from his films, his set designs, photographs, photograms, and "photoplastics," paintings, and an entire photo-essay on his Lichtrequisit einer elektrischen Bühne (Light Prop for an Electric Stage). With its lively, strategic combination of his words and art, *telehor,* though it appeared in journal format, can be considered to be the first substantial monographic publication about Moholy-Nagy.

Why Brno? Why Czechoslovakia? Brno was a center of Modernist culture during the interwar period. Alongside Weimar Germany, it was in Czechoslovakia that Moholy-Nagy's ideas were most widespread during the twenties. Moholy-Nagy's connections to the leftist Czechoslovakian avant-garde dated from 1924–25, when articles by him appeared in the Brno journal *Pásmo* (Zone), published by the city's branch of the left-wing Devětsil artists' society (1923–27). That same year Bedřich Václavek and Devětsil invited him to lecture in Brno on his new book *Painting, Photography, Film*; a grand total of three chapters of the book appeared in *Pásmo*. In 1927 he also contributed material to *Fronta* (Front), another Brno publication.

It was mainly thanks to the efforts of the young Kalivoda that Moholy-Nagy's presence continued to be felt in Czechoslovakia during the 1930s.[2] During the early thirties Moholy-Nagy's writings appeared in at least four Brno publications and Kalivoda was closely involved with all of them.[3] Early in 1933 he arranged for Moholy-Nagy's films to be screened at a festival in Brno. However, this undertaking was thwarted by the authorities, because the films were rejected by the Czechoslovakian Board of Censors. He nonetheless went on to organize further screenings of Moholy-Nagy's films in the city during 1934. The harassment led Kalivoda to express concern that "Brno is increasingly being pushed to the cultural periphery."[4]

As the journals he had previously worked on ceased publication, Kalivoda decided to replace them with two new journals, *Ekran* (Screen), dedicated to avant-garde film, and *telehor*, which was to be international in scope. Kalivoda saw *telehor* as his vehicle for resisting the encroaching provincialism that so preoccupied him. He proposed a thoroughly Moholyan[5] program for *telehor* in its first promotional brochure: an "international journal for optical culture" that was to publish material produced in a wide range of media including film, photography, architecture, painting, sculpture, and theater, as well as "all mechanical arts." He conceived of it, furthermore, as a vehicle to promote

the work of individual figures of the international avant-garde who engaged with new media and whom he saw as serving the overarching goal of transforming society. The first issue was originally to have showcased the work of Hannah Höch, though ultimately it was dedicated to Moholy-Nagy alone: "i could do no better than select the rich and many-sided work of one artist, l. moholy-nagy, whose versatility can scarcely be rivaled among his fellow artists of to-day," intoned Kalivoda in his postscript for the first issue of the new journal. In this text, Kalivoda reiterated the transmedial program outlined in the brochure, highlighting its links to the question of abstract art and its role in the Socialist society he believed would soon take shape. Though Kalivoda had planned up to six editions of *telehor* annually, both *Ekran* and *telehor* ended up as single-issue undertakings.

In 1934 Moholy-Nagy drafted "dear kalivoda," in which he explained his strategic retreat to painting, moving away from an exclusive program of art in new media. This turned out to be *telehor*'s defining text. It comes as no surprise that this tension between Moholy-Nagy's engagement with new and more traditional media was on his mind in 1934, for this is precisely the time when he was preparing a series of exhibitions of his work in Paris and the Netherlands. Preparations for his Paris show in conjunction with the exhibiting society Abstraction-Création in particular, which would be his first exhibition of paintings in a number of years, gave him the opportunity to reflect on his practice. Kalivoda subsequently organized a Moholy-Nagy exhibition at the School of Applied Arts in Bratislava (May 1935), where, at the invitation of Josef Vydra, Moholy-Nagy had held a series of lectures on the new optics in 1931. An expanded version of the show opened at the Künstlerhaus in Brno in June 1935.[6] Consisting of no fewer than 150 works, this was the most extensive of his exhibitions in Europe during his lifetime.[7] It included some twenty paintings, as well as lithographs, photographs, photograms, enlarged photograms, woodcuts, "photoplastics," technical drawings for the Light Prop, theater sets and photographic documentation of his theatrical productions, the prop itself, and his exhibition designs. Moholy-Nagy's preparations for these shows must have facilitated the process of starting to select works for reproduction in *telehor*.[8]

The choice of texts for *telehor* was highly strategic. The foreword is by Zurich art historian and media theorist, Sigfried Giedion, a close friend of Moholy-Nagy. It was followed by three articles addressing the state of contemporary art, with particular reference to Moholy-Nagy's role. These articles recapitulated the argument made in *Painting, Photography, Film*, underlining that light forms the raw material of optical art and tracing out the implicitly developmental arc of optical possibilities (not to mention technical means) available to the contemporary artist, extending from painting, through photography and film to culminate in an art of pure light.

The addition to the *telehor* lineup of "Once a Chicken, Always a Chicken. A Film Script on a Motif from Kurt Schwitters's *August Bolte*" immediately before Kalivoda's postscript not only turned the spotlight on his interest in film, but certainly also appealed to the Czechoslovakian avant-garde's Surrealist sensibilities, while giving readers a sense of Moholy-Nagy's fertile and diverse cinematic imagination during this period. Stills from Development Ltd.'s beautiful "evocation" of this script are included in the last chapter of this book (p. 174).

As mentioned above, *telehor*'s defining text was "dear kalivoda." This seminal status stems from its examination of why he was rescinding on his previous exclusive program of new media art. While he had painted intensively during the early to mid-1920s, Moholy-Nagy abandoned this art form after leaving the Bauhaus, instead pursuing his dream of an interdisciplinary practice that would break down barriers between design, industry, the fine arts, and life itself. His utopian dream of the Gesamtwerk had culminated in his realization of a gallery for the German Werkbund's exhibition in Paris in 1930, for which he arranged to have the Light Prop built. However he was, in some ways, disappointed with his prop and, in any case, regarded it as a mere "model" of the device he really wanted to make. To make matters worse, his stage sets for several Berlin operas and plays met with outright hostility. Furthermore the intensification of the global economic crisis, coupled with the political shift toward the right in Germany, engendered a decline in his interdisciplinary design practice. In the early fall of 1930, during his first stay at the "Maison des Artistes" at La Sarraz,[9] an annual artists' retreat sponsored by the Swiss aristocrat Hélène de Mandrot, Moholy-Nagy resumed painting. He was at a crossroads in his life, his career, and his artistic practice. It was this return to an art form he had previously abandoned that Moholy-Nagy and

Géa Augsbourg: František Kalivoda, Géa Augsbourg, László Moholy-Nagy (left to right), La Sarraz, Switzerland, August 1935. gta Archiv Zürich. Photo Courtesy of gta Archiv © ADAGP (Paris) / SODRAC (Montréal).

Kalivoda discussed in Brno during January of 1934, and which gave rise to "dear kalivoda," drafted around June of that year.

Although he was one of the era's principal advocates and practitioners of alternative media, Moholy-Nagy explains in "dear kalivoda" the constraints that have caused him to revert to production in traditional media:

You have every right to ask, why I surrendered arms, why I am again painting and exhibiting pictures, after once having recognized the real tasks confronting the "painting" of today. This question demands a reply, quite apart from any personal considerations, for it is of vital concern for the rising generation of painters.... Youth has every right to know, why our demands have failed, why our promises have remained unfulfilled.[10]

Moholy-Nagy's responses to these questions, elucidating his retreat from new media art production, resonate with artists working in alternative media, even today: "materially dependent on capital, industry, and workshops ... ," artists are unable to convince these institutions to fund or facilitate the manufacture of their plans. "There are hardly any venues where what is actually achieved can be made available to the public. The realized dream is put on ice and stored for so long that, in its isolation, it evaporates." Then as now, the public is so distracted by the mass media, so bombarded by its content, even cultural content, that "the passionate desire for participation, the longing for direct contact with the forces of artistic creation are transformed into the newspaper reader's 'interest,' an artificial interest leading the reader away from genuine sources of experience..." The ignorance and indifference of the general public in turn leaves the artist bereft of potential allies who could support the realization of plans. Further factors to blame for this state of affairs are, as Moholy-Nagy laments, the "essential dissonance between people and their technological achievements, the clinging to outdated forms of economic organization in spite of changed conditions of production, and the spread of an antibiological sensibility that transforms the lives of employees and employers alike into a ceaseless rush." People just do not have time for art, much less for an art that challenges them to see technology in a different light.

Over and above the prescience of Moholy-Nagy's analysis of why new media art had failed to demonstrate significant results by the 1930s, the most significant aspect of *telehor* is that the question was posed. By raising this issue, the discussion Moholy-Nagy initiates with Kalivoda here, together with the rest of the journal's contents, effectively usher us into the postwar world of media art and theory.

Although the influence of Moholy-Nagy's media theory is not widely recognized, even a superficial perusal of the literature on key twentieth-century media theorists yields intriguing clues as to his importance.[11] For example, Moholy-Nagy's notions on the reproducibility of images influenced debate around Walter Benjamin's seminal essay "Art in the Age of Its Mechanical Reproducibility" (1936).[12] Philosopher György Márkus highlights this point: "for the German discussion [on 'reproduction'] the appearance of the book by László Moholy-Nagy ... in 1925 had a decisive significance.... *Malerei, Photographie, Film* served as the reference point for the ensuing discussion," particularly Moholy-Nagy's prediction of the rise of the "Domestic Pinacotheca," private collections of art reproductions, as Krisztina Passuth was the first to point out.[13] Again, following in Passuth's footsteps, Herbert Molderings cites Moholy-Nagy's "Constructivist photographic aesthetic" as the "theoretical foundation of [Benajmin's] highly influential 'Short History of Photography.'"[14] In his piece on Moholy-Nagy's media theory and its effects, Philippe Simay notes that Moholy-Nagy recognized the way that the apparatus makes or determines cultural epochs and therefore new regimes of experience–before Benjamin and long before Vilém Flusser, and also prior–I would add–to Marshall McLuhan.[15]

In reference to discussions surrounding Sigfried Giedion's pioneering media history *Mechanization Takes Command* (1948), which delved into precisely this issue of the importance of technological innovation in driving the development of "régimes of experience," McLuhan wrote to his friend Giedion in 1945 that "it was, as always, tremendously stimulating to have seen you. What a great thing it will be when your new book is out. I begin to see how the vision in your work is, and can be, applied to ever so many things."[16] *Mechanization Takes Command* (shaped in part by Moholy-Nagy's thinking) helped McLuhan to form his broad view of what can constitute "media."[17]

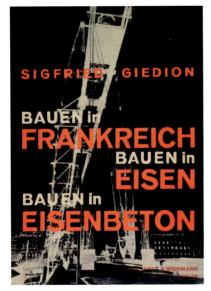

Sigfried Giedion, László Moholy-Nagy in the garden, Doldertal, Zürich, n. d. Photo: Carola Giedion-Welcker (?).

Sigfried Giedion, *Bauen in Frankreich, Eisen, Eisenbeton* (Leipzig: Klinkhardt & Biermann), 1928. Designed by László Moholy-Nagy, employing a tonally reversed photo by himself.

George Morris Jr. (at center), *Shifting with Prisms: Can You See What You Hear? Or Hear with Your Eye?* 1943 (also shown: works by Institute of Design students Nick Savage, Robert Erikson, and Edward Rinker), in László Moholy-Nagy 1947b, pp. 204–5.

Spread with George Morris Jr.'s photograph *Shifting with Prisms,* in *Explorations: Studies in Culture and Communications* 8 (October 1957), "Verbi-Voco-Visual" issue, edited by Marshall McLuhan and Edmund Carpenter eds. Design: Harley Parker. *Explorations* is soon to be reissued by Wipf and Stock.

The close relationship between Giedion and Moholy-Nagy is a particularly salient instance of Moholy-Nagy's impact on twentieth-century media theory. Nowadays Giedion is as famous for his authorship of a book crucial to contemporary architectural thinking (*Space, Time and Architecture*, 1941), as he is for *Mechanization Takes Command*. Before he wrote the introduction to *telehor*, Giedion had cooperated with Moholy-Nagy on a number of projects, the most intensive being the outline for Giedion's first major book *Bauen in Frankreich. Eisen, Eisenbeton* (Building in France, Building in Iron, Building in Ferroconcrete) (1928).[18] Olivier Lugon argues that Giedion's genealogical approach to art history, which did not separate past, present, and future, decisively shaped Moholy-Nagy's thinking.[19] Giedion in turn adopted Moholy-Nagy's idea of a "new optics" as well as his notion of the Gesamtwerk.[20]

Moholy-Nagy's Rilkean view of media as extensions of our sense organs was adopted by McLuhan.[21] Even though he never met Moholy-Nagy, McLuhan read and was apparently teaching with *The New Vision* soon after its second edition appeared in 1938,[22] and he wrote a review of *Vision in Motion* in combination with *Mechanization Takes Command* in 1948 for the *Hudson Review*.[23] Richard Cavell goes as far as to say that Moholy-Nagy's work "played a crucial role in McLuhan's aesthetic."[24] This view is certainly underpinned by McLuhan's choice of an image from *Vision in Motion* as the frontispiece for the 1956 "Verbi-Voco-Visual" edition of the journal he edited with Edmund Carpenter, *Explorations*.

György Kepes, founder of MIT's Center for Advanced Visual Studies and a key instigator of postwar media art, had been Moholy-Nagy's mentee and studio assistant in Berlin and London, and a faculty member under his leadership at Moholy-Nagy's Institute of Design in Chicago. It can be argued that he carried on Moholy-Nagy's project in some ways after the latter's death in 1946.[25] Branden Joseph reports John Cage's assertion that *The New Vision* was "extremely influential to his [Cage's] thinking from the 1930s on and that reading it was what attracted him to teach at the Institute of Design in 1941.[26] Aspects of Moholy-Nagy's thinking on media have reverberated through the work of key postwar media theorists, such as Kittler, Flusser, Deleuze, and Baudrillard.

Even simply listing these names within the context of a discussion of Moholy-Nagy's works serves to span a conceptual bridge in our imaginations, reaching from the mid-1930s crisis of relations between new and traditional media that Moholy-Nagy gave voice to in the texts of *telehor* right to the very heart of late twentieth-century media theory and criticism. The potential of an arc such as this, extending across the decades, spun from an as yet largely unexplored skein of links, is precisely what makes the investigation of Moholy-Nagy's unsystematic but incisive thinking on media so intriguing. There has only been room here to sketch out, in broad strokes, the contours of a fascinating topic that requires more thorough and extensive investigation. A still clearer sense of Moholy-Nagy's importance emerges if one also factors in the profound effect Moholy-Nagy exercised on artistic practices and attitudes in the post–World-War-II era, and the prescience of some of his ideas, which I have outlined in the Introduction and the "Sensory Training" chapter.

Mapping Moholy-Nagy's achievements onto the matrix of twentieth-century art, media art, cinema, alternative education and media theory is the task that I set for myself in this project, which I hope to pursue in further studies. I began this book by citing Moholy-Nagy's own example of the potentially overwhelming nature of sensorial inputs to helping people adapt to the pace of technical change in modernity, and in thereby envisaging a much broader spectrum of senses and media as a basis for artistic work, Moholy-Nagy seems to have had a "sixth sense" about many aspects of the future course of artistic and medial development. Looking back to consider what he had to say about this condition of modernity and about artistic-pedagogical responses to it can afford us valuable insights as we grapple with our own hyperstimulating technological and sensory environment.

other experiments

Photographic experiments may embrace a wide territory: shadow observation of shapes on flat, curved or irregular surfaces, producing less or more emphasized distortions; observation of textures in the form of collages; mirror combinations; positive and negative images; partial enlargement and reduction of suitable subject matters; use of prisms for shifting details of objects, for example, an ear in the place of an eye.

Such experiments can be divided into three sections: light and objects; photographic optics; processing and its manifold combinations. These tasks clearly circumscribed at first can later develop into independent experiments. This is the prerogative of every research worker.

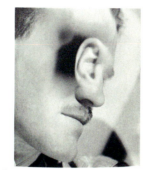

Reproduced by permission of the Theobald Press, Chicago, U.S.A.

October 1957

Polycinema, 2014
Lancelot Coar and Patrick Harrop
(with film program by Oliver Botar and Chris Burke),
after the ideas of László Moholy-Nagy
lasercut Acrylic, mylar, aluminium, LED, data projectors,
servo motors and microcontrollers, fabric, fiberglass,
hardware.
Bauhaus-Archiv, Museum für Gestaltung, Berlin, 2014.

Commissioned Artworks with Artists' Statements

Eduardo Aquino (spmb)

Textspace, 2014
Sound design/composition by Örjan Sandred
Text and sound installations based on the writings of László Moholy-Nagy.
The texts were selected by Oliver Botar and were performed by Oliver Botar and Simone Mahrenholz
Installation view, Plug In ICA, Winnipeg, March 7–June 3, 2014.

Textspace is a narrative/collage of emblematic quotations from Moholy-Nagy's writings, intercalating a female voice (English–with a German accent) and a male voice (German–with a Canadian-English accent). The version of *Textspace* shown at Plug In Institute of Contemporary Art takes the form of an architectural space enveloped by graphic representations of Moholy-Nagy's texts, accompanied by the voices reading the texts. At the Bauhaus Archiv in Berlin, *Textspace*, a collaboration between spmb and Winnipeg composer Örjan Sandred, consists of eight speakers, a camera, a computer (laptop), and an interface with eight outputs. As visitors pass through the installation, a camera identifies their precise location and activates the closest speaker, communicating Moholy-Nagy's ideas in intimate proximity. As a result, each visitor will also be "composing" the soundscape as a function of their relative position. *Textspace* intends to translate Moholy-Nagy's writings into space itself.

Lancelot Coar and Patrick Harrop

Polycinema, 2014
Lancelot Coar and Patrick Harrop
(with film program by Oliver Botar and Chris Burke),
after the ideas of László Moholy-Nagy
lasercut Acrylic, mylar, aluminium, LED, data projectors, servo motors and microcontrollers, fabric, fiberglass, hardware.
Bauhaus-Archiv, Museum für Gestaltung, Berlin, 2014.

Moholy-Nagy's oeuvre addresses the fundamental nature of light as being as much a question of materiality as of the energetic. Particularly during his lifetime, the idea of cinema diverged substantially from the narrative, retinal, and figurative model to which we have been accustomed. For Moholy-Nagy, cinema held the potential to redefine the artistic aspirations of compositional painting and sculpture: a transformation from a static representation, alluding to energy, matter, and time, to a veritable manifestation of these phenomena. Coar is particularly interested in Moholy-Nagy's use of technology and material behaviour to manipulate space and light. Using bending active elliptical frames, Coar produced an interpretation of the Polycinema screenal space through a suspended double ellipsoid surface that received the interactions between a replica of the Light Prop for an Electric Stage and the projection tower within it developed by Harrop. The translucency of the fabric scrim used for the screen allows for multiple and simultaneous interpretations of the cinematic experience within and without the Polycinema. Harrop, an electronic artist and digital fabricator, responds to Moholy-Nagy's obsession with the synthesis and modulation of light as it is mechanically magnified, refracted, and diffused. The boundary between generating (such as film) and manipulating (reflection and transmission) are blurred. The work forms a complete metabolism of material-energetic systems. Moholy-Nagy's oeuvre is of particular relevance now, given his importance for the emergence of projection art. This work joins in the conversation between his influence on our contemporary culture of the digital.

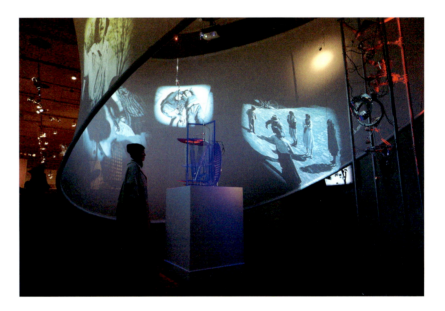

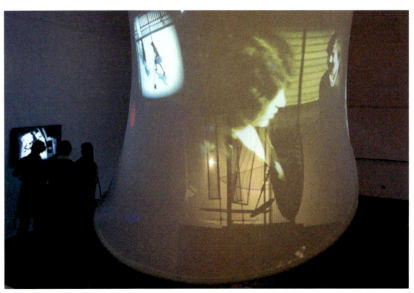

Olafur Eliasson

Your screen-free environment, 2014
12 C-prints.

Your screen-free environment consists of a series of photographs documenting experiments with elliptical mirrors, carried out by Eliasson in his Berlin studio. The artwork is both the experimental action itself and the twelve photographs that resulted from it. In the images, Eliasson can be seen swinging an elliptical mirror around his head, catching glimpses of other, off-camera spaces in the studio.
In the spirit of Moholy-Nagy's investigations of phenomena such as light, space, and motion, these images create an abstract play of perspectives, color, foreground, and background.

Olafur Eliasson

The reflected polar reversal,
Lines for horizons, Geometric lines for horizons,
all 2014
All works unique
Each sphere: partially silvered glass sphere,
paint (black), rubber ring, wood
150 × 40 × 40 cm
Mirror, tripod, steel, motors, control unit,
custom electronics, software

In *The reflected polar reversal*, exhibited at the Bauhas Archiv (and installed with *Lines for horizons* and *Geometric lines for horizons*), a map of the earth has been designed on the surface of a crystal glass sphere. Through a hand-silvering process, the oceans have been given a mirror finish and coated in a layer of black paint, resulting in an outline of the world's landmasses in negative. Peering into the sphere through the empty continents, the viewer encounters distorted reflections of the interior and fragmentary views of her surroundings.

As Olafur Eliasson says, "The earth is spinning and every space upon it is a consequence of this movement. When looking at the world from the inside, looking through the glass, at the back of the earth, you put yourself on the inside of the globe and gaze out from the centre. Looking at Europe from the perspective of its footprint, for example, you see a reflection, centrifugal or not, of what is across the globe. You thereby reflect the other in yourself."

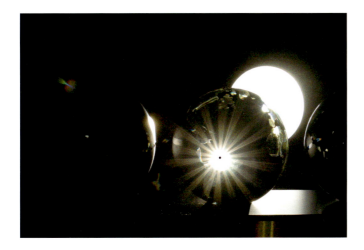
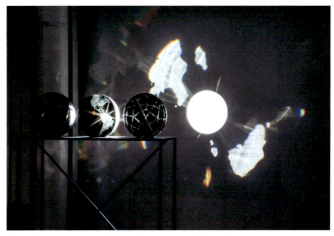

Olafur Eliasson

World illuminator, 2014
Unique
Mirror, tripod, steel, motors, control unit, custom electronics and software

For the Bauhaus Archiv, Olafur Eliasson created *World illuminator*, a site-specific sun-tracking apparatus that redirects sunlight onto a fixed point by adjusting a mirror in concert with the "movement" of the sun across the sky. A round mirror mounted on the sun tracker is programmed to follow the trajectory of the sun in the sky, redirecting the rays into the museum to interact with a work installed there. The artwork is dependent on the weather at the location, changing according to hours of sunlight, cloud coverage, and time of year.

The apparatus belongs to a family of optical devices known formally as *heliostats* – a word deriving from Greek meaning "stationary sun." Eliasson emphasises the sun tracker's ability to make explicit the uniqueness of a position on the earth as it revolves around the sun. The normal "movement" of the sun through a room, after all, is not really movement but, rather, the optical phenomenon that results from the room's location on the rotating earth. The sun tracker thus links the artwork and the viewer to the earth's surface, to the weather environments that determine the sun's visibility, and to the broader planetary cosmos beyond.

In Eliasson's words: "To track the sun is to track yourself, because the sun tracker locates the center of your orbital ellipse, giving your position right now and rendering visible your path. The reflexive potential lies in understanding that we are in a way the 'mirrors'."

Ken Gregory

Prototype Electric Light Machine for a Modern Room, 2014
Machine installation, 3D printed parts, steel, and electronics.

László Moholy-Nagy's Light Prop for an Electric Stage reimagined for installation in the modern home. Order now!

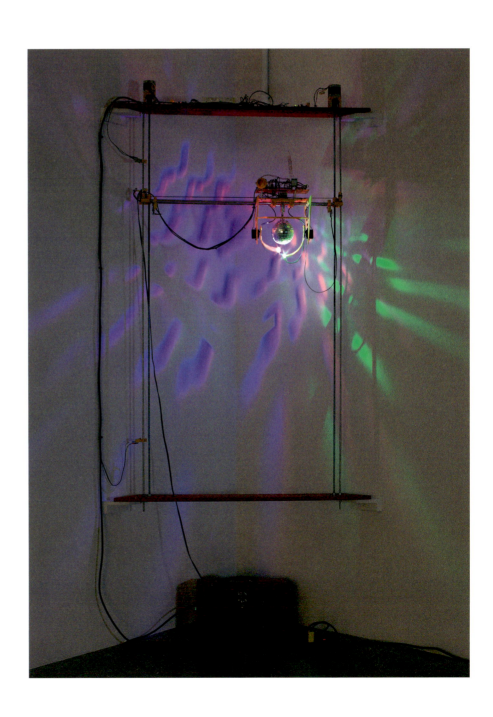

Eduardo Kac

Aromapoetry, 2011
Artist's book, twelve custom-made aromas enmeshed in a nanolayer of mesoporous glass, letterpress text and graphics.

For me, the greatest lesson from Moholy-Nagy is not to be found in the specificity of his formal solutions—for these are, as I see them, his and his only. The greatest lesson lies in his nonconformist spirit, as exemplified by his "Production-Reproduction" essay, in which he states, in my own words, that the challenge is not the reproduction of previously existing relations, but the production (i.e., invention, creation) of new ones. In my *Aromapoetry* I therefore create a new kind of poetry in which the compositional unit (the poem) is made up of smells. I "wrote" the smells by conceiving the poem as an olfactory experience. I then employed multiple chemical procedures to achieve my poetic goals. *Aromapoetry* is a book to be read with the nose.

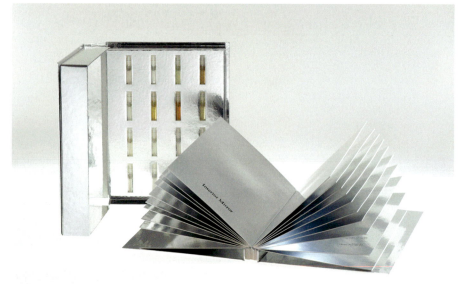

Erika Lincoln

Floe, 2014
Plexiglas, aluminum grid, motors,
electronic components, and metal
Installation view, Gallery 1, Plug In ICA, Winnipeg,
March 7–June 3, 2014.

Floe is comprised of laser-cut Plexiglas arrows combined to form a linked geometric plane. In a gallery space, the plane is hung from from an aluminium grid, which is in turn suspended from the gallery ceiling. Six motors are mounted on the aluminium grid. These motors are attached to the plane via mono-filament, and their rotational movement causes the plane to undulate. The timing of the motor's speed and direction is based on data collected by NASA's Goddard Space Flight Center's Scientific Visualization Studio (data NOAA GFDL CM2.1). As the motors animate the Plexiglas plane, it casts shadows on the walls and floor of the gallery. These shadows wax and wane in response to the motors' timing.

Development Ltd.
(Guy Maddin, Evan Johnson, Galen Johnson, Bob Kotyk and Ryan Simmons)

Once a Chicken…, 2014,
Digital video, 6'39"

Kinoplakat. Sirenenverdichtung, 1925. In Lusk 1980, p. 36 (left).

Still from an earlier state of the film (top right).

Moholy-Nagy's unrealized script, Huhn bleibt Huhn [Once a Chicken, Always a Chicken] struggles in amniotic murk, in placental swirls of geometry and eggs, in convulsions of negated flesh, to will itself into existence, almost succeeding.

Bernie Miller

Zwei Konstruktionsysteme zusammengefügt, 2014
Integration of two systems of construction (assembled from different metals: steel, copper, nickel, aluminum, zinc and plate glass). Reconstruction based on 1922 original by László Moholy-Nagy.

Heuristic research refers to experience-based techniques for problem solving, learning, and discovery. When an exhaustive examination is impractical, heuristic methods are used to accelerate the process. The object of my research here is to seek the art-historical precedents for a basic aspect of my visual arts practice. At first glance my usual work appears to be "sculpture." However, these "sculptural objects" are all at the service of shadows cast by various means and to various ends, which is to say that the actual object does not matter as much as the effect that it produces: it is not an aesthetic object. It is the combination of the object and its effects. When Oliver Botar offered me the opportunity to reconstruct a lost early masterpiece by Moholy-Nagy, I knew it was a perfect fit with my research. Moholy-Nagy's early constructions were concerned with transparency, reflectivity, projection, and shadow casting. As such, they were part of his conception of the dematerialization of the art object into energy, basically a de-emphasis upon the solid object and a re-emphasis, as in my own work, on its effects.

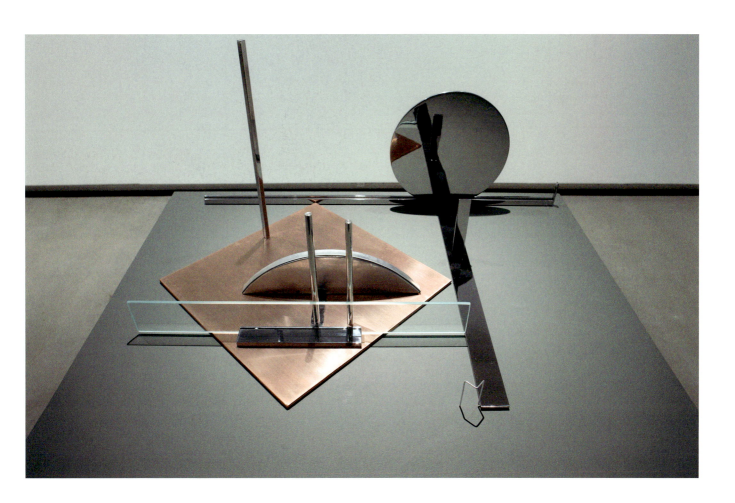

Floris Neusüss and Renate Heyne

Photogram, 2005
made with László Moholy-Nagy's Light Prop
for an Electric Stage at the Bauhaus Archiv,
50 × 50 cm.

Photogram, 2005
made with László Moholy-Nagy's Light Prop
for an Electric Stage at the Bauhaus Archiv,
86.5 × 61 cm.

Photogram, 2005
made with László Moholy-Nagy's Light Prop
for an Electric Stage at the Bauhaus Archiv,
94 × 61 cm.

We set ourselves two challenges: the first explored the possibility of employing the Light Prop as a light modulator in order to generate photograms. We achieved this in 2005 with the black-and-white photograms that are reproduced in this book. The second challenge related to Moholy-Nagy's intention to replace colored pigment in painting with colored light. To this end we deployed the Light Prop, lit with colored lights, as a "painting machine" for producing photograms. Moholy-Nagy lacked the technical prerequisites to achieve this. However, in order to illustrate his intentions, he enlarged some of his black-and-white photograms to the dimensions of his paintings, and displayed them along with his canvases at his 1934 exhibition in Brno, Czechoslovakia.

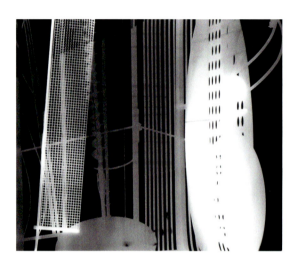

Freya Björg Olafson

Threshold, 2014
Video, 5'28"
Recorded at the Bauhaus-Archiv / Museum für Gestaltung in Berlin with László Moholy-Nagy's Light Prop for an Electric Stage.
View of the storage room of the Bauhaus-Archiv, where the video was made.

In *Threshold* I engage kinaesthetically with Moholy-Nagy's Light Prop for an Electric Stage, responding to its subtle yet repetitive movements. Restricted to a small storage room at the Bauhaus Archiv, where I enjoyed time alone with the Light Prop, I utilized the limitation as a framework. I allowed the movement and sound of the Light Prop to determine my improvisation and experimentation with movement, on site and on camera. Moholy-Nagy was committed to placing humanity in control of the machine rather than the reverse. In *Threshold* my locus of control vacillates between the *machine* leading and/or *my body* initiating, thereby ensuring that kinaesthetic reciprocity fuels the work. The parameters of my practice extend and explore Moholy-Nagy's conception of the Polycinema; including various technologies and video projection techniques such as chromadepth 3-D glasses. Part of a larger project concerned with the interrelationship of art and technology, my works HYPER_, [LIMINAL] and *Threshold* resituate Moholy-Nagy's concerns and predilections within the language and hardware of the twenty-first century.

Chronology

1895	Born László Weisz in Bácsborsod, Hungary.
1913	Moves to Budapest to begin studying law.
1915–18	Serves in the Austro-Hungarian army. Sketches, writes poetry, and short stories.
1918	Joins Lajos Kassák's Budapest "Activist" group (Kassák is the publisher of the journal *MA* [Today]).
1918–19	Briefly attends a private art school.
1919	As a result of his experience of the short-lived Hungarian Soviet Republic, develops a universalist utopianism and a belief in the power of mass communication media. Moves to Vienna where he reconnects with Kassák and the *MA* group in exile.
1920	Settles in Berlin and encounters Raoul Hausmann's and Kurt Schwitters's transmedial Dadaist approaches to art. Learns of empiriocriticism, biocentrism and reform pedagogy through his first wife, Lucia (Schulz) Moholy.
1921	Encounters Russian Constructivism and begins making material constructions and abstract paintings influenced by Kasimir Malevich and Lazar El Lissitzky. Becomes Berlin correspondent for *MA*.
1922	Authors a remarkable series of manifestos and articles that establish his professional agenda and approach for the rest of his career. Has his first exhibition at Galerie Der Sturm in Berlin.
1922–23	Produces the *Emaille* (Enamel) series (known as the "Telephone Pictures"), ordered from an enamel sign maker using graph-paper sketches and standard colors.
1923	Hired to teach at the Bauhaus in Weimar.
1924	Starts work on the Bauhausbücher (Bauhaus Books) series.
1925	*Painting, Photography, Film*, a key manifesto of twentieth-century media art, launches the "New Vision" in photography and film. Also contained in this book was the proposal for the "Polycinema", a forerunner of Expanded Cinema. Moves with the Bauhaus from Weimar to Dessau.
1926–28	Edits the *bauhaus* journal with Walter Gropius.
1928	Leaves the Bauhaus for private design practice in Berlin. Separates from Lucia Moholy.
1929–32	Makes a series of documentary films about urban life.
1930	His mechanized Light Prop for an Electric Stage produces "live" abstract film and moving colored light projections, initiating immersive light art.
1932	Moves in with actress and screenwriter Sibylle Pietzsch (Sibyl Moholy-Nagy). Publication of *The New Vision*, the English edition of his 1929 book *Von Material zu Architektur*.
1933	National Socialists elected in Germany. Birth of his daughter Hattula.
1934	Relocates his studio to Amsterdam.
1935	Moves with his family to London. Largest European exhibition of his oeuvre during his lifetime in Brno, Czechoslovakia.
1936	Publication of an issue of the journal *telehor* dedicated to his work. Birth of his daughter Claudia.
1937	Becomes director of the New Bauhaus in Chicago.
1939	Opens the School of Design (later renamed The Institute of Design).
1943	Participates in the founding of the Hungarian-American Council for Democracy.
1946	Dies of leukemia in Chicago.
1947	Posthumous publication of *Vision in Motion*. Comprehensive memorial exhibition shown at the Museum of Non-Objective Art in New York before touring the United States.

Photothek Berlin, Agentur, Portrait, László Moholy-Nagy, Staatliches Bauhaus Weimar 1924. Modern gelatin silver print from original negative (2005), 23.9 × 17.7 cm.

Artists' Biographies

Eduardo Aquino graduated in architecture and urban studies in Brazil and holds an MFA in open media from Concordia University, Montreal. His long-standing research and creative practice addresses public space, and he has realized projects for galleries and urban spaces in North America, South America, and Europe. Aquino has served as a program and policy consultant on public art and interdisciplinary arts for the Canada Council for the Arts and the Winnipeg Arts Council. He holds a doctorate from the Universidade de São Paulo, for which he realized a project on beachscapes. He is the coauthor of *Complex Order: Intrusions in Public Space* (Winnipeg: Plug In Editions, 2009). An associate professor at the faculty of architecture, University of Manitoba, Aquino teaches a design studio, as well as theory, history, and technology of design, and has received both a National Award from the National Art Foundation, Brazil, and a Design Award from the Royal Architectural Institute of Canada. He is part of the international design team spmb.

Lancelot Coar is assistant professor in the department of architecture and a researcher at the Centre for Architectural Structures and Technology (CAST) at the University of Manitoba, Winnipeg. At CAST Coar explores the unexpected potentials of building materials' behavior, which results in the creation of flexible, dynamic, and unique structural systems. His work has been displayed in museums, galleries, and public settings internationally and he has an extensive publication record. Since 2007 Coar began to develop a community-based design/build studio that has earned several honors. In addition to teaching awards, Coar has also been awarded a number of important grants to pursue his research and teaching. He holds a BS in civil engineering and architectural engineering from Drexel University and a masters in architecture from the University of California, Berkeley.

Development Ltd is a Winnipeg-based four-person collaborative team of writers, filmmakers, and designers formed in 2011 during preparations for Guy Maddin's 2012 *Spiritismes* installation at the Centre Georges Pompidou in Paris. Inspired by the poignant fact that most films made during the last 100 years are now permanently lost, and conceived in response to the infinitely omnivorous data-vacuuming juggernaut of the Internet, **DevLtd** (members **Guy Maddin, Evan Johnson, Galen Johnson & Robert Kotyk**) has tasked itself with making art with a short lifespan, fruit-fly-ephemeral Internet presences, art that wears out with use, fades, self-destructs, and is forgotten. **DevLtd** pledges to return regret and even grief to the practice of digital art-making.

Danish-Icelandic artist **Olafur Eliasson** was born in 1967. His works range from installation and sculpture to photography and film, and have been exhibited worldwide in institutions such as MoMA and Tate Modern, and at the Venice Biennale. Eliasson's projects in public space include *Green river*, realized in various cities between 1998 and 2001; *The New York City Waterfalls*, 2008; and the façades for the Harpa Reykjavik Concert Hall and Conference Centre, with Henning Larsen Architects, 2005–2011. Most recently Eliasson's work has appeared at the Kunstsammlung Nordrhein-Westfallen K20, Düsseldorf, and at the Louisiana Museum of Modern Art, Copenhagen. Established in 1995, his Berlin studio employs about 80 craftsmen, architects, and art historians. In April 2009, in his capacity as professor at the Universität der Künste Berlin, Eliasson founded the Institut für Raumexperimente [Institute for Spatial Experiments]. Working in conjunction with Frederik Ottesen, since 2012 he has directed the social business Little Sun, which produces solar lamps for use in off-grid communities.

Winnipeg artist **Ken Gregory** has been working with do-it-yourself interface design, hardware hacking, audio, video, installation, and computer programming since 1990. His performance and installation work has been shown in Winnipeg, elsewhere in Canada and at many international media and sound art festivals. Career highlights include the exhibition of *wind coil sound flow* at San José's City Hall Rotunda as part of the 2010 San José Biennial, and the acquisition/exhibition of his interactive sound installation *12 motor bells* by the National Gallery of Canada. www.cheapmeat.net

Patrick H. Harrop is an artist, architect, researcher and academic based in Montreal and Winnipeg. A professor at Laurentian University in Sudbury, Ontario, his artistic practice engages with questions of augmented materiality, the modulation of the immaterial phenomena of light and sound through material agency. His practical and theoretical research addresses the philosophy of technology with a particular emphasis on electromechanical hacking, digital fabrication, and contemporary theory. His work has been shown in Montreal, Shanghai, Berlin, and Winnipeg.

Kassel-based **Renate Heyne** studied with Joseph Beuys at the Kunstakademie Düsseldorf. She has worked on Fotoforum Kassel's exhibitions and publications since 1972 and has been artistic assistant to the Experimental Photography Class at the Kunsthochschule Kassel. In 2009 she co-published the catalogue raisonné of Moholy-Nagy's photograms with Floris Neusüss. Since 2001, she has been working with Neusüss on "Leibniz' Lager," an exhibition of photograms of objects on display in various types of museums.

Since the early 1980s, Chicago-based **Eduardo Kac** has pioneered new art forms to create poetry and art that explore the limits of locality, light, language, and life. He has integrated disciplines to present an imaginative view of art's relevance to the contemporary world, a view rooted in the artist's background in philosophy and literature. Widely recognized for his innovative work, he pioneered telecommunications art before the Web, particularly with his telepresence art. His work has focused on the relationships among and between humans, machines, animals, and other life forms. Kac's work explores but goes beyond human language and culture to encompass communication between all living organisms. It embodies a combination of robotics, biotechnology, and networking. He uses communication processes, biological life, and digital networks to create works that explore fundamental human experiences such as the fluidity of language, interactions in dialogue, and awareness of our relative position in the broader community of life. Kac's work has been exhibited internationally at many important venues and is represented in the permanent collections of a number of major museums.

Erika Lincoln is a Winnipeg-based artist working in kinetic sculpture and responsive installation. In her work she mixes objects with communications and timing mechanisms, using visual means to trace connections between human-made systems and natural processes. Her work has been shown at media art festivals and events across Europe and Canada. She has been awarded several grants from major Canadian funding agencies and has participated in artists' residencies at the Banff New Media Institute in Canada and Medialab Prado in Spain. In 2014 she was awarded an Artist in Residence slot with the City of Winnipeg's Climate Change Office.

Toronto-born **Bernie Miller** graduated from the Ontario College of Art in 1974, where he was awarded the Ontario College of Art Medal. He has participated in residency programs at the Cité des Arts, Paris, and the Banff Centre. He was a peer advisor for the Technology Rhetoric and Utopia Residency at the Banff Centre and has contributed articles to numerous publications. His work has been exhibited throughout North America and Europe. Miller has been commissioned to create major public artworks throughout Canada. He coedited *Crime and Ornament: The Arts and Popular Culture in the Shadow of Adolf Loos* with Melony Ward in 2006. Miller served on the board of Plug In ICA. He was represented by Paul Petro Contemporary Art, Toronto. He passed away in 2017.

Kassel-based **Floris Neusüss** studied mural painting in Wuppertal, photography in Munich, and experimental photography with Hans Hajek-Halke at the Kunsthochschule, Berlin. From 1960 on, he participated in the Werkgruppe Körperfotogramme in Berlin, Vienna, and Munich. From 1972 to 2002 he was professor of experimental photography at the Kunsthochschule Kassel. There he founded the Hochschulgalerie as well as the Fotoforum Kassel collection/publishing house. He has been researching the history of the photogram in conjunction with Renate Heyne since 1980. A monograph on this topic was published by DuMont, Cologne in 1990. He published the catalogue raisonné of Moholy-Nagy's photograms in 2009, also with Heyne. Starting in 2001 he and Heyne collaborated on "Leibniz' Lager," an exhibition of photograms of objects on display in various types of museums. He passed away in 2020.

Freya Olafson is a Winnipeg-based intermedia artist who works with video, audio, painting, and performance. She has produced a significant body of work presented in her native Canada, across North and South America, and Europe, and has received the Buddies in Bad Times Vanguard Award for Risk & Innovation as well as funding from national, provincial, and municipal arts councils in Canada. Professionally trained as a classical and contemporary dance performer as well as a visual artist, Olafson obtained an MFA in new media from the Transart Institute / Donau Universität Krems in 2007. She has taken part in a number of residencies throughout North America and Europe. Olafson joined the Department of Dance at York University in July 2017, and subsequently joined the University of Manitoba School of Art as an Assistant Professor in 2021.

Self-portrait, 1944. Kodachrome transparency, 24 × 36 mm.

Notes

Introduction
1 Moholy-Nagy 1925, 35. Translation adapted from Moholy-Nagy 1969, 43.
2 Elcott 2011, 39.
3 Moholy-Nagy, in *Section Allemande* (1930), reprinted in Loers et al. 1991, 270.
4 Moholy-Nagy, 1932, p. 10. The italics are mine.
5 See, for example, Moholy-Nagy, "Geradlinigkeit des Geistes–Umwege der Technik," bauhaus no. 1 (1926), np.
6 Moholy-Nagy 1969, 42.
7 F. T. Marinetti, "Destruction of Syntax–Imagination without Strings–Words-in-Freedom" (1913), in Apollonio 1973, 96.
8 Herbert Molderings, "Eine Welt ohne Schwerkraft," German typescript of his introduction to *Laszlo Moholy-Nagy* (Paris, Berlin, 1997/1998): "der ungarische Konstruktivist Moholy-Nagy gehört zu den grossen Universalkünstler der Moderne."
9 Rubio 2010, 11.
10 Kac 2005, 22.
11 Neusüss, Heyne, with Moholy-Nagy 2009, 19.
12 Moholy-Nagy, "The Contribution of the Arts to Social Reconstruction" (1943), in Kostelanetz 1970, 20.
13 Moholy-Nagy 1932, 15.
14 Moholy-Nagy, quoted in Passuth 1985, 286.
15 Moholy-Nagy, "Space-Time and the Photographer," *The American Annual of Photography* (1943), in Kostelanetz 1970, 61.

Sensory Training
1 From Kurt Schwitters, "Eve Blossom," his own translation of "An Anne Blume" (Source: http://www.costis.org/x/schwitters/eve.htm, accessed July 3, 2014). Originally published in Schwitters 1922. Moholy-Nagy owned a copy of this book, dedicated by Schwitters "Für Mein Lieber Moholy-Nagy 3.1.1922." (PC)
2 "Why Bauhaus Education," *Shelter* (March 1938): 8.
3 Quoted in Sibyl Moholy-Nagy 1950, 44–45.
4 On *Reformpädagogie*, see Scheibe 1978, 139–48. For the clearest statement of Moholy-Nagy's adherence to the German Youth Movement, see Sibyl Moholy-Nagy 1969, xii.
5 See Oliver A. I. Botar, "An Activist-Expressionist in Exile: László Moholy-Nagy 1919–21," in Chapp 1995, 70–86.
6 John Alexander Williams, *Turning to Nature in Germany: Hiking, Nudism, and Conservation, 1900–1940* (Stanford: Stanford University Press, 2007), 135.
7 Quoted in Arthur Kracke, ed. *Freideutsche Jugend. Zur Jahrhundertfeier auf dem hohen Meissner 1913* (Jena: Eugen Diederichs, 1913), 89, 91. See also Diethart Kerbs, ed., *Handbuch der Deutschen Reformbewegungen 1880–1933* (Wuppertal: Peter Hammer, 1998), 13.
8 On *Biozentrik* see Botar 1998, Chapter Two; and Botar and Wünsche 2011, Chapter One.
9 On Lucia Schulz and Barkenhoff, see Oliver A. I. Botar, "The Origins of László Moholy-Nagy's Biocentric Constructivism," in Kac 2007, 325–28.
10 Michael Laws, "Das Wirken des Ordinarius für Physikalische Therapie Paul Vogler (1899–1969) am 'Institut für natürliche Heil- und Lebensweisen' der Berliner Medizinischen Fakultät," PhD diss., Faculty of Medicine, Humboldt-Universität zu Berlin, 1961, 13.
11 Quotation from Fritz Jöde, ed., *Pädagogik des Wesens. Gedanken der Erneuerung aus dem Wendekreis* (Hamburg: Adolf Saal, 1919), 5. For detailed documentation of this paragraph, see Botar 2007, 331ff (see note 9).
12 Dietlind Brehme, et al., eds., *Chronik der Schule Schwarzerden. Geschichte einer Frauensiedlung in der Rhön 1927–1987* (Schwarzerden/Rhön: Schwarzerden/Rhön e.V., 1989), 12.
13 Quoted in Marion E. P. de Ras, *Körper, Eros und weibliche Kultur. Mädchen im Wandervogel und der Bündischen Jugend 1900–1933* (Pfaffenweiler: Centaurus, 1991), 162.
14 See Botar 2007, 329–30 (see note 9).
15 On Schwarzerden, see Ortrud Wörner-Heil, *Von der Utopie zur Sozialreform: Jugendsiedlung Frankenfeld im hessischen Ried und Frauensiedlung Schwarze Erde in der Rhön 1915 bis 1933* (Darmstadt: Hessische Historische Kommission; Marburg: Historische Kommission für Hessen, 1996); and Brehme et al. 1989 (see note 12).
16 De Ras 1991, 160 (see note 13); and Ulrich Linse, *Zurück, o Mensch, zur Mutter Erde: Landkommunen in Deutschland, 1890–1933* (Munich: Deutscher Taschenbuch Verlag, 1983), 159.
17 Lucia Moholy, "Autobiographical Notes" (Lucia Moholy Papers, Bauhaus-Archiv, Berlin; Mappe 135, 1178–1167), pp. 9–10. See also Laws 1961 (see note 10).
18 Quoted in Worner-Heil 1996, 506 (see note 15).
19 Paul Vogler quoted in Laws 1961, 77 (see note 10).
20 *Mitteilungen des Bundes Sozial Angewandter Gymanistik und Korperpflege e.V. (Schwarzerde)* no. 1 (July 1930), p. 5.
21 Moholy-Nagy 1929, 17.
22 Moholy-Nagy 1932, 14.
23 For the 1924 date of the portraits, see the list of her photographs in the Lucia Moholy Papers, Bauhaus-Archiv, Berlin, 12.433/8894, and the card in her negative card file, also in the Lucia Moholy Papers. The photos are sometimes dated to 1927.
24 Moholy-Nagy to Jacoby, Weimar, 20 January 1925. (Courtesy of the Jacoby/Gindler Stiftung, Berlin.)
25 Moholy-Nagy's response to Kállai's article in *i10* 1, no. 6 (June 1927): 234, note; and in Moholy-Nagy 1929, 15. On the planned book, see Moholy-Nagy's letter to van Doesburg, 26 August 1924; the Bauhausbücher prospectus, indicating that this (along with the other listed books) was "in preparation" (reprinted in Wingler 1977, 130–31.), and Moholy-Nagy's letter to Jacoby, 22 January 1927, in which he indicates that the book will be sent to the printer as soon as he receives the revised version of the article as a manuscript for it. (Heinrich Jacoby/Elsa Gindler Stiftung, Berlin)
26 Moholy-Nagy 1929, 10.
27 Ibid., 11.
28 Alain Findeli, "Die Pädagogische Ästhetik von Laszlo Moholy-Nagy," in Engelbrecht and Hahn 1988, 33.
29 Moholy-Nagy 1929, 14.
30 On Lucia Moholy's role, see Moholy 1972, 69.
31 *De Stijl*, vol. 5, no. 7 (July 1922).
32 Haus's analysis, with a quotation from Mach's text from *Die Analyse der Empfindungen und das Verhhältnis des Physischen* (Jena 1900) in Haus 1978, 59.
33 Andreas Haus, "Sinnlichkeit und Industrie," in Von Moos 1983, 108–9.
34 Haus 1978, 60ff. On art education reform, see Wingler 1977.
35 Moholy-Nagy 1938, 23.
36 Moholy-Nagy 1938, 24. The text, as printed, is garbled. I have corrected the first use of "enteroceptive" to the correct "exterceptive" and the second to the correct "interoceptive." While Sherrington published his sensory classification system as early as 1906, it seems to have been in England and/or the United States that Moholy-Nagy encountered it, for it is not used in Moholy-Nagy 1929, 21.
37 *MA* (June 1, 1921), 90. The text is dated "Milan, 11 January 1921."
38 For a thorough analysis of the hand as a motif in Moholy-Nagy's and especially György Kepes's oeuvres, see Orosz 2013, 403–11.
39 Moholy-Nagy 1938, 32.
40 Wick 2000, 277–78.
41 Moholy-Nagy 1938, 26.
42 Ibid., 32.
43 Ibid., 27.
44 Ibid.
45 Ibid., 93.
46 Moholy-Nagy encountered the American educational reformer and philosopher John Dewey, for whom this idea was the cornerstone of his thinking. On Moholy-Nagy and Dewey, see Findeli 1995, 177–82.
47 Moholy-Nagy 1929, 13
48 Sibyl Moholy-Nagy 1969, xvi–xvii.
49 Moholy-Nagy 1929, 69; see also Moholy-Nagy 1938, 6.
50 Sibyl Moholy-Nagy, 1969, xvii–xvii.
51 "Aufruf zur elementaren Kunst. An die Künstler der Welt," *De Stijl* 4, no. 10 (October 1921). Signed by Raoul Hausmann, Hans Arp, Iwan Puni, and Moholy-Nagy.
52 First published in *De Stijl* 4, no. 9 (September 1921).
53 Hausmann, "Versuch einer kosmischen Ontographie," in Niebisch 2013, 74ff. See also Niebisch's introduction, 19–20.
54 Moholy-Nagy 1947b, 185.
55 Moholy-Nagy, "Photography Is Manipulation of Light" (1928), in Haus 1980, 48. On this topic see Botar 2004.
56 Moholy-Nagy 1967, 27–32.
57 See Botar 2004.
58 Andreas Haus and Michel Frizot, "Figures of Style: New Vision, New Photography," in Frizot 1998.
59 See ibid. and Botar 2004.
60 Moholy-Nagy 1947b, 197.
61 Moholy-Nagy 2013, 29. If Szilágyi is correct, and Moholy-Nagy didn't begin to take photographs until ca. 1924, it may be that he was playing with, what was for him, a completely new medium. Szilágyi 2011, 35.
62 Haus 1980, 11.
63 Molderings 2008, 23–24.
64 Hausmann, "Wir sind nicht die Photographen" (1921), in Erlhoff 1982, 39.
65 See, for example, *Raoul Hausmann* (Saint-Étienne: Musée d'Art Moderne; and Rochechouart: Musée Départemental), 1994.

Production–Reproduction
1 Haus 1978, 58–60.
2 Moholy-Nagy in Passuth 1985, 289–90. Neusüss has made the suggestion that these are gramophone needles. Neusüss, Heyne, with Moholy-Nagy 2009, 88.
3 Moholy-Nagy, "zu dem film: moholy-nagy zeigt ein lichtspiel schwarz–weiss–grau," typescript, n.d., stamped "moholy-nagy berlin-chbg" (ca. 1930–33), Ryerson and Burnham Archives, The Art Institute of Chicago Libraries, Inv. No. unknown. I saw a copy in the archives of Hattula Moholy-Nagy, Ann Arbor MI.
4 Gabriel Jutz, "'Produktion–Reproduktion': Echos von László Moholy-Nagys Medientheorie in der Geschichte von Film und Medienkunst," in Bru, Nuijs, and Hjartarson 2012, 397.
5 On this, see the chapter "Sensory Training."
6 Lucia Moholy, in Moholy 1972, 59.
7 Moholy-Nagy, "Photoplastische Reklame," in *Offset, Buch und Werbekunst* 7 (1926): 386–88. See also Loers, "Moholy-Nagys 'Raum und Gegenwart' und die Utopie vom dynamisch-konstruktiven Lichtraum," in Loers et al. 1991, 41.
8 Iris Fischer and Eckhardt Köhn, eds., *Lichtbildwerkstatt Loheland: Fotografien einer neuen Generation Weib* (Berlin: Bauhaus-Archiv, 2007), 41–44.
9 On publications about photogram technique, see Neusüss, Heyne, with Moholy-Nagy 2009, 16–17.
10 See Neusüss, Heyne, with Moholy-Nagy 2009, for the dating of the photograms by their size and paper type.
11 Moholy-Nagy, letter to Gropius, 16 December 1935, cited in Haus 1980, 51.
12 Moholy-Nagy, "Light: A Medium of Plastic Expression," *Broom* 4 (March 1923): 283–84.
13 Ibid.
14 Ibid.
15 Moholy-Nagy, "Neue Gesaltung in der Musik. Möglichkeiten des Grammophons," *Der Sturm* no. 14 (July 1923).
16 "Von der Pigmentmalerei bis zu der in den Raum geworfenen farbigen Lichtgestaltung," in *Pásmo* 1, no. 11 (1924–25): 9. This article also appeared in *Katalog der Zehnten Jahresausstellung L. I. A.* (Leipzig: E.R. Wunderlich, 1925), 40–44.
17 Moholy-Nagy, "Musico-Mechanico, Mechanico-Optico," *Musikblätter des Anbruch* 8, nos. 8–9 (1936): 367.
18 Stuckenschmidt 1978, 7.
19 Hans Heinz Stuckenschmidt, "Mechanisierung der Musik: Die Interpretation bedeutet die Zerstörung der Musik" (The Mechanization of Music: Interpretation Entails the Destruction of Music), *MA*, "Musik und Theaternummer" 9 (September 15, 1924), unpag.
20 Ibid.
21 Levin 2003, 47.
22 Ibid., 46.
23 Raoul Hausmann, "Optofonetika," *MA* 7, no. 1 (October 15, 1922), unpag.
24 Alexander László, *Die Farblichtmusik* (Wiesbaden: Leipzig, Breitkopf & Härtel, 1925), 71.
25 On Moholy-Nagy and László, see Jörg Jewanski, "'Your taste and mine are meeting each other …' Künstlerische und biographische Parallelen zwischen László Moholy-Nagy und Alexander László," in Jäger and Wessing 1997, 215–24.
26 Moholy-Nagy 1929, 20–22.
27 Ibid., 20.
28 Moholy-Nagy 1969, 24.
29 Levin 2003, 48.
30 Moholy-Nagy, *telehor* 1, nos. 1–2 (1936): 39.
31 Sibyl Moholy-Nagy 1950, 68, 84. There must have been some carelessness involved because, sometime after 1935, just like the original soundtrack for *Grosstadt-Zigeuner*, all prints of the film had to

be destroyed due to copyright infringement related to the sound technology. A print turned up at the British Film Institute in 2019.
32 Moholy-Nagy 1947b, 168.
33 On Grierson and Moholy, see Sahli 2006, 143, and Senter 1975, 47.
34 On McLaren's and others' use of the technique, as well as the technique of scratching into records, see, for example, Jutz 2012, 403ff (see note 4). See also Levin 2003, 64–65.
35 On this, see Jultz 2012, 401ff (see note 4).

Gesamtwerk
1 Moholy-Nagy 1925, 12–13.
2 See Botar 2007a. See also Walter Gropius, "Idee und Aufbau des Staatlichen Bauhauses," in *Staatliches Bauhaus in Weimar,* edited by Walter Gropius (Weimar: Staatliches Bauhaus, 1923), in which Gropius employs the term *Gesamtwerk*. In my view it is incorrect, as Wilson-Smith does, to translate Gropius's "Gesamtwerk" as "total work of art," thereby eliding their sense difference. Wilson-Smith 2007, 51. Kassák introduced his notion of the "collective individual" in his text "Aktivizmus" (Activism), given as a lecture on February 20, 1919, and published in *MA* 4, no. 4 (1919).
3 Zoltán 2010, 14.
4 On this intellectual context, see, for example Szabó 1981, 20–25.
5 On Moholy-Nagy and the Galileo Circle, see Botar 2007a, 19–20.
6 Franz Eckelt. "The Internal Policies of the Hungarian Soviet Republic," in Iván Völgyes, ed. *The Hungarian Soviet Republic, 1919. An Evaluation and a Bibliography* (Stanford, CA: Hoover Institution Press, 1970), 61.
7 Koczó 1968, 155–65.
8 Kassák, "Activism." The English translation is by John Bátki in Benson and Forgács 2002, 220 and 223.
9 Lajos Kassák, letter to Hans Curjel (in German), dated "Budapest 13.V.1966" (Hans Curjel papers of the Deutsches Literaturarchiv / Schiller-Nationalmuseum Marbach a. N., Handschriftenabteilung).
10 Moholy-Nagy, letter to Sigfried Giedion (in English), 3 November 1939 (Sigfried Giedion papers, ETH, Zürich). Seen at Hattula Moholy-Nagy archive, Anna Arbor, MI.
11 Botar 2007a, 147–49.
12 See Botar 2007a, 108–19; and Passuth 1985, 37.
13 See, for example, Kai-Uwe Hemken, "World Harmony and Power System. 'The Book of New Artists' (1922) as a visual Manifesto of Hungarian Constructivism," in Hemken 1991, unpag.
14 Ibid.
15 László Moholy-Nagy, "Richtlinien für eine Synthetische Zeitschrift," *Pásmo* 1, nos. 7–8 (1924–25): 5. The plan is dated "1922" in the text.
16 Hemken 1991.
17 See the contract between Moholy-Nagy and the Bauhaus, 31 March 1923. Bauhaus file, Thüringische Hauptstaatsarchiv, Weimar. See also Wahl 2008, 299.
18 Lucia Moholy claims that their early texts were the result of "eine Art symbiotischer Arbeitsgemeinschaft." Lucia Moholy 1972, 11.
19 László Moholy-Nagy and Alfréd Kemény, "Dynamisch-konstruktiven Kraftsystem," in *Der Sturm* 13, no. 12 (December 1922): 186. The remaining articles were credited to Moholy-Nagy alone: "Produktion – Reproduktion," in *De Stijl* 5, no. 7 (July 1922): 98–101; "Light: A Medium of Plastic Expression," *Broom* 4 (March 1923): 283–84; "Vita az új tartalom és az új forma problémájáról" (Debate on the problem of the new content and the new form), *Akasztott Ember* 1, nos. 3–4 (December 1922): 3–4; "Neue Gestaltung in der Musik. Möglichkeiten des Grammophons," *Der Sturm* 14, no. 7 (July 1923), 102–6; "Richtlinien für eine Synthetische Zeitschrift," in *Pásmo* 1, nos. 7–8 (1924–25): 5. Note that this latter plan is dated "1922" in the text itself.
20 Wilhelm Ostwald was a chemist who, along with the physicist Ernst Mach, exercised a powerful influence on the doctor and philosopher Alexander Bogdanov. Ostwald and Mach promoted "Energeticism," which was opposed to the atomic theory of matter, proposing "energy" as the "stuff" of the universe. Einstein later resolved this dichotomy between matter and energy by demonstrating their equivalence in his famous formulation "$E = mc^2$." On Ostwald's extensive influence in Hungary before World War I, see Szabó 1981, 20–21.

21 Walter Gropius, "On Laszlo Moholy-Nagy," in Oliver Botar, "Moholy-Nagy and the Hungarian-American Council for Democracy: Documents." *Hungarian Studies Review* 15, no. 1 (Spring 1988): 85.
22 I saw a copy of the German original in the archive of Hattula Moholy-Nagy, Ann Arbor, Michigan. For an English translation, see Passuth 1985, 392–94. See also Passuth 1982, 42–43, on the synthetic conception of the Bauhausbücher series.
23 While his biocentrism is rooted in the period before he was hired to the Bauhaus, heavy-duty biologistic terminology was first inserted into Moholy-Nagy 1927.
24 Moholy-Nagy 1929, 8–10. This book appeared in English as Moholy-Nagy 1932. Moholy-Nagy's usage of «Gesamtkomplex» owes much to Raoul Francé's notion of Zoësis, defined as the sum of all sense experiences. See Francé 1921, 16.
25 Wilson-Smith 2007, 49.
26 Tafuri is quoted in ibid., 61–62.
27 Kókai, "Film und Filmprojekte in der Wiener Avant-Garde Zeitschrift Ma (1920–1925)," in Bru, Nuijs, and Hjartarson 2012, 379–93.
28 Hemken 1991.
29 On their friendship, see Botar 2007b, 93. It was likely that Moholy-Nagy came into contact with the Institute through With.
30 Peer Moritz, "Berthold Bartosch: Trick- und Animationsfilmer," in *CineGraph – Lexikon zum deutschsprachigen Film* (Munich: Text + Kritik im Richard Boorberg Verlag, , 1984ff), http://www.berthold-bartosch.de/lexikon_cinegraph01.htm.
31 Jeanpaul Goergen, "Schaffende Hände. Zur Gründung des 'Instituts für Kulturforschung e.V.' vor 80 Jahren," in *Filmblatt* 5, no. 12 (Winter 1999–2000): 5.
32 Andreas Haus, Nike Elena Arnold, Aline Helmcke, Frank Hopper, Frédéric Krauke and Walter Lenertz, *Dynamik der Gross-Stadt. Ein filmisches Experiment nach László Moholy-Nagy* [Dynamics of the big city. A filmic experiment after László Moholy-Nagy], 2006, Three-channel DVD projection. The work was shown in *Sensing the Future* both in Winnipeg and in Berlin.
33 See Oliver A. I. Botar, "Films by László Moholy-Nagy," *Journal of the Society of Architectural Historians* 67, no. 3 (2008): 460–62.
34 Botar 2004.
35 On this project, see Jaeggi 2007 and Joachim Driller, "Bauhäusler zwischen Berlin und Paris: Zur Planung und Einrichtung der 'Section allemande' in der Ausstellung der Société des artistes décorateurs Français 1930." In: Ewig, Gaehtgens, and Noell 2002, 255ff.
36 See *Section allemande* 1930.
37 Ibid., unpag., and W.S., "Die deutsche Werkbundausstellung in Paris," in *Düsseldorfer Nachrichten* (May 21, 1930).
38 Siegfried Giedion, "Der deutsche Werkbund in Paris," in *Neue Zürcher Zeitung* (June 17, 1930). See also Max Osborn's review "Gropius und die Seinen. Die deutsche Ausstellung in Paris," *Vossischen Zeitung* (May 22, 1930). Thanks to Klaus Weber for making these reviews available to me.
39 A postcard dated May 19, 1923, from Moholy-Nagy to Dorner suggests that they had known each other since Moholy-Nagy's early visits to Hannover in late September 1922 and early January 1923. Archive of the Sprengel Museum, Hannover.
40 Alexander Dorner, "Gedanken zur französisch-deutschen Ausstellung in Paris," in *Hannoverscher Anzeiger* (July 6, 1930).
41 W.S., "Die deutsche Werkbundausstellung in Paris," *Düsseldorfer Nachrichten* (May 31, 1930).
42 Dorner, "Gedanken zur französisch-deutschen Ausstellung in Paris" (see note 40).
43 Alexander Dorner, "Was sollen heute Kunstmuseen?" (1924), in Rischbieter 1962, 198.
44 See, e.g., Monika Flacke-Knoch, *Museumskonzeptionen der Weimarer Republik. Die Tätigkeit Alexander Dorners im Provinzialmuseum Hannover* (Marburg: Jonas-Verlag, 1985), 65–77; and Gebert and Hemken, in Gärtner et al. 2009, 140ff.
45 Joachim Büchner, "Laszlo Moholy-Nagy – Alexander Dorner 'Raum der Gegenwart,'" in Moeller 1988, 89. On the "Raum der Gegenwart," see also Flacke-Knoch 1985 (see note 44) and Wilts 2004, 110–21.
46 Dorner 1947, 15.
47 Ibid., 27.
48 Gebert and Hemken in Gärtner et al. 2009, 146.
49 Ines Katenhausen, "Alexander Dorners und László Moholy-Nagys 'Raum der Gegenwart'" im Provinzialmuseum Hannover," in Gärtner et al. 2009, 133.
50 Moholy-Nagy 1925, 15.

51 Veit Loers, "Moholy-Nagy's 'Raum der Gegenwart' und die Utopie von Dynamisch Konstruktiven Lichtraum," in Loers, et al. 1991, 37.
52 See Gebert and Hemken in Gärtner et al. 2009.
53 Moholy-Nagy 1947b, 360–61.
54 Passuth 1985, 45.

Immersion / Participation
1 See, for example, Frieling 2008.
2 Botar 2007a, 170ff.
3 Sibyl Moholy-Nagy 1969, xiii.
4 On Bogdanov and the avant-garde, see Jarolsav Andel, "The Constructivist Entanglement: Art Into Politics, Politics Into Art," in Richards, et al. 1990, 225–26, and Charlotte Douglas, "A Lost Paradigm of Abstraction: Alexander Bogdanov and the Russian Avant-Garde," in Petrova 2001.
5 Botar 2007b, 192ff.
6 My translations are from the typescript in the Raoul Hausmann Archiv, Berlinische Galerie, Berlin. (#1251).
7 The translation is my own.
8 Moholy-Nagy 1925, 35. He developed these ideas in other publications, for example, in *telehor* 1, nos. 1–2 (1936).
9 Raoul Hausmann and László Péri, "Die Absichten des Theaters PRÉ," in *Der Sturm* 13, no. 9 (September 1922): 138.
10 Kirby 1971, 150.
11 Moholy-Nagy, "Theater, Zirkus, Varieté," in Moholy-Nagy, Molnár, and Schlemmer 1925, 54.
12 Ibid., 54–55.
13 Ibid., 53.
14 Ibid., 62.
15 Moholy-Nagy, "Typo-Photo," *Typographische Mitteilungen, Sonderheft: Elementare Typographe* (October 1925): 202.
16 Moholy-Nagy 1929, 205.
17 Barbara Lesák, "Visionary of the European Theatre," in Phillips 1989, 39.
18 *G* no. 4 (March 1926): 92. On Moholy going to and exhibiting his proposal for a Mechanical Eccentric at Kiesler's show, see Passuth 1985, 46.
19 "Railway Theater," in Friedrich Kiesler, ed., *Internationale Ausstellung neuer Theatertechnik* (Vienna: Kunsthandlung Würthle & Sohn, 1924), 11.
20 Andor Weininger, "Das Kugeltheater," in *bauhaus*, no. 3 (1927): 2. The translation into English by Jürgen Riehle (with my minor adjustments) is from: Svestka and Jánszky Michaelsen, eds. 1991, 113.
21 On disorientation in Modernist art of the period, see Botar 2013a, 172–83.
22 Moholy-Nagy 1925, 23.
23 Klaus Weber, "Kinetisches konstruktives System 1922," in Droste and Fiedler 1988, 374, and Lesák 1988, 168; Botar 2007a, 170–77; Olivier Lugon, "Le vieux pont, l'historien et le nouveau photograhie," in Bon, Lugon and Simay 2013, 19.
24 Bodo-Michael Baumunk, "Luna-Park und Metropol," in Korff and Rürup 1987, 412.
25 Moholy-Nagy, "Filmváz: A nagyváros dinamikája," in *MA* 9, nos. 8–9 (September 15, 1924), unpag.
26 Baumunk, 411 (see note 24).
27 Lesák 1988, 54.
28 See Bajac et al. 2010, 60–61, and Barbara Haskell, *Joseph Stella* (New York: Whitney Museum of American Art, 1994), 40ff.
29 Slater 2010, 11–12.
30 Apollonio 1973, 197–98.
31 Max Burchartz, "Luna Park," in *G* (June 1924): 138–39. Translation by Steven Lindberg with Margareta Ingrid Christian in Mertins and Jennings 2010.
32 Lesák 1988, 52.
33 Mark Dessauce, "Against the Style," in *Casabella* (September 1993). As coeditor of the Bauhausbücher, Moholy-Nagy had planned to publish volumes by Burchartz, Kiesler, and Lönberg-Holm around 1926, if not earlier.
34 Nancy Troy in Lehman et al. 1986, 139–40.
35 Ibid.
36 Kac 2007, 109.
37 See the chapter "Gesamtwerk" in the present book, and Oliver A. I. Botar, "Films by László Moholy-Nagy," in *Journal of the Society of Architectural Historians* 67, no. 3 (2008): 460–62.
38 Sibyl Moholy-Nagy 1950, 84.
39 On the handheld camera that LMN used (introduced, coincidentally, in 1926) see Jeanpaul Goergen, "Light Play and Social Reportage: László Moholy-Nagy and the German Film Avant-Garde," in Rubio 2010, 204.

40 Charles Metain, *G* no. 5 (March 1926): 225.
41 Jeanpaul Goergen, in Rubio 2010, 212.
42 Moholy-Nagy 1929, 14.

Projection Spaces
1 Moholy-Nagy in *telehor* 1, nos. 1–2 (1936): 30.
2 Krisztina Passuth was the first to suggest this, even if only indirectly, in Passuth 1985, 48.
3 For examples of works such as this, see the chapter "Transparency / Reflection / Motion" in the present volume.
4 Raoul Hausmann and Viking Eggeling, "Zweite präsentistische Deklaration. Gerichtet an die internationalen Konstruktivisten," in *MA* (March 15, 1923), reprinted in Erlhoff 1982, 85.
5 Moholy-Nagy 1925, 37; and Moholy-Nagy 1969, 45.
6 Roh 1930, 3.
7 Moholy-Nagy, "zu dem film: moholy-nagy zeigt ein lichtspiel schwarz–weiss–grau," typescript, n.d., stamped "moholy-nagy berlin-chbg" [ca. 1930–33], Ryerson and Burnham Archives, The Art Institute of Chicago Libraries, Inv. No. unknown. I saw a copy in the private archives of Hattula Moholy-Nagy, Ann Arbor, MI.
8 Moholy-Nagy, "In Defense of Abstract Art," in *Journal of Aesthetics and Art Criticism* 4, no. 2 (1945): 75.
9 Elcott 2011, 237. On Moholy-Nagy's complicated relationship to this term, see 237–40.
10 Neusüss in Neusüss, Heyne, with Moholy-Nagy 2009, 22.
11 Moholy-Nagy 1929, 90–91; and Moholy-Nagy 1938, 86–87.
12 Moholy-Nagy in *telehor* 1, nos. 1–2 (1936): 37. I have adapted the English translation.
13 Moholy-Nagy 1938, 84, caption for fig. 72.
14 Raoul Hausmann, "Prezentizmus" (Presentism), *MA* (February 1, 1922).
15 Moholy-Nagy 1927, 30 and elsewhere.
16 Moholy-Nagy 1947b, 206. For an earlier history of the awareness of the electromagnetic spectrum among artists, especially the Futurists, see Henderson 2013, 18.
17 See Vergo 2012, 284–86. On this relationship, see the chapter "Immersion / Participation" in the present volume.
18 For a thorough study of one of these, see Rave and Heusinger von Waldegg 1983.
19 Joyce Tsai, "Excavating Surface: On the Repair and Revision of László Moholy-Nagy's *Z VII* (1926)" in Saletnik and Schuldenfrei 2009, 147–48.
20 Moholy-Nagy, "Problems of the Modern Film," in *Korunk* (1930) in Passuth 1985, 315. This version is revised by me on the basis of the Hungarian and German originals.
21 Lusk 1980, 92. See also Hight 1995, 169.
22 Moholy-Nagy 1925, 32.
23 See, for example, Jan Sahli's treatment of the subject (Sahli 2006, 129–33).
24 Moholy-Nagy 1927, 41.
25 Moholy-Nagy in *telehor* 1, nos. 1–2 (1936): 40. The text is dated to "1928–30." The English translation provided is adapted by me using the German original.
26 Hight 1995, 166–69.
27 Kittler 1999, 124.
28 Sibyl Moholy-Nagy 1969, xvii.
29 Hapkemeyer in Hapkemeyer and Stasny 2000, 131.
30 For a review of the literature on the use of film in theatrical productions, see Elcott 2011, 282, note 249.
31 Jörg Jewanski, "The Visions of Oskar Fischinger and Alexander László in 1935/36 about a New Way of Visualizing Music," and Jeanpaul Goergen, "Oskar Fischinger in Germany 1900 to 1936," in Keefer and Goldemund 2013, 135 and 43. Raumlichtkunst has recently been reconstructed by the Center for Visual Music in Los Angeles, with spectacular results, for example, at the Whitney Museum of American Art in New York, June–October 2012.
32 Jeanpaul Goergen, "Light Play and Social Reportage: László Moholy-Nagy and the German Film Avant-Garde," in Rubio 2010, 201, 204.
33 Sahli 2006, 132, note 74; and an invitation to the screening I've seen in the Thomas Derda collection, Berlin.
34 Moholy-Nagy in Moholy-Nagy, Molnár, and Schlemmer 1925, 51.
35 Walter Gropius, "Vom modernen Theaterbau, unter Berücksichtung des Piscatortheaterneubaus in Berlin," *Die Scene* 18 (1928): 4, quoted in Noam Elcott, "Rooms of our time: László Moholy-Nagy and the Stillbirth of Multi-Media Museums," in Todd 2011, 34.
36 Moholy-Nagy, "dear kalivoda," *telehor* 1, nos. 1–2 (1936): 30.
37 Engelbrecht 2009, 476.
38 Moholy-Nagy, "Lichtrequisit einer Elektrischen Bühne," *Die Form* (June 7, 1930): 297. Sibyl Moholy-Nagy recalls that the mechanic Otto Ball constructed the device in a dingy machine shop on Alexanderplatz. Sibyl Moholy-Nagy 1950, 64–65.
39 Alexandra Käss, "Knoten, Relationen und der seltsame Fall des 'Licht-Raum Modulators' von László Moholy-Nagy," in Broch et al. 2007, 127.
40 Moholy-Nagy 1925, 36.
41 Hapkemeyer in Hapkemeyer and Stasny 2000, 131.
42 Moholy-Nagy, "Lichtrequisit einer Elektrischen Bühne," 298 (see note 39).
43 Ibid, 298.
44 Moholy-Nagy in Moholy-Nagy, Molnár, and Schlemmer 1925, 55.
45 Sahli 2006, 135.
46 Elcott 2011, 40.
47 Ibid., 294.
48 Quoting terms used by Elcott in ibid.
49 On Van Doesburg's conception of cinematic light-space, see Elcott 2011, 256–63.
50 Elcott, quoting Étienne de Beaumont in: Elcott 2011, 272. Beaumont is not referring to Moholy-Nagy's film here, but Elcott cleverly imbricates his comment into his own argument concerning that film.
51 Moholy-Nagy, Molnár, and Schlemmer 1925, 44–45.
52 Klaus Weber made this observation to me. On Moholy-Nagy's use of translucent projection screens in his set designs, see Gerald Köhler, "Zum Raum wird hier das Licht: Der szensiche Theaterkosmos von László Moholy-Nagy," in Pfeiffer and Hollein 2009, 96–100.
53 Sigfried Giedion, "Der Deutsche Werkbund in Paris," *Neue Zürcher Zeitung* (June 17, 1930), quoted in Elcott 2011, 273.
54 Klaus Weber shared with me his copies of Gropius's collection of reviews of this show.
55 "Trolitan is the tradename of the Dynamit Nobel Corporation of West Germany for a phenol-formaldehyde resin virtually identical to Bakelite.… Production of Trolitan in Germany began in 1926 with the expiration of Bakeland's patent … for Bakelite." Properties of Bakelite: "1. Sheets of Bakelite are hard, opaque, and infusible. 2. Bakelite is black and cannot be pigmented.… 3. Bakelite will resist high heat–to 400–600 F." From "Common Plastic Materials Used by Moholy-Nagy," No author indicated, undated. I saw a copy of the typescript in the archive of Hattula Moholy-Nagy, Ann Arbor, MI. The heat-resistance would have been important given the temperatures that would have been produced within the Light Prop's Trolit and flashed glass housing.
56 Jacob Gebert and Kai-Uwe Hemken, "Raum der Gegenwart: Die Ordnung von Apparaten und Exponaten," in Gärtner et al. 2009, 150. On Malina, see Czeglédy and Kopeczky 2010. Thanks to Hattula Moholy-Nagy for discussing the issue of flashing with me.
57 On this topic see the chapter "Production / Reproduction" in the present volume. See also Engelbrecht 2009, 193; Noam Elcott, "Darkened Rooms: A Genealogy of Avant-Garde Filmstrips from Man Ray to the London Film-Makers' Co-op and Back Again," in *Grey Room* 30 (Winter 2008): 26; and Jeanpaul Goergen, "Films, Projects, Proposals: Commented Filmography 1921–1934," in Rubio 2010, 243.
58 Elcott refers to Hight here in Elcott 2011, 280.
59 On this, see the chapter "Gesamtwerk" in the present volume; and Oliver A. I. Botar, "Taking the Kunst out of Gesamtkunstwerk: Moholy-Nagy's Conception of the Gesamtwerk," in Rubio 2010, 159–68.
60 The drawings are reproduced in Gärtner et al. 2009, 140–41.
61 This is strongly suggested in the last, descriptive paragraphs of Moholy-Nagy, "Új filmkísérletek," in *Korunk* 8, no. 3 (1933): 231–37 (translation in Passuth 1985, 323). See also Moholy-Nagy's color photographs of a children's "underwater" shadow play at the School of Design, Chicago, 1940–42, in Fiedler and Moholy-Nagy 2006, 102–3.
62 See "Artists' Statements" in the present volume.
63 Moholy-Nagy, in *telehor* 1, nos. 1–2 (1936): 30.
64 *Forum* no. 3 (1932) and Kálmán Brogyányi, *A fény művészete* (The Art of Light), Bratislava/Pozsony, 1932.
65 Sibyl Moholy-Nagy 1969, xvii.
66 Sibyl Moholy-Nagy 1950, 64.

Transparency / Reflection / Motion
1 "Space-Time Problems in Art," in *American Abstract Artists*, 1946.
2 Moholy-Nagy 1947a.
3 With 1997.
4 Moholy-Nagy 1947a.
5 Findeli 1988, 7–8.
6 Hilberseimer 1922.
7 Moholy-Nagy 1938, 115.
8 Moholy-Nagy to Franz Roh, 23 March 1934
9 Moholy-Nagy 1947a.
10 Ernst Kallai, "Moholy-Nagy," in *Sammlung Marzona* (Bielefeld, 1926), quoted in Elcott 2011, 228.
11 Moholy-Nagy 1947b, 252.
12 Moholy-Nagy 1938, 86.
13 Moholy-Nagy 1947b, 237.
14 Moholy-Nagy 1947a.

Art as Information / Information as Art
1 Moholy-Nagy 1969, 26.
2 A text by Moholy-Nagy of 1925 quoted in Sibyl Moholy-Nagy 1950, 28. The translation is, presumably, also by her.
3 Sibyl Moholy-Nagy 1950, 28. On the Constructivist background to the EM series, see Passuth 1985, 32.
4 Moholy-Nagy, "Emaille im February 1924," *Der Sturm* 15 (February 1924): 1.
5 Moholy-Nagy, "Zeitgemässe Typographie: Ziele, Praxis, Kritik," in *Gutenberg Festschrift* (Mainz: Gutenberg Gesellschaft, 1925), 307.
6 Lazar El Lissitzky, "Topography of Typography," *Merz* no. 4 (July 1923).
7 This paragraph: Moholy-Nagy 1925, 112–13, here 13.
8 Charles R. Gibson, *The Romance of Modern Electricity* (London: Seeley & Co., 1907); Charles R. Gibson, *A modern villamosság*, trans. Rezső Hajós (Budapest: Franklin-Társulat, 1913).
9 On this topic, see Botar, "Four Poems of 1918 by László Moholy-Nagy," in *Hungarian Studies Review* 21, nos. 1–2 (Spring–Fall 1994): 103–12.
10 For more discussion of his debt to Francé, see Botar 2004 and Oliver A. I. Botar, "The Origins of László Moholy-Nagy's Biocentric Constructivism," in Kac 2007, 315–44.
11 Note that five works are listed in the catalogue of the February 1924 exhibition at *Der Sturm*. Three are currently in the Museum of Modern Art collection (1, 1a, 1b), and one is in the Langen Foundation collection in Germany (1). One was shown in an exhibition of modern Western artists in Russia in the late 1920s (probably 2). This one may have gone missing. Another, with a different design, was offered for sale at Galerie Gmurzynska in 1975. No. 92 in the catalogue, it is here marked as being "Em 3" and signed, dated (1923), and titled on the verso. (*The 1920s in Eastern Europe* [Cologne: Galerie Gmyrzynska, 1975], 121, 133.) (A sixth version was the color reproduction in *telehor*, on the color reproduction of which he lavished attention.)
12 Sibyl Moholy-Nagy 1950, 17.
13 Moholy-Nagy, "Emaille in Februar 1924."
14 Moholy-Nagy 1947a, 79.
15 Ernő Kállai, "Ladislaus Moholy-Nagy," *Jahrbuch der Jungen Kunst* (1924): 188.
16 Roters 1969, 166.
17 Manovich 2002, xxxi.
18 Klemens Gruber, "Das Intermediale Jahrhundert: Die Saison 1922/23," in Schoenmakers et al. 2009.
19 The quotation is from: Eduardo Kac, "Aspects of the Aesthetics of Telecommunications," 1992: http://www.ekac.org/telecom.paper.siggrap.html. See also: Eduardo Kac, "The Aesthetics of Communications," in Kac 2005, 16–21.
20 Moholy-Nagy, "Von der Pigmentmalerei bis zu der in den Raum geworfenen farbigen Lichtgestalutng," in *Katalog der Zehnten Jahresausstellung L. I. A.* (Leipzig: E. R. Wunderlich, 1925), 35–47.
21 After its initial publication in 1925 it subsequently appeared in reworked variants published in German, Hungarian, English, and other languages throughout Europe as well as in Russia, Japan, and the United States.

***telehor* 1936 and the Crisis of Media Art**
1 A good deal of the text in this section was developed in conjunction with Klemens Gruber, with whom I edited the facsimile edition of *telehor*, and with whom I cowrote the essay accompanying that re-edition.

2   On Kalivoda, see Botar and Gruber 2013.
3   Ibid.
4   Quoted in Zuzana Marhoulová, "František Kalivoda organizátor brněnské avantgardy," master's thesis, Masarykova univerzita, Brno, 2004, 19.
5   Ibid., 68.
6   Brno was a bicultural city, with a substantial population of German speakers as well as Czechs. This was the German art center.
7   "Künstlerhaus, mährischer kunstverein, brno-brünn, 1.VI.1935–16.VI.1935. výstava–ausstellung l. moholy-nagy," two-page typescript list of works in the exhibition, Kalivoda papers, Muzeum města Brna.
8   Engelbrecht 2009, 498–99.
9   Baudin 1998, 316–19.
10   From a typescript version of the response, the copy of which is in the archive of Hattula Moholy-Nagy (received from Alain Findeli), 1 and 3.
11   Gabriel Jutz has recently remarked on just this, in her excellent article: "'Produktion–Reproduktion': Echos von László Moholy-Nagys Medientheorie in der Geschichte von Film und Medienkunst," in Bru, Nuijs, and Hjartarson 2012, 399–400.
12   Benjamin would have been particularly aware of Moholy-Nagy once his friend Sybille Pietzsch became Moholy-Nagy's wife. On Pietzsch, her first husband, Carl Dreyfuss, and their friend Benjamin, see Rüttgens-Pohlmann 2008.
13   György Márkus, "Walter Benjamin and the German 'Reproduction' Debate,'" http://www.rae.com.pt/Caderno_wb_2010/Markus%20Benjamin%20and%20german%20reproduction%20debate.pdf, 353; Krisztina Passuth, "Moholy-Nagy et Walter Benjamin: Une rencontre," in Cahiers du Musée Georges Pompidou 5 (1980): 398–409.
14   Molderings 2008, 160. See also Passuth, in ibid.
15   Philippe Simay, "Double Vue: Moholy-Nagy et le pont transbordeur," in: Bon, Lugon, and Simay 2013, 40–41.
16   McLuhan to Sigfried Giedion, Assumption College, Windsor, ON, 22 December 1948. (Giedion Papers, gta Zurich)
17   On Giedion and McLuhan, see Richard Cavell, McLuhan in Space: A Cultural Geography (Toronto: University of Toronto Press, 2002), 33ff.
18   Reto Geiser, "Erziehung zum Sehen. Kunstvermittlung und Bildarbeit in Sigfried Giedions Schaffebn beidseits des Atlantiks," and Gregor Harbusch, "Bauen in Frankreich, 1928," both in Harbusch and Oechslin 2010, 151 and 184, respectively.
19   Olivier Lugon, "Neues Sehen, Neue Geschichte: László Moholy-Nagy, Sigfried Giedion und die Ausstellung Film und Foto," in ibid., 95, 101–3. See also Sibyl Moholy-Nagy 1950, 75.
20   Sigfried Giedion, Bauen in Frankreich, Eisen, Eisenbeton (Leipzig: Klinkhardt & Biermann, 1928), 3.
21   Rainer Maria Rilke had proposed this idea a couple of years before Moholy-Nagy, in 1919, though it is not certain that Moholy-Nagy read Rilke on this. Rainer Maria Rilke, "Ur-Geräusch" in Das Inselschiff 1, no. 1 (1919/1920): 14–20. Quoted and translated as "Primal Sound" in Kittler 1999, 42.
22   McLuhan scholar Gerald O'Grady related this to me in a telephone conversation that took place between Singapore (School of Art, Design & Media at Nanyang Technological University in Singapore) and Winnipeg (School of Art, University of Manitoba) in fall 2011.
23   McLuhan to Giedion, Toronto, 1 July 1948 (Giedion papers, gta Archiv, Zurich). See Marshall McLuhan, "Encyclopaedic Unities," The Hudson Review (December 1948): 599–602.
24   Cavell 2002, 111 (see note 17). On Moholy-Nagy and McLuhan, see also Richard Kostelanetz 1970, 214; and Jeanine Fiedler and Ben Buschfeld, "Von der Virtualität der Warhnemung im 20. Jahrhundert–Ein Gespräch zwischen László Moholy-Nagy und Marshall McLuhan," in Jäger and Wessing 1997, 181–88.
25   Orosz 2013. In Orosz's view, the notion that Kepes carried on Moholy-Nagy's project after the latter's untimely passing is greatly exaggerated. While I appreciate the importance of the long-overdue establishment of Kepes's independent profile, and while Orosz demonstrates that there are significant differences between their projects, the extent to which they shared ideas and ideals is also striking.
26   Branden W. Joseph, Beyond the Dream Syndicate: Tony Conrad and the Arts After Cage (Cambridge, MA: Zone Books, 2011), 160.

Reference List

Apollonio, Umbro, ed. (1973) *Futurist Manifestos*. London: Thames and Hudson.

Bajac, Quentin, et al. (2010) *Dreamlands: Des parcs d'attractions aux cités du futur*. Paris: Centre Pompidou.

Baudin, Antoine. (1998) *Hélène de Mandrot et la Maison des Artistes de La Sarraz*. Lausanne: Editions Payot.

Benson, Timothy, and Éva Forgács, eds. (2002) *Between Worlds: A Sourcebook of Central European Avant-Gardes, 1910–1930*. Cambridge, MA: The MIT Press.

Bergdoll, Barry, and Leah Dickerman, eds. (2009) *Bauhaus 1919–1933: Workshops of Modernity*. New York: MOMA.

Bock, Hans-Michael, ed. (1984ff.) *CineGraph–Lexikon zum deutschsprachigen Film*. Munich: edition text + kritik im Richard Boorberg Verlag.

Bogner, Dieter, ed. (1988) *Friedrich Kiesler: Architekt, Maler, Bildhauer 1890–1965*. Vienna: Löcker.

Bon, François, Olivier Lugon, and Philippe Simay. (2013) *Le pont transbordeur de Marseille, Moholy-Nagy*. Paris: Ophrys.

Borchardt-Hume, Achim. (2006) *Albers and Moholy-Nagy: From the Bauhaus to the New World*. London: Tate Publishing.

Botar, Oliver A. I. [1998] (2001) "Prolegomena to the Study of Biomorphic Modernism: Biocentrism, László Moholy-Nagy's 'New Vision' and Ernő Kállai's Bioromantik," PhD diss., University of Toronto. Ann Arbor, MI: UMI Research Press.

_____. (2004) László Moholy-Nagy's 'New Vision' and the Aestheticization of Scientific Imagery in Weimar Germany," *Science in Context: Writing Modern Art and Science* 17, no. 4: 525–56.

_____. (2007a) *Technical Detours: The Early Moholy-Nagy Reconsidered*. New York: Art Gallery of The Graduate Center, The City University of New York and The Salgo Trust for Education.

_____. (2007b) *Természet és technika: Az újraértelmezett Moholy-Nagy 1916–1923* [Nature and Technology: Moholy-Nagy Reconsidered]. Budapest: Vince Kiadó.

_____. (2010a) "László Moholy-Nagy, a Biocentric Artist?" in Botar and Moholy-Nagy 2010, 47–59.

_____. (2010b) "László Moholy-Nagy's Synthesekonzept von 1922," in Jaeggi, et al. 2010, 81–93.

_____. (2010c) "Taking the Kunst out of Gesamtkunstwerk: Moholy-Nagy's Conception of the Gesamtwerk," in Rubio 2010, 159–68.

_____. (2011a) "Defining Biocentrism," in Botar and Wünsche 2010, 15–46.

_____. (2011b) "Moholy-Nagy and Biocentrism," in Iguchi 2011, 208–13.

_____. (2013a) "Le dérèglement sensoriel ou la formation des sens pour la modernité: l'art de l'ilinx et l'avant-garde européenne," in Lampe ed. 2013, 172–83.

_____. (2013b) "László Moholy-Nagy et la vue aérienne," in Lampe ed. 2013, 136–43.

Botar, Oliver A. I., and Klemens Gruber, eds. (2013) "Melancholy for the Future," in *telehor, László Moholy-Nagy*, 7–29. Zurich: Lars Müller Publishers.

Botar, Oliver A. I., and Hattula Moholy-Nagy, eds. (2010) *Hungarian Studies Review, Special Volume: Proceedings of the Conference "László Moholy-Nagy: Translating Utopia into Action"* 37, nos. 1–2, 47–59.

Botar, Oliver A. I., and Isabel Wünsche, eds. (2011) *Biocentrism and Modernism*. Farnham, UK: Ashgate.

Broch, Jan, et al., eds. (2007) *Netzwerke der Moderne: Erkundungen und Strategien*. Würzburg: Königshausen & Neumann.

Bru, Sascha, Laurence Nuijs, and Benedikt Hjartarson, eds. (2012) *Regarding the Popular: Modernism, the Avant-Garde and High and Low Culture*. Berlin: De Gruyter.

Chapp, Belena, ed. (1995) *László Moholy-Nagy: From Budapest to Berlin, 1914–1923*. Newark: University Gallery, University of Delaware.

Clark, Bruce, and Linda D. Henderson, eds. (2002) *From Energy to Information: Representation in Science and Technology, Art and Literature*. Stanford, CA: Stanford University Press.

Czeglédy, Nina, and Róna Kopeczky, eds. (2010) *The Pleasure of Light: György Kepes, Frank Malina / A Fényjátékosok Kepes György, Frank Malina*. Budapest: Ludwig Múzeum–Museum of Contemporary Art.

David, Catherine, and Corinne Diserens, eds. (1991) *László Moholy-Nagy*. Marseilles: Musées de Marseille and Réunion des musées nationaux.

Dorner, Alexander. (1947) *The Way Beyond Art: The Work of Herbert Bayer*. New York: Wittenborn, Schultz.

Droste, Magdalena, and Jeannine Fiedler, eds. (1988) *Experiment Bauhaus*. Berlin: Bauhaus-Archiv.

Elcott, Noam. (2011) *Into the Dark Chamber: Avant-garde Photograms and the Cinematic Imaginary*. Charleston: BiblioBazaar.

Engelbrecht, Lloyd C. (2009) *Moholy-Nagy: Mentor to Modernism*, 2 vols. Cincinnati: Flying Trapeze Press.

Engelbrecht, Lloyd C., and Peter Hahn, eds. (1988) *50 Jahre New Bauhaus: Bauhausnachfolge in Chicago*. Berlin: Bauhaus-Archiv and Argon.

Erlhoff, Michael, ed. (1982) *Raoul Hausmann: Sieg Triumph Tabak mit Bohnen*, vol. 2 of *Texte bis 1933*. Munich: edition text + kritik.

Eskildsen, Ute, and Robert Knudt, eds. (1995) *Laszlo Moholy-Nagy: Fotogramme 1922–1943*. Munich: Schirmer/Mosel.

Ewig, Isabel, Thomas W. Gaehtgens, and Matthias Noell, eds. (2002) *Das Bauhaus und Frankreich 1919–1940*. Berlin: Akademie Verlag.

Fiedler, Jeannine, and Hattula Moholy-Nagy, eds. (2006) *László Moholy-Nagy: Color in Transparency. Photographic Experiments in Color 1934–1946*. Göttingen: Steidl and Bauhaus-Archiv.

Findeli, Alain. (1995) *Le Bauhaus de Chicago: L'oeuvre pédagogique de László Moholy-Nagy*. Sillery PQ: Éditions Septentrion.

Finkeldey, Bernd, Kai-Uwe Hemken, and Rainer Stommer, eds. (1992) *Konstruktivistische Internationale: Schöpferische Arbeitsgemeinschaft 1922–1927. Utopien für eine europäische Kultur*. Stuttgart: Hatje Cantz.

Foster, Stephen C., ed. (2006) *Hans Richter Activism: Modernism and the Avant-Garde*. Cambridge, MA: The MIT Press.

Francé, Raoul H. (1921) *Bios: Die Gesetze der Welt*, 2 vols. Munich: Franz Hanfstaengl.

Frieling, Rudolf. (2008) *The Art of Participation*. New York: Thames and Hudson.

Frizot, Michel, ed. (1998) *A New History of Photography*. Cologne: Könemann.

Gärtner, Ulrike, et al., eds. (2009) *Kunst Licht Spiele: Lichtästhetik der klassischen Avantgarde*. Bielefeld: Kerber.

Grau, Oliver, ed. (2002) *MediaArtHistories*. Cambridge, MA: The MIT Press.

_____. (2003) *Virtual Art: From Illusion to Immersion*. Cambridge, MA: The MIT Pess.

Gruber, Klemens, and Barbara Wurm, eds. (2009) "Digital Formalism: Die kalkulierten Bilder des Dziga Vertov." Special issue of *Maske und Kothurn* 55, no. 3.

Hapkemeyer, Andreas, and Peter Stasny, eds. (2000) *Ludwig Hirschfeld-Mack. Bauhäusler und Visionär*. Stuttgart: Hatje Cantz.

Harbusch, Gregor, and Werner Oechslin, eds. (2010) *Sigfried Giedion und die Fotografie: Bildinszenierungen der Moderne*. Zurich: GTA Verlag.

Haus, Andreas. (1978) *Moholy-Nagy: Fotos und Fotogramme*. Munich: Schirmer und Mosel.

_____. (1980) *Moholy-Nagy: Photographs and Photograms*. New York: Pantheon.

Hemken, Kai-Uwe, ed. (1991) *Buch neuer Künstler* (Facsimile edition). Baden: Lars Müller.

Henderson, Linda Dalrymple. (2013) *The Fourth Dimension and Non-Euclidean Geometry in Modern Art*, 2nd ed. Cambridge, MA: The MIT Press.

Hight, Eleanor M. (1995) *Picturing Modernism: Moholy-Nagy and Photography in Interwar Germany*. Cambridge, MA: The MIT Press.

Iguchi, Toshino, ed. (2011) *Moholy in Motion*. Kyoto: The National Museum of Modern Art.

Jaeggi, Annemarie. (2007) *Werkbund Exhibition Paris 1930: Living in a High Rise*. Berlin: Bauhaus-Archiv.

Jaeggi, Annemarie, et al., eds. (2010) *bauhaus global. Gesammelte Beiträge der Konferenz bauhaus global vom 21. bis 26. September 2009*. Berlin: Gebr. Mann Verlag.

Jäger, Gottfried, and Gudrun Wessing, eds. (1997) *Über Moholy-Nagy*. Bielefeld: Kerber Verlag.

Kac, Eduardo. (2005) *Telepresence and Bio Art: Networking Humans, Rabbits, & Robots*. Ann Arbor: University of Michigan Press.

_____, ed. (2007) *Signs of Life: Bio Art and Beyond*. Cambridge, MA: The MIT Press.

Keefer, Cindy, and Jaap Goldemund, eds. (2013) *Oskar Fischinger 1900–1967: Experiments in Cinematic Abstraction*. Amsterdam: EYE Filmmuseum and Los Angeles: Center for Visual Music.

Kiesler, Friedrich, ed. (1924) *Internationale Ausstellung neuer Theatertechnik*. Vienna: Kunsthandlung Würthle &Sohn.

Kirby, Michael. (1971) *Futurist Performance*. New York: Dutton.

Kish, John, ed. (1987) *The Hungarian Avant-Garde, 1914–1933*. Storrs, CT: W. Benton Museum of Art.

Kittler, Friedrich. (1990) *Discourse Networks 1800–1900*. Stanford, CA: Stanford University Press.

_____. (1999) *Grammaphone, Film Typewriter*. Stanford, CA: Stanford University Press.

Koczó, Margit. (1968) "Die ungarische Räterepublik," PhD diss., Universität Wien.

Korff, Gottfried, and Reinhard Rürup, eds. (1987) *Berlin, Berlin. Die Ausstellung zur Geschichte der Stadt*. Berlin: Nikolai Verlag.

Kostelanetz, Richard, ed. (1970) *Moholy-Nagy: An Anthology*. New York: Praeger Publishers.

Lampe, Angela, ed. (2013) *Vues d'en Haut*. Metz: Centre Pompidou-Metz.

Lehman, Arnold L., et al., eds. (1986) *Oskar Schlemmer: The Baltimore Museum of Art*. Baltimore: Baltimore Museum of Art.

Lesák, Barbara. (1988) *Die Kulisse explodiert. Friedrich Kieslers Theaterexperimente und Architekturprojekte 1923–1925*. Vienna: Löcker Verlag.

Levin, Thomas Y. (2003) "'Tones from out of Nowhere': Rudolph Pfenninger and the Archaeology of Synthetic Sound," *Grey Room* 12 (Summer): 33–79.

Loers, Veit, et al., eds. (1991) *László Moholy-Nagy*. Stuttgart: Gerd Hatje.

Lusk, Irene-Charlotte. (1980) *Montagen ins Blaue: Laszlo Moholy-Nagy Fotomontagen und -collagen, 1922–1943*. Giessen: Anabas.

McLuhan, Marshall. (1964) *Understanding Media: The Extensions of Man*. New York: McGraw-Hill.

Manovich, Lev. (2002) *The Language of New Media*. Cambridge, MA: The MIT Press.

Marchessault, Janine. (2005) *Marshall McLuhan: Cosmic Media*. London: Sage Publications.

Marchessault, Janine, and Susan Lord, eds. (2007) *Fluid Screens, Expanded Cinema*. Toronto: University of Toronto Press.

Margolin, Victor. (1997) *The Struggle for Utopia: Rodchenko, Lissiztky and Moholy-Nagy, 1917–1946*. Chicago: University of Chicago Press.

Mertins, Detlef, and Michael W. Jennings, eds. (2010) *G: An Avant-Garde Journal of Art, Architecture, Design and Film, 1923–1926*. Los Angeles: Getty Research Institute.

Moeller, Magdalena M., ed. (1988) *Die Abstrakten Hannover–Internationale Avantgarde 1927–1935*. Hannover: Sprengel Museum.

Moholy, Lucia. (1972) *Marginalien zu Moholy-Nagy. Dokumentarische Ungereimtheiten / Moholy-Nagy: Marginal Notes, Documentary Absurdities*. Krefeld: Scherpe Verlag.

Moholy-Nagy, László. (1925) *Malerei, Photographie, Film*. Munich: Albert Langen Verlag.

_____. (1927) *Malerei, Fotografie, Film*. 2nd ed. Munich: Albert Langen Verlag.

_____. (1929) *Von Material zu Architektur*. Munich: Albert Langen Verlag.

_____. (1932) *The New Vision: From Material to Architecture*. New York: Brewer, Warren and Putnam.

_____. (1938) *The New Vision: Fundamentals of Design, Painting, Sculpture, Architecture*. New York: W. W. Norton & Co.

_____. (1947a) *The New Vision and Abstract of an Artist*, 4th ed. Translated by Daphne M. Hofmann. New York: George Wittenborn Inc.

_____. (1947b) *Vision in Motion*. Chicago: Paul Theobald and Company.

_____. [1927] (1967). *Malerei, Fotografie, Film*. 2nd ed. of 2nd. ed. Mainz: Florian Kupferberg.

_____. [1927] (1969) *Painting, Photography, Film*. 2nd ed. Translated by Janet Seligman. Cambridge, MA: The MIT Press.

_____. (1979) *A festéktől a fényig* [From Pigment to Light]. Edited by Erzsébet Sugár. Bucharest: Kriterion.

_____. [1936] (2013) *telehor*. Edited by Klemens Gruber and Oliver A. I. Botar. Zurich: Lars Müller Publishers.

Moholy-Nagy, László, Farkas Molnár, and Oskar Schlemmer. (1925) *Die Bühne im Bauhaus*. Munich: Albert Langen Verlag.

Moholy-Nagy, Sibyl. (1950) *Moholy-Nagy: Experiment in Totality*. New York: Harper and Brothers.
———. (1969) *Moholy-Nagy: Experiment in Totality*, 2nd. ed. Cambridge, MA: The MIT Press.
Molderings, Herbert. (1998) *Laszlo Moholy-Nagy*. Paris: Photo-Poche 77.
———. (2008) *Die Moderne der Fotografie*. Hamburg: Philo Fine Arts.
Neusüss, Floris M., and Renate Heyne, eds., with Hattula Moholy-Nagy. (2009) *Moholy-Nagy: The Photograms*. Stuttgart: Hatje Cantz.
Niebisch, Arndt, ed. (2013) *Raoul Hausmann, Dada Wissenschaft: Wissenschaftliche und technische Schriften*. Berlin: Philo Fine Arts.
Orosz, Márton. (2013) "A látás reviziója: Művészet mint humanista tudomány Kepes György korai életművében" [The Revision of Vision: Art as a Humanist Science in the Early Oeuvre of György Kepes], PhD diss., Eötvös Loránd University, Budapest.
Packer, Randall, and Ken Jordan, eds. (2001) *Multi-Media from Wagner to Virtual Reality*. New York: Norton.
Passuth, Krisztina. (1982) *Moholy-Nagy*. Budapest: Corvina.
———. (1985) *Moholy-Nagy*. London: Thames and Hudson.
Petrova, Yevgenia, ed. (2001) *The Russian Avant-Garde: Representation and Interpretation*. St. Petersburg: Palace Editions.
Pfeiffer, Ingrid, and Max Hollein, eds. (2009) *László Moholy-Nagy Retrospektive*. Munich and New York: Prestel.
Phillips, Lisa, ed. (1989) *Frederick Kiesler*. New York: Whitney Museum of American Art.
Rave, Horst, and Joachim Heusinger von Waldegg. (1983) *Laszlo Moholy-Nagy, Z IX, 1924*. Mannheim: Städtische Kunsthalle.
Rees, A. L., et al., eds. (2011) *Expanded Cinema: Art, Performance, Film*. London: Tate Publishing.
Richards, Andrew, et al., eds. (1990) *Art into Life: Russian Constructivism 1914–1932*. New York: Rizzoli.
Rischbieter, Henning, ed. (1962) *Die zwanziger Jahre in Hannover: Bildende Kunst, Literatur, Theater, Tanz, Architektur, 1916–1933*. Hannover: Kunstverein.
Roh, Franz. (1930) *L. Moholy-Nagy 60 Fotos*. Berlin: Klinkhardt & Biermann.
Roters, Eberhard. (1969) *Painters of the Bauhaus*. New York: Frederick A. Praeger.
Rubio, Oliva María, ed. (2010) *László Moholy-Nagy: The Art of Light*. Madrid: La Fábrica Editorial.
Rüttgens-Pohlmann, Hannelore. (2008). *Kunstwerk eines Lebens: Sibyl Moholy-Nagy*. Oldenburg: BIS-Verlag der Carl von Ossietzky Universität.
Sahli, Jan. (2006) *Filmische Sinneserweiterung, László Moholy-Nagys Filmwerk und Theorie*. Marbug: Schüren.
Saletnick, Jeffrey, and Robin Schuldenfrei, eds. (2009) *Bauhaus Construct: Fashioning Identity, Discourse and Modernism*. London and New York: Routledge.
Section allemande, Exposition de la Société des artistes décorateurs, Grand Palais, 14 Mai–13 Juillet. Berlin: Verlag Herman Reckendorfhaus, 1930.
Senter, Terrence A. (1975) "Moholy-Nagy in England: May 1935–July 1937," master's thesis, University of Nottingham.
Scheibe, Wolfgang. (1978) *Die Reformpädagogische Bewegung. Eine einführende Darstellung*. Weinheim: Beltz.
Schoenmakers, Henri, et al., eds. (2009) *Theater und Medien. Grundlagen–Analysen–Perspektiven*. Bielefeld: Transkopf Verlag.
Schwitters, Kurt. (1922) *Anna Blume, Dichtungen*. Hannover: Paul Steegemann Verlag.
Slater, Christian. (2010) *Entangled: Technology and the Transformation of Performance*. Cambridge, MA: The MIT Press.
Stuckenschmidt, Hans Heinz. (1978) *Musik am Bauhaus*. Berlin: Bauhaus-Archiv.
Svestka, Jiři, and Katherine Jánszky Michaelsen, eds. (1991) *Andor Weininger: From Bauhaus to Conceptual Art*. Düsseldorf: Kunstverein für die Rheinlande und Westfalen.
Szabó, Júlia. (1981) *A magyar aktivizmus művészete 1915–1927* [The Art of Hungarian Activism, 1915–1927]. Budapest: Corvina.
Szilágyl, Sándor. (2011) "Anti-Fotográfia. Fotográfia mint a művészi kommunikáció medium Moholy-Nagy László optico-pedagógiai rendszerében" [Anti-Photography: Photography as a Medium of Artistic Communication in Moholy-Nagy's Optico-Pedagogical System], PhD diss., Pécsi Tudományegyetem, Pécs.
Todd, Tamara, ed. (2011) *Screen/Space: The Projected Image in Contemporary Art*. Manchester and New York: Manchester University Press.
Urorskie, Andrew V. (2014) *Between the Black Box and the White Cube: Expanded Cinema and Post-War Art*. Chicago and London: University of Chicago Press.
Van Doesburg, Theo. (1985) *Grondbegrippen van de nieuwe beeldende kunst*. Nijmegen: SUN.
Vergo, Peter. (2012) *The Music of Painting: Music, Modernism and the Visual Arts from the Romantics to John Cage*. London: Phaidon Press.
Von Moos, Stanislaus, ed. (1983) *Avant Garde und Industrie*. Delft: Delft University Press.
Wahl, Volker, ed. (2001) *Die Meisterratsprotokolle des Staatlichen Bauhauses Weimar 1919 bis 1925*. Weimar: Verlag Hermann Böhlaus Nachfolger.
Weibel, Peter. (1996) *Jenseits von Kunst*. Vienna: Passagen Verlag.
Wick, Rainer. (2000) *Teaching at the Bauhaus*. Stuttgart: Hatje Cantz.
Wilson-Smith, Matthew. (2007) *The Total Work of Art: From Bayreuth to Cyberspace*. New York and London: Routledge.
Wilts, Bettina. (2004) *Zeit, Raum und Licht. Vom Bauhaustheater zur Gegenwart*. Weimar: VDG, Verlag und Datenbank für Geisteswissenschaften.
Wingler, Hans. (1978) *The Bauhaus*. Cambridge: The Cambridge University Press.
Wingler, Hans, ed. (1977) *Kunstschulreform 1900–1933*. Berlin: Gebr. Mann.
Zoltán, Péter. (2010) *Lajos Kassák, Wien und der Konstruktivismus 1920–1926*. Frankfurt and New York: Peter Lang.
Züchner, Eva, ed. (1994) *Der Deutsche Spiesser ärgert sich. Raul Hausmann 1886–1971*. Stuttgart: Hatje Cantz.

Index

Aquino, Eduardo, 13, 15, 180; spmb 166
Akasztott Ember, 12
Antheil, George, 47
Aromapoetry, 27, 172
Avenarius, Richard, 20–21, 31, 41

Barkenhoff, 18
Bauhaus, 17, 20, 21, 26, 27, *36,* 44, 47, 59, 62, 67–68, 87, *88,* 101, 103, 112, *136–37,* 160, 179
bauhaus (journal), *157,* 179
Bauhaus-Archiv/Museum für Gestaltung, 6–7, 15, *43, 125, 127,* 166, *176, 177,* 177
Bauhausbücher (book series), 46, *67,* 68, 86, *156,* 179
Bayer, Herbert, *76,* 78, 154, *156*
Benjamin, Walter, 12, 161
Berger, Otti, 26, *26*
Berlin, 9, 17–19, 31, 33, *36–37,* 43, 47, 60–62, *68,* 76–77, 81, 92, 101, 106, 153, 179
Berliner Stilleben (*Berlin Still Life*), 10, 23, *39, 53,* 77, 97
biocentrism, biophilosophy, 12, 17–18, 59, 179
Bogdanov, Alexander, 11, 31, 41, 67, 81
Book of New Artists (*Buch neuer Künstler; Új művészek könyve*), 60, *63*
Bratislava (Pozsony or Pressburg), *127,* 160
Brno (Brünn), *100, 129, 158,* 159, 160–61, *176,* 179
Broom, 44, *45,* 46
Buchhold, Marie, 18–19, *19*
Budapest, 59–60, *60–61,* 152–53, 179
Bühne im Bauhaus, Die, 28, 86–87, 116
Bund Entschiedener Schulreformer (Association of Determined School Reformers), 19, 20
Burchartz, Max, 94

Cage, John, 12, 81, 162
Chicago, 26, *95, 108, 134,* 162, 179, 181
Clausen, Franciska, 43, 46, *47*
Coar, Lancelot, 13, 104, *165, 167, 167,* 180
Communism, 59–60
Constructivism, 11, 17, 32, 59, 62, 66, 68, 78, 81, 86, 151, 161, 179
Contes d'Hoffmann (*The Tales of Hoffmann*), *Les,* 104, *107,* 112, *114–15,* 117, *122*
Corbusier, Le 62
Crellin, Naomi, 13, 116, *124–25*
Cürlis, Hans, 76

Das deutsche Lichtbild, 32
Dénes, Mihály, *152,* 153, 159
Deutscher Werkbund (German Werkbund), 77–78, 112–13, *121,* 160
Development Ltd. 15, 160, 174, *174,* 180
Devětsil, 159
digital, 12–13, 112, 116, *124, 125,* 154, 167, 180, 181
Doesburg, Theo Van, 69, *80,* 117, *155, 156*
Dorner, Alexander, 78–79, 113, 123
"Dynamisch-konstruktives Kraftsystem" (Dynamic–Constructive Energy System), *80,* 81, 86–88, 97
"Dynamic of the Metropolis" ("Dynamik der Gross-Stadt"; "A nagyváros dinamikája"), *68, 70–71, 72–75,* 76–77, 86, 92, *92,* 106, *110*

Eggeling, Viking, *30,* 76, 113, 123, *155*
Ekran (Screen), 159–60
Eliasson, Olafur, 15, *168–70, 168–70,* 180
Empiriokritizismus; empiriocriticism, 20–21, 31, 41, 67–68, 179
Enamel series (*Konstruktionen in Emaille,* "Telephone Pictures," *EM* series), 12, *150,* 151, 153–54, 179
Esprit Nouveau, 62
Expanded cinema, 12, 86, 179
Explorations, 162, *163*

Film und Foto Exhibition (FIFO), 1929; 32, *32,* 77, *77*
film, and cinema, 9, 26, 32–33, 38, *38,* 42–44, 46, 47, 53–54, *56–57,* 76–77, 86, *90, 95,* 97, *98, 101–6, 110,* 112–13, *115,* 116–17, *116,* 122–23, *127, 148,* 152, 160, *174,* 179, 180–86

Fischinger, Oskar, 54, *57,* 112
Flusser, Vilém, 161–62
Floe, 173, *173*
Francé, Raoul Heinrich, 21, 27, *28,* 31, 41, 153
Freideutsche Jugend (Free German Youth), 17–19, 43
Futurism: 11, *21,* 26, 46, 62, 66, 87, 94, 96

Galileo Circle (Galilei Kör), 59, 153
Gesamtkunstwerk, 59, 69, 76, 79, 154
Gesamtwerk, 59–80, 97, 112, 126, 154, 160, 162
Giedion, Sigfried, 12, 33, 78, 122, 160–62, *162*
Gilbert, Charles, 152
Gregory, Ken, 13, 123, 171, *171,* 180
Grierson, John, 54
Gropius, Walter, *17,* 59, 62, 67–68, 69, 77–78, 106, 112, *114, 115,* 122, 126, *156, 157*
Grossstadt-Zigeuner (*Metropolitan Gypsies*), 77, 97, *98*
Günther, Bertha, *42,* 43–44
Gutenberg Festschrift, 153, *153*
Gyros, 32, 96, *148*

hand sculptures, 26, *27*
Harrop, Patrick, 13, 104, *165, 167, 167,* 181
Hausmann, Raoul, 11, 21, 26–27, *30–31,* 31–33, 38, 41, 42, 53–54, *55,* 81, *82,* 86, 101, *102,* 103, 179
Heyne, Renate, 15, 43, *43, 127,* 176, *176,* 181
Hirschfeld-Mack, Ludwig, 103–4, *105,* 106, 113
Höch, Hannah, 31, 160
Holzhauser, Karl Martin, 15, 113, *116*
Hungary, 11, 179; as Soviet Republic, 59–60, 153, 179

i10, 32, *32*
immersion, 13, 21, 81–100, 126
Institut für Kulturforschung (Institute for Cultural Research), 76

Jacoby, Heinrich, 19–20, *20, 130*
Jäger, Gottfried, 15, 113
Jugendbewegung (Youth Movement), 17, 19, 42

Kac, Eduardo, 12–15, 27, 96, 154, 172, *172,* 181
Kalivoda, František, *56,* 153, *158,* 159–61, *160*
Kállai, Ernő (Ernst), 153
Kassák, Lajos, 11, *18,* 31, *52,* 59, 60–62, *62–65,* 66–67, 68, *68–69, 92, 96,* 102, 103, 154, *155,* 179, *190*
Kaufmann von Berlin, Der, 104, 112, *113*
Kemény, Alfréd, 11, 21, 67, *80,* 81, 89, 96–97
Kepes, György, *22,* 117, 154, 162
Kiesler, Friedrich, *68–69,* 89, 92, 94, 106
Kinetic-Constructive System. Structure with movement tracks for play and conveyance ("Kinetisches konstruktives System. Bau mit Bewegungsbahnen für Spiel und Beförderung") (Also: "Structure"), 9, 67, *82, 84–86,* 86–88, *88–89,* 92, 96
Klages, Ludwig, 17–18
Korn, Arthur, 152, *152*
Kunstblatt, Das, 27

László, Alexander, 53, *55,* 104, 112
Lebensphilosophie (life philosophy), 59
Lebensreformbewegung (life reform movement), 11, 12, 17, 43, 59, 60, 66
Lensing, Jörg, 15
light painting, Lichtgestaltung, Lichtmalerei, 46, *95,* 96, 101, 112–13, 116, 117, 122, 126, 144
Light Prop for an Electric Stage ("Lichtrequisit einer elektrischen Bühne"), 9, 42–43, *43,* 79, 86, 103, 112, 118, 121, *124–27,* 148, 153, 159, 160, 171, 176, *176, 177, 177,* 179
Light-Space Modulator (*Licht-Raum Modulator*), see: Light Prop for an Electric Stage
Lichtspiel Schwarz Weiss Grau (*Lightplay Black White Grey*), 42, 117
Lincoln, Erika, 13, 173, *173,* 181
Lissitzky, Lazar el 43, *64,* 69, 78, *80,* 96, 152, *155,* 179
Loheland, 18, 20, 43, 46
Luna Park, 26, 92, 94

MA (Today), *18, 20,* 26, *30,* 31, 32, 47, 53, *53, 55,* 60–62, 66, *68,* 76, *93,* 101, *102,* 103, *129, 155,* 179
Mach, Ernst, 20, 41
McLaren, Norman, 54, *57*
McLuhan, Marshall, 12, 161–62, *162*
Maddin, Guy, 15, 174, *174,* 180
Malerei, Photographie, Film (*Painting, Photography, Film*), 9, *14,* 32, 86, 101, 161
Malevich, Kasimir, *64,* 94, 102, 179
Man with a Movie Camera, 97, 112
Man Ray, 43, 44
Marcus, Ernst, 31, 33
Marseilles, vieux port (Marseilles: Old Port), *38,* 77, *90,* 97
media, 9–13, 46, 60, 62, 67, 76, 78, 101–2, 152, 159–65; traditional hierarchy, 12, 69
Miller, Bernie, 13, 175, *175,* 181
Marinetti, F. T., 11, *20, 26,* 32, 96
mechanische Exzentrik, 27, *28, 121*
modernity, 9, 11, 59, 81, 94, 106, 162
Moholy, Lucia (née Schulz), *1,* 11, *17,* 18–20, *18–20,* 41, 43, 67, *80, 114,* 117, *122,* 153, 179
Moholy-Nagy, Sibyl, 27, 31, 54, 81, 97, 106, 153, 179
Molnár, Farkas, *28, 82,* 86, *86,* 88, *88–89, 121, 156*
Monument to the Third International, 96, *96*
Müller-Freienfels, Robert, 21, 41
Musikblätter des Anbruch, 47, *53*

National Film Board of Canada, 54
Natter, Christoph, 20, *20*
Neue Sachlichkeit (New Objectivity), 32, 66, 151
Neue Wege der Photographie, 32
Neusüss, Floris, 11, 15, 43, *43,* 104, 27, 176, *176,* 181
New Bauhaus, 26–27, *134,* 179
New Vision, The, 8, *26, 28,* 32, *32,* 38, 44, 77, 96, 102, 117, *143,* 154, 162, 179

Olafson, Freya, 13, 177, *177,* 182
Once a Chicken…, 160, 174, *174*
optophonetics, 13, 32, 53, 54, *55–56,* 67, 101, 103

Pädagogische Reformbewegung (Pedagogical Reform Movement), 17–18
painting, 11, 32, 33, 42–44, 62, 67, 81, 94, 96, 101–4, 113, 130, 132, *136,* 138–46, *139–45,* 151, 154, 161, 167, 176, 179
participation, 13, 79, 81–100, 126, 161
Pásmo (Zone), *63,* 66, *70,* 76, 154, 159
pedagogy, 9, 18–21, 43, 66, 68, 179
Péri, László, *41, 82,* 86
Pfenninger, Rudolf, 54, 56
photography, 12, *22,* 32–33, *32–33,* 38, 42, *43–45,* 67, 77–78, 102, *136,* 151, 161
photogram, 14, 15, 22, 24, 41, *42–44,* 42–44, 48, *50, 100,* 102, 104, *107, 115,* 117, 122–23, 126, *127,* 159–60, 176, *176*
Pictorialism, 151
Piscator, Erwin, *58,* 104, 106, 112, *112, 114–15*
Plug In Institute of Contemporary Art, 15, 166, *173,* 180, 181
Polycinema, 9, 13, 86, 104, 106, 112, *114,* 177, 179
Potsdamer Platz, 9, *10,* 106
"Production / Reproduction," 11, 41–58, 92, 126
Proletkult (movement), 21
projection / "Projection Spaces," 42, 79, 88, 101–28, 167, 175, 177, 179
Prototype Electric Light Machine for a Modern Room, 123, *171*
Proun Room, 81, 96
Provinzialmuseum, Hannover, 78
Puni, Ivan, 31, *155*

Railway Theater, 89, 94
Raumbühne (Spatial Stage), 89
Raum der Gegenwart, 78–79, *78,* 123–24, *124, 125*
Readymade, 151
record player (gramophone), 41, 42, *46,* 53, 67, 151–53
reflected polar reversal, The, 169, *169*
Richter, Hans, 76, 102, 113, 123
Rodchenko, Alexander, 68, 69

Roma/Sinti, 97
Ruttmann, Walter, 76, 113, 123
Schad, Christian, 43
Schlemmer, Oskar, *28, 82,* 86, *89,* 96, 112, *121, 156*
Schwarzerden, 18–19, *18–19,* 38, 46
Schwerdtfeger, Kurt, 103
Schwitters, Kurt, 11, 96, 179
sculpture, 26, *26, 32,* 67, 81, 86, *90,* 101, 102, 116, 126, 136, *137,* 167, 175
"Section allemande," *Exposition de la Société des artistes décorateurs, 76,* 77–78, *115,* 118
Sebök, István, 84–85, 88, 104, 113, *114–16, 118–19, 121, 124*
senses, the; 9, 17, 20–21, 26–27, 31, 67, 81, 88, 106, 154, 162, interoceptive, 21, 92, 97; kinesthesial, 97; proprioceptive, 88, 92, 97; sensory exercises, 9; sensory training, 17–40, 41, 43, 59, 67, 81, 162; tactilism, *20, 26, 26,* 32
Sherrington, Charles Scott, 21
simultaneity, 9
Spherical Theater, 89, 92
Staatsoper am Platz der Republik, 104, *107, 114, 122*
Stijl, De 40, 41, 46, 81
Stieglitz, Alfred, 32
Stuckenschmidt, H. H., 47, *53*
Sturm, Der, 46, *46, 80,* 81, *82, 151,* 179
Stuttgart, *32,* 76
Suprematism, 11

tactile chart, 26, *26*
Tatlin, Vladimir, *96,* 97
technology, 9, 11, 13, 27, 31, 41, 47, 53, 62, 67–68, 130, 152–54, 161
Tektologiia (tectology), 31, 81
Telefonhirmondó (Telephone Herald), 152, 153
telehor, 13, 33, *56,* 102, *107,* 123, 153–54, *153, 158,* 159–64, 179
television, 9, 13, 103, 153, 159
Textspace, 166, *166*
"Theater, Zirkus, Varieté" (Theater, Circus, Variety Theater), 87
Third Comintern Congress, Moscow, 81
Threshold, 177, *177*
Tönendes ABC (Sounding alphabet), 54, *56*
Totaltheater, 112, *114,* 122
transparency, translucency; 43, 104, 112, 116, 117, 122, 123, 126, 129–50, 175, *182*
Tschichold, Jan, *46,* 154

U-Theater, *86,* 88

Václavek, Bedřich, 159
Vertov, Dziga, 97, 112, 154
Victory Over the Sun, 94
Vogler, Elisabeth, 18, *19*
Vogler, Heinrich, 18–19
Vogler, Paul, 18–19
Vogler, Paula, 18, *18,* 67
Von Material zu Architektur, 8, 19, 21, 27, 31, 53, 68, 96, 154, 179

Weimar, 32, *80, 137,* 153, 179
Weininger, Andor, 89, *92*
Wendekreis, 18, 19
Wilfred, Thomas, 42, 103, 104
World illuminator, 170, *170*
Wyneken, Gustav, 18

X-ray, 32, 33, *34,* 67, 103, *104*

Yeadon, Peter, 13, *86, 89*
Your screen-free environment, 168, *168*

*Z*wei Konstruktionsysteme zusammengefügt (aus verschieden Metallen: Stahl, Kupfer, Nickel, Aluminium, Zink und Kristallglas montiert) [Integration of two systems of construction (assembled from different metals: steel, copper, nickel, aluminum, zinc and plate glass)], 96, *175; Metal Sculpture, 136*

Locations, Image Credits and Copyright Information

Guide to the Captions:
Unless otherwise indicated, all works are by László Moholy-Nagy.

n.d. = not dated or date unknown

Unless significant, inscriptions and markings on artworks are not provided

Unless otherwise indicated all reproduced photographs are gelatin silver prints.

Unless otherwise indicated, scans and film stills are by Oliver Botar.

Unless otherwise indicated, digital image files are courtesy of Hattula Moholy-Nagy, the Salgo Trust for Education, or from the archive of Oliver Botar.

Unless otherwise indicated, all photos are by William Eakin.

When otherwise unavailable, information caption information is from or checked against the following published sources: Botar 2007b, 2007c; Borchardt-Hume 2006; David and Diserens 1991; Loers et al. 1991; Droste and Fiedler 1988; Fiedler and Moholy-Nagy 2006; Lusk 1980; Neusüss and Heyne with Moholy-Nagy 2009; Orosz 2013; Passuth 1982; Pfeiffer and Hollein 2009; Rubio 2010 (See Reference List)

Every effort has been made to trace copyright holders for both artworks and copy photographs reproduced in this volume. We apologize for any errors or oversight in this matter.

Abbreviations:
Photo = photographer
BHA = Bauhaus-Archiv, Museum für Gestaltung, Berlin
CA = Collection of the Artist(s)
HMN = Hattula Moholy-Nagy
IVAM = Institut Valencià d'Art Modern – Centre Julio González, Valencia
LMN = László Moholy-Nagy
PC = Private Collection
SM = Kurt and Ernst Schwitters Stiftung, Sprengel Museum, Hannover
ST = The Salgo Trust for Education, New York
TSUK = Theaterwissenschaftliche Sammlung, Universität zu Köln

Image Credits:
p. 19 (bottom left), 24, 25, 49, 50, 105 (top; bottom left), 108, 110 (top), 111 (top), 137 (bottom left), 146 (bottom), 148, 149 (top left), 182, 191: HMN © VG Bild-Kunst, Bonn
p. 8, 64, 65, 96, 102 (top; bottom right), 190 (bottom): Collection of Miklós Müller and Jan E. Keithly
p. 9, 152 (bottom): Photos: Weltspiegel. PC
p. 10, 23 (bottom left, right), 27 (left), 28 (top), 33 (top), 39, 42 (middle), 42 (bottom left), 46 (top), 53, 55 (bottom), 70, 71, 91 (bottom), 94 (top), 98, 99, 111 (bottom), 112, 126 (top), 127, 128 (top), 136, 149 (top right), 157 (top right, middle right, bottom right): ST © VG Bild-Kunst, Bonn
p. 1, 14 (top), 28 (bottom), 41 (top), 47 (top), 57 (bottom), 60, 61 (bottom), 82 (top left; bottom right), 83 (top), 102 (bottom left), 163 (top): PC
p. 14 (bottom), 22 (top), 48, 84 (top), 114 (middle), 120 (middle right), 121 (bottom), 133 (top left), 142 (bottom): BHA. Photos: Markus Hawlik, courtesy of BHA © VG Bild-Kunst, Bonn
p. 16 (top), 18 (top; bottom 2nd from right), 19 (bottom right), 20 (top), 122, 123: BHA. Photos courtesy of BHA © Lucia Moholy: VG Bild-Kunst, Bonn 2014
p. 17, 20 (bottom), 23 (top), 29, 36 (top; bottom), 48 (bottom right), 76 (top), 104 (top), 107 (bottom right), 109, 116 (bottom left), 118 (top right), 120 (bottom left; bottom right), 131 (bottom), 134 (bottom), 135: BHA. Photos courtesy of BHA © VG Bild-Kunst, Bonn
p. 16 (bottom), S. 18 (middle): PC © Lucia Moholy: VG Bild-Kunst, Bonn 2014
p. 18 (bottom left), 27 (right), 56 (top right), 76 (bottom), 77, 165 (middle), 175. Photos courtesy of BHA
p. 21 (top), 26 (bottom), 32, 37, 46 (middle), 63, 72–75, 83 (bottom), 86 (top), 91 (top), 104 (bottom), 107 (top), 113, 126 (middle), 130 (top), 142 (top), 145 (middle), 146 (top), 149 (bottom), 153, 162 (bottom): PC © VG Bild-Kunst, Bonn
p. 19 (top): © Stiftung der deutschen Frauenbewegung, Kassel; HL-K-27
p. 21 (bottom), 30/31: Collection Lorenz and Ildiko Czell, Munich, courtesy of derda berlin / rare books + fine art
p. 22, 44 (bottom left), 51 (bottom), 100 (bottom), 107 (bottom left): Museum Folkwang, Essen. Photo: Museum Folkwang © VG Bild-Kunst, Bonn
p. 26 (top): BHA. Photo: Hartwig Klappert, courtesy of BHA
p. 33 (bottom), 52 (top): ST
pp. 34/35: Photo p. 44: F.M. Duncan; Photo p. 45: Atlantic; Photo p. 60: AGFA; Photo p. 61: Schreiner/Weimar; Photo p. 56: Observatory Arequipa; Photo p. 57: Atlantic. ST © VG Bild-Kunst, Bonn
p. 36 (top left), 37 (bottom), 40 (bottom), 42 (middle), 43 (bottom), 51 (top), 84 (bottom), 92 (bottom), 93 (top right), 108 (top left), 134 (top): HMN. Photo: Peter Schaelchli, courtesy of ST © VG Bild-Kunst, Bonn
p. 40 (top): derda berlin / rare books + fine art
p. 42 (top): Loheland Stiftung, Kuenzell, Germany. Photo: Loheland Stiftung
p. 42 (bottom right), 117, 124 (bottom), 125 (top), 126 (bottom left), 166, 171, 173: CA
p. 43 (top): Kirkland Collection, London © VG Bild-Kunst, Bonn
p. 44 (top), 55 (top), 101, 104 (middle), 129: HMN
p. 44 (bottom right): Kunstsammlung Dresdner Bank – eine Marke der Commerzbank AG © VG Bild-Kunst, Bonn
p. 45 (top left, bottom), 46 (middle), 66: M. Szarvasy Collection, New York © VG Bild-Kunst, Bonn
p. 45 (top right): HMN. Photo courtesy of ST © VG Bild-Kunst, Bonn
p. 47 (bottom): Kunstmuseet Brundlund Slot, Denmark. Photo: Kunstmuseet Brundland Slot © VG Bild-Kunst, Bonn
p. 48 (bottom left), 115 (top), 119: derda berlin / rare books + fine art. Photos courtesy of derda © VG Bild-Kunst, Bonn
p. 52: (bottom): Collection Lorenz and Ildiko Czell, Munich, courtesy derda berlin / rare books + fine art. For Picasso: © ProLitteris
p. 54: PC. For Léger: © VG Bild-Kunst, Bonn
p. 56 (top left): ST © Kalivoda Brno Museum, etc.
p. 58, 85, 100 (middle right), 116 (top), 118 (top right): TSUK. Photos: TSUK © VG Bild-Kunst Bonn
p. 56 (bottom): Muzeum města Brna © VG Bild-Kunst, Bonn
p. 61 (top): Stiftung Saarländische Kulturbesitz, Saarbrücken. Photo: Stiftung Saarländische Kulturbesitz © VG Bild-Kunst, Bonn
p. 62: M. Szarvasy Collection, New York © Kassák Múzeum, Budapest
pp. 68/69: Collection Lorenz and Ildiko Czell, Munich © VG Bild-Kunst, Bonn
pp. 78/79: Photos courtesy of Kai-Uwe Hemken
p. 80 (top): M. Szarvasy, New York
p. 82 (top right): Berlinische Galerie, Berlin. Photo: Berlinische Galerie © VG Bild-Kunst, Bonn
p. 86 (bottom), 87, 89 (bottom): CA. Images courtesy of the artist
p. 88 (top): BHA. Photo courtesy of BHA © Estate of T. Lux Feininger
p. 88 (bottom), 92 (top), 93 (top left), 94 (bottom), 95, 133 (top right), 137 (middle left), 150 (top): © VG Bild-Kunst, Bonn
p. 89 (top middle): TSUK
p. 90: Photo p. 182: Max Krajewsky; Photo p. 183: Weltspiegel; Photo p. 122: Berliner Illustrierte Zeitung; Photo p. 123: Eckner, Weimar. PC
p. 93 (bottom): Magyar Fotógráfiai Múzeum, Kecskemét © VG Bild-Kunst, Bonn
p. 100 (top): National Gallery of Art, Washington, DC, Gift of Richard Zeisler 2007.112.1. Photo: National Gallery of Art © VG Bild-Kunst, Bonn
p. 103: BHA, Donation from the Estate of Margaret Leischner. Photo: Hartwig Klappert, courtesy of BHA © VG Bild-Kunst, Bonn
p. 105 (bottom right): BHA. Photo courtesy of BHA © Kaj Delugan
p. 114 (top): TSUK © Lucia Moholy: VG Bild-Kunst, Bonn 2014
p. 114 (bottom left): TSUK © Walter Gropius: VG Bild-Kunst, Bonn 2014
p. 114 (bottom right): CA. All rights reserved © 2004
p. 115 (bottom), 120 (top), 121 (top): BHA. Photo courtesy of BHA. For Walter Gropius © VG Bild-Kunst, Bonn 2014
p. 116 (bottom right): Kunsthalle Bielefeld © VG Bild-Kunst, Bonn
p. 118 (bottom right): SM © VG Bild-Kunst, Bonn
p. 124 (top left): Sprengel Museum Hannover
p. 124 (top right), 125 (bottom): PC. Photo: Oliver Botar, taken with permission
p. 125 (middle): PC. Photo: Oliver Botar © VG Bild-Kunst, Bonn
p. 126 (bottom right): National Gallery of Canada, Ottawa. Acquisition number NGC 40572. Photo © NGC © VG Bild-Kunst, Bonn
p. 128 (bottom left): Miklós Müller and Jan Keithly © VG Bild-Kunst, Bonn
p. 128 (bottom right): Museum Wiesbaden. Photo: Museum Wiesbaden © VG Bild-Kunst, Bonn
p. 130 (bottom): Kunstmuseum Gelsenkirchen. Photo: Kunstmuseum Gelsenkirchen, M. Schmüdderich © VG Bild-Kunst, Bonn
p. 131 (top): Solomon R. Guggenheim Museum, New York. Photo: Guggenheim Museum. © VG Bild-Kunst, Bonn
p. 132 (left): Sammlung Etta und Otto Stangl im Kunstmuseum Stuttgart © VG Bild-Kunst, Bonn
p. 132 (right): Kunstmuseum Winterthur © VG Bild-Kunst, Bonn
p. 133 (bottom): BHA. Erworben mit Unterstützung des Deutschen Sparkassen- und Giroverbands. Photo: Markus Hawlik, courtesy of BHA © VG Bild-Kunst, Bonn
p. 137 (top): Brandenburgisches Landesamt für Denkmalpflege und Archäologisches Museum / Messbildarchiv. Photo courtesy of BHA © VG Bild-Kunst, Bonn and Brandenburgisches Landesamt für Denkmalpflege
p. 137 (bottom right): The Museum of Modern Art, New York © VG Bild-Kunst, Bonn
p. 138 (bottom), S. 139 (right): SM. Photo: Sprengel Museum, Stuttgart © VG Bild-Kunst, Bonn
p. 138 (top): Solomon R. Guggenheim Museum, New York. Solomon R. Guggenheim Founding Collection 47.1157. Photo: Guggenheim Museum © VG Bild-Kunst Bonn
p. 139 (left): László Moholy-Nagy, *Sil I*, Scottish National Gallery of Modern Art, Edinburgh. Purchased 1977. Photo: SNGMA © VG Bild-Kunst, Bonn
p. 140: BHA. Photo: Hermann Kiessling, courtesy of BHA © VG Bild-Kunst, Bonn
p. 141, 147: IVAM, Valencia © VG Bild-Kunst, Bonn
p. 144 (top left): McMaster Museum of Art, Levy Bequest Purchase, 1995. Photo: McMaster Museum of Art © VG Bild-Kunst, Bonn
p. 143, 144 (top right): HMN. Photo courtesy of HMN © VG Bild-Kunst, Bonn
p. 144 (bottom): BHA. Photo: Atelier Schneider, courtesy of BHA © VG Bild-Kunst, Bonn
p. 145 (top): Queensland Art Gallery © VG Bild-Kunst, Bonn
p. 145 (bottom): Solomon R. Guggenheim Museum, New York. Solomon R. Guggenheim Founding Collection 47.1063. Photo: Guggenheim Museum © VG Bild-Kunst, Bonn
p. 150 (top and middle): Museum of Modern Art, New York. HMN
p. 152 (top, middle): Wikipedia Commons, Public Domain
p. 155: Collection Lorenz and Ildiko Czell, Munich. Courtesy of derda fine arts, etc. For Arp and Puni © ADAGP (Paris / SODRAC (Montreal). For Archipenko, Grosz and LMN © VG Bild-Kunst Bonn. For Kassák © Kassák Múzeum, Budapest.
pp. 156/157: derda fine arts, etc. For LMN and Bayer © VG Bild-Kunst, Bonn
p. 158 (top): Photos: Jaroslav Bouček. HMN
p. 158 (bottom): National Gallery of Art, Washington, DC. PC © VG Bild-Kunst, Bonn
p. 162 (top): Familie Giedion, Zürich. Reproduced with permission.
p. 163 (bottom): PC © Estates of Marshall McLuhan and Edmund Carpenter. Note: Explorations has been reissued by Wipf and Stock: https://wipfandstock.com/
p. 165: Photo: Oliver Botar
p. 167: © Photo: Lancelot Coar
pp. 168–170: CA. Photos courtesy of Eliasson Studio, Berlin
pp. 169 (bottom left), 170 (top, bottom left): © Photos: SHIMURAbros
p. 172: CA. Photos courtesy of Eduardo Kac
p. 174: CA. Film stills courtesy Guy Maddin / Development Ltd.
p. 176: BHA. Photo courtesy of the artists
p. 177: CA. Photo and video stills courtesy of the artist
p. 179: BHA. Photo courtesy of BHA © bpk Berlin

Acknowledgments

Supplementing the acknowledgments in the Prefaces and the Introduction, we would also like to thank:

Lenders to the exhibitions in Winnipeg and Berlin: Center for Visual Music, Los Angeles; Criterion Films; Lorenz and Ildiko Czell, Munich; derda berlin / rare books + fine art; Dan and Natalia Hug, Cologne; the IVAM, Institut Valencia d'Art Moderna; the Kunsthalle Bielefeld; the Kunstmuseet Brundlund Slot, Aabenraa; the Kunstmuseum Gelsenkirchen; the Kunstmuseum Winterthur; the Kurt und Ernst Schwitters Stiftung, Sprengel Museum Hannover; McMaster University Museum of Art, Hamilton, ON; Hattula Moholy-Nagy, Ann Arbor, MI; The Moholy-Nagy Foundation, Ann Arbor, MI; Miklós Müller and Jan Keithly, New York; Musée d'art contemporain de Montréal; Musée national des beaux-arts du Québec, Quebec City; National Film Board of Canada, Montréal; The National Gallery of Canada, Ottawa; the Museum Folkwang Essen; the Museum Wiesbaden; the National Gallery of Art, Washington; The Salgo Trust for Education, New York; M. Szarvasy, New York; the Scottish National Gallery of Modern Art, Edinburgh; the Solomon R. Guggenheim Museum, New York; the Stiftung Saarländischer Kulturbesitz Saarlandmuseum Saarbrücken; the Theaterwissenschaftliche Sammlung, Universität zu Köln and a private collector.

We are also very grateful to all the artists involved in the project including the team of Malou Airaudo, Sascha Hardt, Jörg U. Lensing, Thomas Neuhaus, Gudula Schröder and Jürgen Steger (Düsseldorf); Eduardo Aquino (Winnipeg); the team of Nike Arnold, Andreas Haus, Aline Helmcke, Frédéric Krauke and Walter Lenertz (Berlin); Lancelot Coar (Winnipeg); Naomi Clare Crellin (Baltimore); Olafur Eliasson (Berlin); Ken Gregory (Winnipeg); Patrick Harrop (Winnipeg); the team of Karl Martin Holzhauser and Gottfried Jäger (Bielefeld); the team of Evan Johnson, Galen Johnson, Bob Kotyk, Guy Maddin, and Ryan Simmons (Winnipeg); Eduardo Kac (Chicago); Erika Lincoln (Winnipeg); Bernie Miller (Winnipeg); Javier Núñez and Francisco Javier Navarro de Zuvillaga (Madrid); Freya Olafson (Winnipeg); Örjan Sandred (Winnipeg) and Peter Yeadon (New York).

Thanks are due to the following persons in Winnipeg: Joanna Black, Jim Bugslag, Noam Gonick, Andrew Kear, Sotirios Kotoulas, Christine Lylyk, Marcelle Lussier, Simone Mahrenholtz, Evan Marnoch, Kanchana Sankaranarayanan, Brenda St. Hilaire, Shep Steiner, Marlene Stern, Ralph Stern, George Toles, Liv Valmestad, Meeka Walsh, Micheline Watson,

Thanks to Eva Badura-Triska (Vienna), Eileen Baral (Port Washington, NY), Esther Butterworth (Zurich), Todd Connel (Wichita, KS), Therese Costes and Michael Matthews (Berlin), Csilla Csorba (Budapest), Else Eckert (Berlin), Sjarel Ex (Rotterdam), Éva Forgács (Los Angeles), Ihor Holubitzky (Hamilton, ON), Andreas Hug (Ann Arbor, MI), Katalin Keserü (Budapest), Michael Maginness (Berlin), Cristina Mulinas (Valencia), Martina Mullis (Zurich), Keonaona Peterson (Southbridge, MA) Doina Popescu (Toronto), Edit Sasvári (Budapest), Anna Schiestl (Zurich), Béla Tarr (Budapest), Nadine Unterharrer (Zurich), Daniel Weiss (Zurich).

I have had the privilege of conducting fruitful discussions on topics related to this project with Nicholas Baer (Berlin), Jonah Corne (Winnipeg), Noam Elcott (New York), Klemens Gruber (Vienna), Patrick Harrop (Winnipeg), Andreas Haus (Wehrheim/Berlin), Kai-Uwe Hemken (Kassel), Toshino Iguchi (Tokyo), Angela Lampe (Paris), Rodney Latourelle (Berlin), Márton Orosz (Budapest), Krisztina Passuth (Budapest), Esther Polonyi (Berlin/ New York), Oliva Rubio (Madrid), Sándor Szilágyi (Budapest), Karole Vail (New York), Monika Vrecar (Berlin/ Winnipeg) and Klaus Weber (Berlin).

Thank you to the helpful staff at: Architecture and Art Library, University of Manitoba; Art Gallery of Ontario, Toronto; Department of Advertising and Graphic Design, Museum of Modern Art, New York; Elektrotechnikai Múzeum, Budapest; George Eastman House, Rochester, NY; The Getty Research Institute Library, Los Angeles; Image Centre, Ryerson University, Toronto; Institut Valencià d'Art Modern, Valencia; Kassák Múzeum / Petőfi Irodalmi Múzeum, Budapest; Library and Archives Canada, Ottawa; Los Angeles County Museum of Art; Muzeum města Brna; Musée National d'Art Moderne, Centre Georges Pompidou, Paris; Museum Folkwang, Essen; Office of Research Services, University of Manitoba; Országos Széchényi Könyvtár, Budapest; San Francisco Museum of Modern Art; Santa Barbara Museum of Art; Solomon R. Guggenheim Museum, New York; Sprengel Museum, Hannover; Telefónia Múzeum, Budapest, Univerzitná knižnica v Bratislave.

Lancelot Coar and Patrick Harrop thank the following students, who assisted with the construction of the Polycinema. Without their collaboration, the realization of this project would not have been possible: Apollinaire Au, Nish Balakrishnan, Jaya Beange, Christopher Burke, Jason Hare, Kyle Janzen, Nathan Johns, Zoé Lebel, and Ryan Marques.

The Bauhaus-Archiv / Museum für Gestaltung thanks the following for their contributions to the exhibition in Berlin: Leif Christensen for lighting design, L2 M3 Kommunikationsdesign for graphic design and Bernd-Michael Weisheit and his team for the installation.

Please forgive any omissions. Thank you to all the individuals and institutions who have made this project happen.

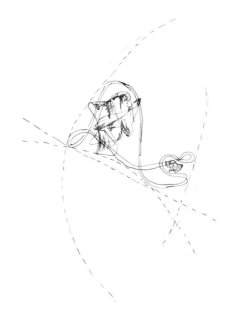

Through Canada, graphite and ink on paper, 1941, 21,5 × 28 cm.

Recipient of the prestigious Moholy-Nagy Award, Oliver A. I. Botar is professor of Art History and Associate Director of the School of Art, University of Manitoba in Winnipeg, Canada. His PhD (Toronto) was on Biomorphic Modernism and Biocentrism. The nexus of Biocentrism-Modernism, the Hungarian avant-garde, László Moholy-Nagy, the Bauhaus, and the origins of new media art have been research focuses. He has lectured, published, and curated exhibitions in Canada, the United States, Europe, and Japan. He is author of *Tehchnical Detours: The Early Moholy-Nagy Reconsidered* (2006) and a book on Andor Weininger's Canadian sojourn, as well as numerous articles, book chapters, and exhibition catalogues. He is co-editor of *Biocentrism and Modernism* (with Isabel Wunsche), 2011), and *telehor* (with Klemens Gruber, 2013). Botar also works on Canadian Modernism, and is currently working on a book on settler art in Winnipeg.

Also published by Lars Müller Publishers:
telehor, Facsimile Reprint of the 1936 Original, 2013
avant-garde transfers 1
Edited by Klemens Gruber and Oliver A. I. Botar
ISBN 978-3-03778-253-8

Sensing the Future:
Moholy-Nagy, Media and the Arts

Author: Oliver A. I. Botar
Editing of artists' statements: Oliver A. I. Botar
Assistance: Christine Lylyk
Design: Integral Lars Müller / Lars Müller
and Nadine Unterharrer
Typesetting: Integral Lars Müller / Esther Butterworth
Coordination: Rebekka Kiesewetter
Copyediting: Helen Ferguson
Proofreading: Keonaona Peterson, Rebekka Kiesewetter
Assistance LMP: Anna Schiestl
Translations G-E, Index: Allison Plath-Moseley
Lithography: Ast & Fischer, Wabern
Printing and binding: Graspo, Zlín, the Czech Republic
Paper: Hello Fat Matt, 1.1, 135 g/m²

First published on the occasion of the exhibition:
Sensing the Future: Moholy-Nagy, Media and the Arts
Plug In ICA, Winnipeg, March 8–June 1, 2014
Bauhaus-Archiv/Museum für Gestaltung, Berlin,
October 8, 2014–January 12, 2015

© 2023 Lars Müller Publishers, Hattula Moholy-Nagy
and Oliver A. I. Botar
Works by László Moholy-Nagy © 2023 ProLitteris, Zürich

No part of this book may be used or reproduced
in any form or manner whatsoever without prior written
permission, except in the case of brief quotations
embodied in critical articles and reviews.

Lars Müller Publishers
Zürich, Switzerland
www.lars-mueller-publishers.com

ISBN 978-3-03778-746-5

Printed in the Czech Republic

bauhaus-archiv
museum für gestaltung

PLUG IN
INSTITUTE OF
CONTEMPORARY ART

THE SALGO TRUST
for EDUCATION

The Moholy-Nagy Foundation

SSHRC ≡ CRSH

UNIVERSITY
OF MANITOBA